De musica and *Sententiae*

Medieval Institute Publications is a program of
The Medieval Institute, College of Arts and Sciences

Western Michigan University

Aribo
De musica and *Sententiae*

Edited and translated by
T. J. H. McCarthy

TEAMS • Varia

MEDIEVAL INSTITUTE PUBLICATIONS
Western Michigan University
Kalamazoo

Manufactured in the United States of America
This book is printed on acid-free paper.

Library of Congress Cataloging-in-Publication Data

Aribo, Scholasticus, active 1068-1078, author.
De musica and sententiae / Aribo ; edited and translated by T. J. H. McCarthy.
pages cm -- (Teams varia)
Latin, with facing English translation.
ISBN 978-1-58044-196-4 (pbk. : alk. paper)
1. Music theory--History--Early works to 1800. I. McCarthy, Thomas John Henry. II. Aribo, Scholasticus, active 1068-1078. De musica. 2014. III. Aribo, Scholasticus, active 1068-1078. De musica. English. 2014. IV. Title. V. Series: Varia (Kalamazoo, Mich.)
MT5.5.A75 2014
781--dc23

2014033175

P 5 4 3 2 1

Contents

J. A. Caldwell

Figures

Preface

This edition of Aribo's *De musica* follows on from the 1784 edition by Dom Martin Gerbert and the 1951 edition by Joseph Smits van Waesberghe. Gerbert laid the foundations for the modern study of medieval music theory with the publication of his *Scriptores ecclesiastici de musica sacra potissimum*, a three-volume collection of the music theory works he had studied on his European travels. In the twentieth century the study of medieval music theory was given new impetus by Smits van Waesberghe, who throughout his prolific career published critical editions of numerous important works. Smits van Waesberghe's editions of the treatises by John, Aribo, and Guido of Arezzo helped to establish the *Corpus scriptorum de musica* series, which has since been the means of bringing many medieval music treatises to print.

The time that has elapsed since Smits van Waesberghe's 1951 edition has seen not only the rise of new approaches to the study of music history but also the discovery of new manuscripts of *De musica*. These developments, which have helped shed considerable light on Aribo's intentions and context, warrant a new critical edition and the first translation of his treatise.

The older historiography on Aribo is dominated by the researches of Smits van Waesberghe, who, in a series of scholarly publications, traced Aribo's career to Lotharingia and portrayed him as a leading member of a so-called Liège school of music theory. Subsequent research has substantially revised this interpretation and scholars now situate Aribo within the learned tradition of musical studies that flourished in the monasteries and cathedral schools of southern Germany.

The complexity of *De musica* has previously been discussed by Gabriela Ilnitchi, who sees in the treatise a sophisticated organization of Christological allegories deriving from Eriugenian mystical and hierarchical philosophy.[1] My own research, which has proceeded independently, has resulted in very different conclusions about Aribo and his treatise. Nevertheless, where I disagree with Ilnitchi, it is only after having considered her work carefully. The impact of eleventh-century church reform movements is central to the present edition, translation, and introduction. The treatise's practical orientation stems from the importance of music to religious life, its dissemination reflects the institutional networks that were the backbone of contemporary intellectual life, while its erudite character is testimony to Aribo's knowledge of divine and secular literature. *De musica* is a product not just of a music theory tradition but of the wider and deeper intellectual tradition of eleventh-century Germany.

In preparing this edition and translation of *De musica* it has been my privilege to work at numerous libraries and manuscript departments in Europe and the United States, and I should like to record my thanks to the staff of those libraries. In particular, I wish to thank David Coppen (Sibley Music Library of the Eastman School of Music in Rochester, NY) and Sonja Führer (Stiftsbibliothek of the Archabbey of St. Peter in Salzburg) for making me welcome at their respective institutions. I must also record the helpfulness of Dr. Friedrich Buchmayr (Stiftsbibliothek, St. Florian) and Dr. Christoph Mackert (Universitätsbibliothek, Leipzig).

I have benefited from the kindness and encouragement of some distinguished scholars with whom I discussed aspects of this project: Constant Mews (Monash University), John Haines (Toronto), John Magee (Toronto), and Christopher Page (Cambridge). Virginia Newes kindly provided many helpful comments. I must also express my gratitude to Tom Krol, Theresa Whitaker, and Patricia Hollahan of Medieval Institute Publications who, with unfailing good humor, worked hard with me to address the various stylistic and type-setting challenges presented by this edition and translation.

My friends and colleagues in Dublin, Toronto, and Florida have also been generous with their support and ideas: Andrew Johnstone, Massimiliano Vitiello, Pascale Duhamel, and David Rohrbacher. Carrie Beneš, my wife, has been unfailingly generous in her support, taking time from her own Italian studies to read my introduction and translation, thereby saving me from many errors and barbarisms.

I count myself fortunate to continue to benefit from the learned advice of Professor John Caldwell, who supervised my doctoral research and who has been a constant support in subsequent years. So too has Professor I. S. Robinson, who taught me as an undergraduate and, while supervising my first steps in the study of Aribo, generously gave of his time to correct the errors of my ragged pen.

NOTES

1. Ilnitchi, *Play of Meanings*.

Abbreviations

AH	Guido Maria Dreves, Clemens Blume, and H. M. Bannister, eds. *Analecta hymnica medii aevi.* 55 vols. Leipzig, 1886–1922.
Aribonis De musica	Aribo. *De musica.* Edited by Joseph Smits van Waesberghe. *Aribonis De musica.* Corpus scriptorum de musica 2. Rome: American Institute of Musicology, 1951.
CAO	René-Jean Hesbert, ed. *Corpus antiphonarium officii.* 6 vols. Rerum ecclesiasticarum documenta. Series Maior. Fontes 7–12. Rome: Herder, 1963–79.
DA	*Deutsches Archiv für Erforschung des Mittelalters*
MBDS	*Mittelalterliche Bibliothekskataloge Deutschlands und der Schweiz.* 4 vols. Munich: C. H. Beck, 1918–79.
MBÖ	*Mittelalterliche Bibliothekskataloge Österreichs.* 4 vols. Vienna: Adolf Holzhausen, 1915–66.
MGH	Monumenta Germaniae Historica
Briefe	Die Briefe der deutschen Kaiserzeit
Libelli	Libelli de lite imperatorum et pontificum
NecG	Necrologia Germaniae
SS	Scriptores (in Folio)
SSrG	Scriptores rerum Germanicarum in usum scholarum separatim editi
SSrG NS	Scriptores rerum Germanicarum, Nova Series
Pesce, *Guido*	Dolores Pesce, ed. and trans. *Guido d'Arezzo's "Regule rithmice, Prologus in antiphonarium" and "Epistola ad Michahelem": A Critical Text and Translation.* Wissenschaftliche Abhandlungen 73. Ottawa: Institute of Mediaeval Music, 1999.
PL	J.-P. Migne, ed. *Patrologiae cursus completus. Series Latina.* 221 vols. Paris, 1844–55.

RISM B	Joseph Smits van Waesberghe, P. Ernstbrunner, Pieter Fischer, Christian Mass, Michel Huglo, Christian Meyer, N. C. Phillips, A. Rausch, and C. Ruini, eds. *The Theory of Music from the Carolingian Era up to 1400: Descriptive Catalogue of Manuscripts.* Répertoire International des Sources Musicales, Series B 3/1–6. Duisburg: G. Henle, 1961–2003.
TK	Karl-Heinz Schlager, ed. *Thematischer Katalog der ältesten Alleluia-Melodien aus Handschriften des 10. und 11. Jahrhunderts, ausgenommen das ambrosianische, ält-römische und ält-spanische Repertoire.* Erlanger Arbeiten zur Musikwissenschaft 2. Munich: W. Ricke, 1965.

Biblical references are given according to the Vulgate.

Sigla

B	Brussels, Bibliothèque Royale, MS 10162/66, fols. 81v–84r
D	Darmstadt, Universitäts- und Hochschulbibliothek, Cod. 1988, fols. 170v–178r
D1	fols. 171v–174v
D2	fols. 176r–177r
D3	fol. 177rv
D4	fols. 177v–178r
D5	fol. 179r
D6	fols. 170v–171r
D7	fol. 175rv
F	Frankfurt am Main, Stadt- und Universitätsbibliothek, Fragm. lat. IX 75
K	Kassel, Landesbibliothek und Murhardsche Bibliothek der Stadt Kassel, 4º MSS Math. 1, fols. 32v–33v
L	Leiden, Rijksuniversiteit Bibliotheek, BPL 194, fols. 39v–41r
Lz	Leipzig, Universitätsbibliothek, Cod. 431, fols. 157r–161r
Lz1	fols. 157r–160v
Lz2	fols. 160v–161r
M_1	Munich, Bayerische Staatsbibliothek, Clm 14663, fols. 28r–29r
M_2	Munich, Bayerische Staatsbibliothek, Clm 14965a, fols. 7v–8r, 31r–32v
M_3	Munich, Bayerische Staatsbibliothek, Clm 29770, Frag. 3, 2 fols.
R	Rochester (NY), Eastman School of Music, Sibley Music Library, ML 92/1200, fols. 11r–42r
S	Salzburg, Stiftsbibliothek St. Peter, Cod. a. V. 2, fols. 114v–145r
Sf	St. Florian, Stiftsbibliothek, Cod. XI 35, fol. 1rv
V	Vienna, Österreichische Nationalbibliothek, Cod. 787, fols. 57v–59v, 70rv
V1	fols. 57v–59r

V2 fol. 59rv
V3 fol. 70rv
W Wolfenbüttel, Herzog-August Bibliothek, 334 Gud. Lat. 8º, fols. 57r–61r, 101v, 103r–104v, 106r–110v, 127v–128v
W1 fols. 57r–61r
W2 fol. 101v
W3 fols. 103r–104v
W4 fols. 106r–110v
W5 fol. 127v
W6 fol. 128rv

Introduction

Historical Context

Aribo's *De musica*, written between 1070 and 1078, is a treatise concerned with the workings of the liturgical music that Aribo and his contemporaries called Gregorian chant. It is one of several chant treatises written in the German monastic and cathedral schools of the eleventh century by authors such as Abbot Bern of Reichenau (d. 1048) and his pupil Herman (1013–54), Abbot William of Hirsau (d. 1091), Frutolf of Michelsberg (d. 1103), and Theoger of Metz (ca. 1050–1120). These authors, and others unnamed, received and developed each others' ideas about music. The teaching contained in Abbot Bern's influential treatise *Prologus in tonarium* was developed and modified by Herman of Reichenau in his *Musica*. Bern and Herman's "Reichenau theory" was transmitted to the monastery of St. Emmeram in Regensburg where the learned monk William incorporated it into his own music treatise. Reichenau theory, as well as William's own, then travelled from St. Emmeram to the monastery of Michelsberg in Bamberg. Here the monk Frutolf, prior and schoolmaster of Michelsberg, incorporated into his *Breviarium de musica* both Herman's and William's work. When William was called to be abbot of the Swabian monastery of Hirsau in 1069, he brought with him the teaching of the Reichenau theorists. That legacy was transmitted to William's pupil Theoger, who became abbot of St. Georgen in the Black Forest and ended his days as the nominal bishop of Metz. Aribo too was part of this scholarly network, which can aptly be termed the "south German circle" of music theorists.[1]

Aribo's lifetime was dominated by concepts of monastic and church reform. An understanding of these related movements is vital to the study of *De musica* and the motivations of its author. Throughout the second half of the tenth century and for the first three-quarters of the eleventh, the reform associated with the Lotharingian monastery of Gorze and those monasteries it influenced—particularly St. Maximin in Trier—had been the dominant type of monastic reform in the German kingdom.[2] The communal life espoused by Gorze had found favor at the imperial court: characterized by strict discipline, this life stressed devotion to regular prayer and the proper execution of the liturgy, as well as emphasizing the importance of scholarship and learning.[3] The Saxon emperor Henry II was particularly impressed by the discipline of the Gorze movement and considered it vital to the spiritual and intellectual well-being of his kingdom. He sought to spread its influence among the imperial monasteries under his jurisdiction by the appointment of reforming abbots.[4]

Unlike the contemporary reform movement emanating from the Burgundian monastery of Cluny, the Gorze reform had no clearly-defined network of mother and daughter houses. Monasteries were bound together by looser bonds of friendship and formed associations based upon the house from which they had received their commonly held customs. The communities prayed for each other and remembered each other's dead in their necrologies (lists of deceased brethren). The friendship links that existed between monasteries also facilitated the transmission of books and ideas. A good example is that of Reichenau and St. Emmeram in the eleventh century: their friendship links are evident in the appointment of the Reichenau monk Burchard as abbot of St. Emmeram in 1030, the transmission of works by Bern and Herman of Reichenau in St. Emmeram manuscripts, and the commissioning of Herman to write a festal office for the canonization of Wolfgang of Regensburg (d. 994) at St. Emmeram in 1052.[5]

The Gorze movement was superseded in the final quarter of the eleventh century by the reform associated with the Swabian monastery of Hirsau.[6] The central figure in this movement was Abbot William of Hirsau, a distinguished scholar and former monk of St. Emmeram.[7] In 1075 William travelled to Rome where he met Pope Gregory VII (1073–85). Gregory's enthusiasm for monastic reform—and particularly the reform associated with Cluny—had a lasting effect on William. Over the next few years William's contact with the Gregorian papacy and Cluny increased. In 1078, at the persuasion of Gregory's legate, Abbot Bernard of St. Victor in Marseilles, William introduced a modified version of Cluniac customs to Hirsau. Daughter houses were quickly established and became bases for the reform of other monasteries according to the customs of Hirsau. Although the Hirsau reform possessed a more defined structure than that of Gorze, it benefitted from and used the friendship networks that had been built up by the earlier reform.

The Hirsau movement in Germany became closely linked with the papal reform movement, which had begun in earnest in 1046 with the intervention of Henry III of Germany (r. 1039–56) in the politics of the Roman church.[8] The papal reformers were especially concerned to counter the corrupting influence of the secular world, an influence that in their eyes had gravely damaged the spiritual and temporal welfare of the church. Pope Gregory VII was especially impressed by the monastery of Cluny, which epitomized freedom from secular interference, and took advantage of his meeting with Abbot William to encourage him to emulate Cluny within the German kingdom. By the 1070s, however, the claims of the reform papacy, coupled with Gregory's interference in German politics, had brought it into conflict with King Henry IV (r. 1056–1106), who wished to preserve his traditional rights of control over the imperial church. The Hirsau reform network was vital to papal strategy in this conflict, which divided the church and people of the empire (the kingdoms of Germany, Italy, and Burgundy). The conflict resulted in the first pamphlet war of the Middle Ages, as papal and royalist partisans sought to justify their respective positions.[9] It also had special significance for Aribo who, as we shall see, seems to have been torn between loyalty to his patron, the royalist Bishop Ellenhard of Freising (1052–78), and his friendship with the staunch Gregorian William of Hirsau.[10]

Musical Context

Music was central to the medieval church's public worship: it was the essential medium of the Mass and the Divine Office (the daily round of prayer offered in monastic and secular foundations).[11] It is not surprising, therefore, that so important an activity should elicit a considerable body of theory, just as rhetoric (necessary for the art of writing) and astronomy (necessary for the calculation of the liturgical year) elicited their own theoretical corpuses.

The first steps towards codifying Western ecclesiastical music were taken by Carolingian scholars, who sought to explain how their liturgical music worked.[12] They had no theoretical vocabulary of their own and so looked to the past for the tools they needed. They looked primarily to Boethius (ca. 480–ca. 525), who they assumed was relevant to Gregorian chant. (Boethius had attempted in his *De institutione musica* to synthesize ancient Greek music theory for the Romans of his day, who could no longer read Greek.) Thus in his treatise *Musica disciplina*, Aurelian of Réôme (fl. 840–50) applied Boethius's mathematical proportions to the intervals and adopted the names of the ancient Greek *tonoi* (modes or modal patterns) for the eight medieval modes.[13] Aurelian's example was followed by his successors, who appropriated other theoretical concepts from *De institutione musica*.[14] Nevertheless, the process of analyzing and classifying Gregorian chant using a theoretical vocabulary derived from antiquity was not always successful. In the late tenth century an influential Italian theorist named Odo (frequently confused with Abbot Odo of Cluny) wrote of certain chants in which notes "contravened the rules by being too high or too low." He did not correct them "since universal usage unanimously defended them," but merely "marked them as unusual…in order that nobody enquiring into the truth of the rule might be in doubt."[15]

Abbot Bern of Reichenau, writing in the first third of the eleventh century, was heir to nearly two hundred years of Carolingian music theory. His *Prologus in tonarium*, a remarkable synthesis of Carolingian sources, took important steps towards a coherent understanding of how Gregorian chant worked. The importance of *Prologus in tonarium* is reflected in the wide dissemination it enjoyed in eleventh- and twelfth-century Germany.[16] Abbot Bern's work was continued and modified in important respects by his pupil Herman of Reichenau. Herman's theory then formed the basis for the treatises of William of Hirsau, Aribo, Frutolf of Michelsberg, and their contemporaries. This theory was concerned above all with music as the science of singing. It was concerned with singing the chant of the liturgy flawlessly, an important point since perfection in prayer through music was the only portal through which mortals could approach the ineffable mystery of the divine. But it was also concerned with teaching an understanding of music, so that errors in chants could be corrected and new chants written in a proper manner. Frutolf of Michelsberg commented in his *Breviarium de musica* that music "is the science of singing well through long reflection and constant practice." "To sing well," he further elaborated, was to "use the modes and intervals correctly through legitimate movement, to form correct chants through appropriate singing and, after proper ascent and descent, to bring them to an appropriate end."[17]

The practical orientation of south German music theory was shaped by the Gorze reform. When Bern was appointed abbot of Reichenau in 1008 by Emperor Henry II, he was appointed to restart the reform that had begun in the last quarter of the tenth century, but that had faltered at the beginning of the eleventh.[18] Coming as he did from the Gorze tradition of monasticism—which stressed the equivalence of strenuous liturgy and good monastic discipline—Abbot Bern was concerned with the practical aspects of reform in his monastery. This concern is reflected in all of his scholarly works, which focus exclusively on the liturgy and music. Similarly, Bern's pupil Herman of Reichenau composed all his works to serve the needs of monastic life.[19] This practicality is a consistent feature of the south German treatises, including Aribo's *De musica*.

Figure 1. The ancient Greek *systema teleion* and the south German gamut

Ancient Greek Greater Perfect System		Ancient Greek Lesser Perfect System		South-German gamut		
nete hyperboleon				$^{a}_{a}$		
paranete hyperboleon	*hyperboleon*			g		
trite hyperboleon				f	*excellentes*	
nete diezeugmenon				e		
paranete diezeugmenon		nete synemmenon		d		d
trite diezeugmenon	*diezeugmenon*	paranete synemmenon	*synemmenon*	c	*superiores*	c
paramese		trite synemmenon		b		♭
mese		mese		a		a (*synemmenon* tetrachord)
lichanos meson	*meson*	lichanos meson	*meson*	G		
parhypate meson		parhypate meson		F	*finales*	
hypate meson		hypate meson		E		
lichanos hypaton		lichanos hypaton		D		
parhypate hypaton	*hypaton*	parhypate hypaton	*hypaton*	C		
hypate hypaton		hypate hypaton		B	*graves*	
proslambanomenos		proslambanomenos		A		
				Γ		

The South German Musical System

It is necessary here to provide a brief description of the musical system used by Aribo and his contemporaries. The range of notes in use was essentially two octaves: the first series of seven pitches (.A.–.G.) being repeated at the higher octave (.a.–.g.). From the late tenth century gamma (.Γ.) was added at the bottom and another pitch, which was an octave higher than .a. was added at the top.[20] This note was usually written in manuscripts as $.^{a}_{a}.$, in order to avoid confusion with the note an octave below. The Italian theorist Guido of Arezzo also used the notes $.^{b}_{b}.$, $.^{c}_{c}.$, and $.^{d}_{d}.$ above $.^{a}_{a}.$, which he called the *superacutae* (literally "above the high notes"), but this practice was not consistently adopted by eleventh-century German theorists. This system became known as the gamut of notes, a name deriving from the combination of gamma and ut. Guido of Arezzo and others used gamma as the starting point of the hexachord .Γ.A.B.C.D.E. In Guido's famous mnemonic solmization system built around the hymn "Ut queant laxis,"[21] each note of this hexachord could be given the solmization syllable *ut, re, mi, fa, sol, la,* respectively. Thus the lowest note of the note system could be known as gamma or ut, and this eventually led to the contraction "gamut." The gamut was laid out as follows:

Figure 2. The gamut

.Γ. .A. .B. .C. .D. .E. .F. .G. .a. .b. .c. .d. .e. .f. .g. .$\genfrac{}{}{0pt}{}{a}{a}$.

German theorists understood the octave (.A.–.G.) as a set of two tetrachords, which were conjunct around the note .D. (that is, .D. was the fourth note of the first tetrachord, .A.B.C.D., and first note of the second tetrachord, .D.E.F.G.). This arrangement was repeated at the higher octave, .a.–.g. These tetrachords were called the tetrachords of the *graves, finales, superiores,* and *excellentes.*

Figure 3. The tetrachords of the *graves, finales, superiores,* and *excellentes*

finales *excellentes*

.Γ. .A. .B. .C. .D. .E. .F. .G. .a. .b. .c. .d. .e. .f. .g. .$\genfrac{}{}{0pt}{}{a}{a}$.

graves *superiores*

This system is very neatly laid out because each of the tetrachords has the interval form tone-semitone-tone. The tetrachords are thus symmetrical in their ascent (*intensio*) and descent (*remissio*): singing from .D. to .G. involves singing the intervals of tone, semitone, and tone, as does singing from .G. to .D. This scheme for the tetrachords held obvious advantages over an older scheme that was frequently given in Carolingian sources. The older tetrachords, which are also mentioned by Herman of Reichenau and Aribo, were conjunct around the notes .E. and .e.[22] Unlike the eleventh-century tetrachords, the older ones were not symmetrical in form and thus were of limited usefulness for singing.

The species of *diatessaron* (the melodic interval of a fourth), *diapente* (the melodic interval of a fifth), and *diapason* (the melodic interval of an octave) were also part of the system. The species were types of fourth, fifth, and octave. The different types or species refer to the different interval forms that these melodic intervals could have depending on where they occurred in the gamut. To sing from .A. to .D. (the first species of *diatessaron*) involves singing the intervals of tone, semitone, and tone; to sing from .B. to .E. (the second species of *diatessaron*) involves singing the intervals of semitone, tone, and tone. The standard eleventh-century practice, which was worked out by Herman of Reichenau, was that there were four species of *diatessaron*, four species of *diapente*, and eight species of *diapason*. The species of *diatessaron* and *diapente* are as follows:

Figure 4. The species of *diatessaron*

First species	.A.	.B.	.C.	.D.				*tone-semitone-tone*
Second species		.B.	.C.	.D.	.E.			*semitone-tone-tone*
Third species			.C.	.D.	.E.	.F		*tone-tone-semitone*
Fourth species				.D.	.E.	.F.	.G.	*tone-semitone-tone*

Figure 5. The species of *diapente*

First species	.D.	.E.	.F.	.G.	.a.				*tone-semitone-tone-tone*
Second species		.E.	.F.	.G.	.a.	.b.			*semitone-tone-tone-tone*
Third species			.F.	.G.	.a.	.b.	.c.		*tone-tone-tone-semitone*
Fourth species				.G.	.a.	.b.	.c.	.d.	*tone-tone-semitone-tone*

The beauty of this system is that the species of *diatessaron* and *diapente* combine to form the species of *diapason*.

Figure 6. The species of *diapason*

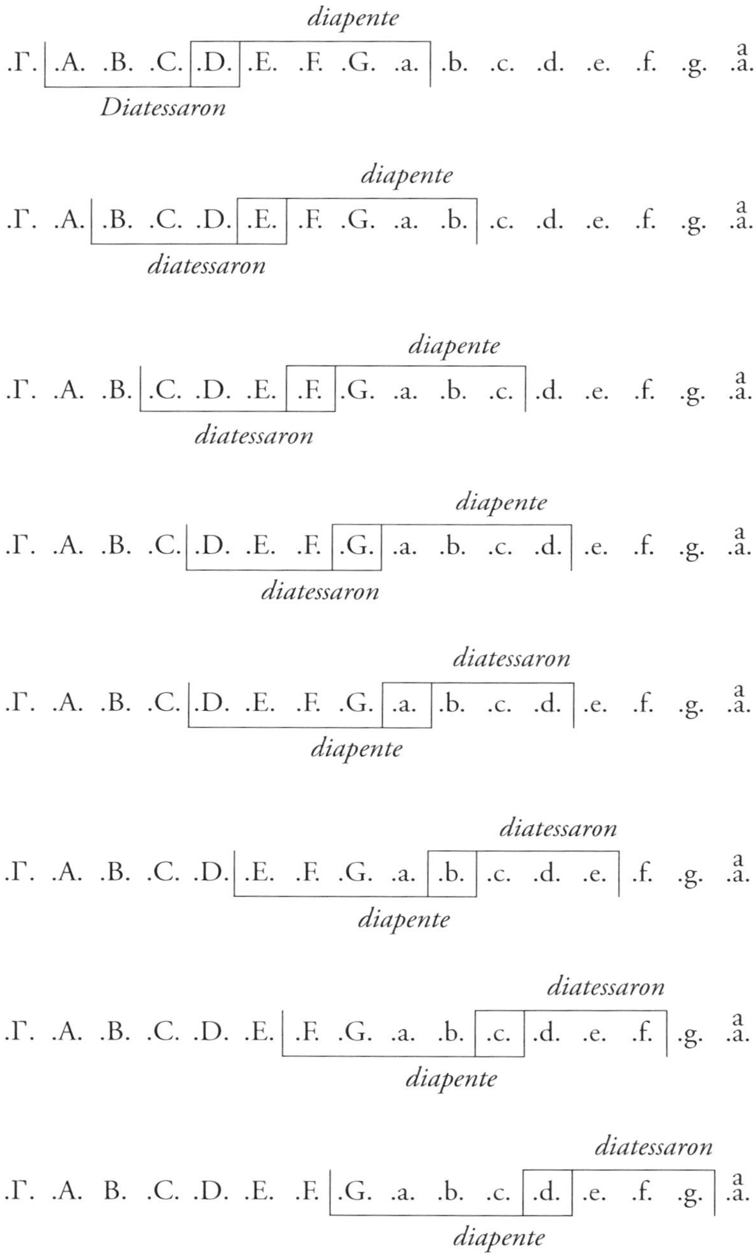

The German theorists were not interested in the species merely because they formed a pleasing symmetrical pattern; the real utility of the species was that they formed the modes. The modes were of central importance to the theorists because the whole repertory of Gregorian chant was classified by mode. According to Aribo and his contemporaries, there were four modes, and they used the Latin terms *modus* or *tropus* to refer to them. The final notes or keynotes of these four modes were, respectively, the notes .D., .E., .F., and .G. The theorists called these four keynotes *protus* (literally, "in the first position"), *deuterus* ("in the second position"), *tritus* ("in the third position"), and *tetrardus* ("in the fourth position").[23] Each of the four modes could be subdivided with reference to high and low ambit, or range, into two "tones." The higher version of a given mode occupied the ambit of an octave above the mode's final (or keynote) and was called authentic; the lower version occupied the octave ambit extending from a fourth below the final to a fifth above it and was called plagal. There were, therefore, four modes and eight tones. To give an example: in the mode with the final .D. (*protus*), the authentic version (or first tone) runs from .D. to .d.; the plagal version (or second tone) from the .A. to .a. The German theorists used the Latin term *tonus* to describe these octaves, and they identified the eight tones with different systems of nomenclature. Sometimes they referred to them ordinally (first to eighth), sometimes descriptively (as authentic *protus*, plagal *tritus*, and so forth), and sometimes with the Latinized forms of the old Greek names *dorius*, *frigius*, *lidius*, and *mixolidius* to indicate authentic *protus*, *deuterus*, *tritus*, and *tetrardus*, respectively, adding the prefix *hypo-* to indicate the appropriate plagal versions. Thus the system of modes was laid out as follows:

Figure 7. The nomenclature of the modes

Ordinal name	*Descriptive name*	*Greek name*	*Range*	*Final*
The first tone	Authentic *protus*	Dorian	.D.–.d.	.D.
The second tone	Plagal *protus*	Hypodorian	.A.–.a.	.D.
The third tone	Authentic *deuterus*	Phrygian	.E.–.e.	.E.
The fourth tone	Plagal *deuterus*	Hypophrygian	.B.–.b.	.E.
The fifth tone	Authentic *tritus*	Lydian	.F.–.f.	.F.
The sixth tone	Plagal *tritus*	Hypolydian	.C.–.c.	.F.
The seventh tone	Authentic *tetrardus*	Mixolydian	.G.–.g.	.G.
The eighth tone	Plagal *tetrardus*	Hypomixolydian	.D.–.d.	.G.

At this point it is worthwhile to return to the species. As we have seen, the species of *diatessaron* and *diapente* combine to form the species of *diapason*. The order in which they are combined affects the resulting octave: if, for example, in combining the first species of *diatessaron* and *diapente* the *diatessaron* comes first, then the resulting octave will be .A.–.a.; if, however, the *diapente* comes first, then the resulting octave will be .D.–.d. From this it will be seen that the eight species of *diapason* that result from the varying combination of the species of *diatessaron* and *diapente* are none other than the eight tones. A tone, therefore, is just a species of octave that differs from the other tones in the form of its intervals.

There is one final appendage to this system. The south German theorists frequently speak of a tetrachord named *synemmenon*. This Greek word means "conjunct" and the tetrachord consists of .a.♭.c.d. In certain tones, particularly in authentic *protus* and in *tritus*, the theorists encountered many melodies with the pitch .♭. The interpolation of the *synemmenon* tetrachord instead of the usual *superiores* tetrachord allowed these melodies to be incorporated within the system.

The Author

Our knowledge of Aribo must largely be inferred from the internal evidence of his treatise and the manuscripts in which it circulates.[24] Aribo dedicated *De musica* to Ellenhard, bishop of Freising from 1052 to 1078. In the letter of dedication that precedes *De musica*, Aribo describes Ellenhard as "his lord . . . the most worthy of bishops" (Domno suo Ellenhardo presulum dignissimo). A little later on he praises Ellenhard's musical abilities, commenting on "the diligence observed in your singing" (ut cantilenarum uestrarum obseruata diligentia affatim uobis perhibent testimonia), which is probably a reference to the singing at the cathedral in Freising. One of the two surviving full recensions of *De musica*—copied during the twelfth century at the monastery of Admont—describes Aribo as *scholasticus*, that is, schoolmaster (Incipit musica Aribonis scholastici).[25] Taken together, these three references not only imply that Aribo was a member of the cathedral chapter at Freising but that he was schoolmaster at the cathedral school. This interpretation is supported by the evidence of *De scriptoribus ecclesiasticis*, an encyclopedia of Christian writers from antiquity to the twelfth century.[26] Its author—possibly Wolfger of Prüfening, fl. 1130–73—was well informed and had collected materials on his travels throughout southern Germany. He was particularly interested in music, for he wrote biographies of many members of the south German circle, including Aribo. It is evident that he had read *De musica* carefully, because he quoted accurately from it in his biography of Aribo. He also gave Aribo the epithet "Cirinus" (a name that had belonged to another Aribo who was bishop of Freising in the eighth century) and ended by quoting a couplet not found in any of the surviving manuscripts of *De musica*:

> Therefore, he offered this treatise to his bishop, to whom he wrote it, as he says:
>
> Aribo the musician has composed this treatise,
> And given it as a gift to his own bishop.
>
> (Hunc itaque tractatum pontifici suo obtulit, cui et scribit, sicut ait:
> Aribo tractatum depinxit musicus istum,
> Atque dedit dono pontifici proprio.)[27]

The author, therefore, identifies Aribo beyond doubt as a subject of the bishop of Freising. Furthermore, the couplet he quoted is stylistically consistent with other couplets from *De musica*.[28] This, combined with the dedicatory purpose of *De musica*, suggests that the author of *De scriptoribus ecclesiasticis* may well have seen the copy of *De musica* that Aribo presented to Ellenhard. It was certainly not unusual for dedicatory copies of works to contain decoration and verses not present in other copies: the presentation copy of Donizo of Canossa's *Vita* of Countess Matilda of Tuscany (1046–1115) contains panegyrical verses not found in other manuscripts.[29]

If Aribo was a canon of Freising, there is good evidence to suggest that he did not remain so all his life. The call of the reformers persuaded many cathedral clergy to enter monasteries in an attempt to escape from the corrupting effects of the secular world. Instances of a simoniac bishop or a contested episcopal election in which an anti-reforming candidate was imposed upon a reform-minded chapter often led to division, resignations by chapter members, and their subsequent flight to monasteries loyal to the papacy and church reform. Examples of this phenomenon are provided by Bernold, canon of Constance, who retired to the monastery of St. Blasien deep in the Black Forest, and Master Henry, *scholasticus* of Augsburg, who in 1077 fled to the monastery of St. Magnus at Füssen after Henry IV imposed one of his royal chaplains, Siegfried, upon a chapter that had already elected a reforming candidate.[30]

What little evidence survives about Ellenhard of Freising suggests that he was a royalist and familiar of King Henry IV.[31] One narrative account, from the hostile chronicle of Benediktbeuern, accuses him of tyranny, familiarity with the king, and unlawful deposition of the abbot in favor of his own candidate.[32] The chronicler's hostility is explained by Benediktbeuern's recent change in status: in 1065 Archbishop Adalbert of Hamburg-Bremen, exploiting the king's minority and seeking to win political friends, had reduced it from an imperial monastery to a proprietary monastery of the bishop of Freising. Ellenhard's status as a supporter of Henry IV is confirmed by the administrative sources: royal diplomas show that he served the king faithfully in the years leading up to the Council of Worms in 1076, when Henry IV called for the abdication of Pope Gregory VII.[33]

Aribo's inclinations, however, seem to have been towards reform. This can be deduced from his references to Abbot William of Hirsau. Aribo and William corresponded over the question of organ-pipe measurements; indeed, *De musica* contains a set of measurements that William "communicated" to Aribo (quam mecum communicauit). Aribo describes William as "the greatest among musicians, without doubt the Orpheus and Pythagoras of the moderns," but—more importantly—he tells us that William has loved him "beyond any worthiness that my poverty may possess."[34] This self-effacing remark is characteristic of the close friendships based upon shared membership of monastic communities that became increasingly evident in the aftermath of eleventh-century monastic reforms.[35]

Aribo's relationship with William of Hirsau helps with the interpretation of another, seemingly cryptic, comment in *De musica*. When introducing William's organ-pipe measurements Aribo says that William, "formerly a monk of St. Emmeram in Regensburg," was "now venerable abbot elsewhere" (Domnus Willihelmus prius Emmerammensis Ratisponę monachus, nunc autem alibi abbas uenerandus).[36] This comment raises the following question: if Aribo knew William so well, why was he so reticent to say that William was abbot of Hirsau? There was a delay of over a year from the time William was named abbot of Hirsau (1069) to the time when he received abbatial benediction (Ascensiontide 1071). This, however, was probably not the reason for Aribo's vagueness: it is more likely that Aribo was being discreet in his reference to Hirsau, perhaps to avoid aggravating Ellenhard of Freising. A further possible suggestion is that Aribo—in a move that paralleled the cases of Bernold of St. Blasien and Henry of Augsburg—had left Freising for Hirsau. If this is so, then the words "now venerable abbot elsewhere" were also intended rhetorically: they are a seemingly vague and deliberately humble reference to Aribo's presence at Hirsau. They are of the same character as the words "one of us" (quidam de nostris), which the imperial chaplain Wipo repeatedly used to describe himself in his biography of Henry IV's grandfather, Emperor Conrad II, or the description "a certain work" (scriptum cuiusdam), which Bernold of St. Blasien used in his chronicle to refer to one of his own treatises.[37]

Three additional pieces of circumstantial evidence support this interpretation. First, the thirteenth-century abbot and music theorist Engelbert of Admont describes Aribo as *scolasticus aurelianensis*, which literally means "school master of Orléans."[38] This is an obvious mistake, as there is nothing French either about the name Aribo or his treatise. It is more likely that the identification stems from a scribal corruption of Aurelius, the patron saint of Hirsau and a frequently used synonym for the monastery in eleventh-century sources.[39] The description *scolasticus* could well derive from the Admont copy of *De musica*, which Engelbert probably used.[40] But he must also have had access to another source, no longer extant, that connected Aribo with Hirsau. Second, three manuscripts that are very close to the earliest tradition of *De musica* are from monasteries associated with the Hirsau reform: the full copies from Admont (reformed from the Hirsau daughter-house of St. Georgen in 1115) and St. Peter's in Salzburg (reformed from Admont in 1116), and the excerpted version from SS. Ulrich and Afra in Augsburg (reformed from St. Georgen in 1109).[41] Finally, the eleventh-century necrology from the cathedral in Freising records the death of an "Aribo pr[es]b[ite]r et fr[ater]," which implies someone who was both priest and monk.[42] As it was customary to remember former community members in necrologies, it is tempting to suggest that this is a reference to the author of *De musica*.

This interpretation of Aribo's career cannot be proven conclusively. Nevertheless, the balance of the evidence, coupled with what is known of Aribo's religious and social context, suggests it as a plausible hypothesis. As I have argued elsewhere, Aribo seems to have been torn between his personal loyalty to Ellenhard of Freising and his spiritual commitment to reform.[43] *De musica* would not have been dedicated to Ellenhard had Aribo seen him as objectionable. Yet Aribo's bond to one of the foremost Gregorians in southern Germany, coupled with the reference to Hirsau's patron St. Aurelius, the manuscript tradition of *De musica*, and the Freising necrology points to a link with the Hirsau reform.

Dating

The terminus ante quem of *De musica* is 1078, the year its dedicatee, Ellenhard of Freising, died. The terminus post quem is fixed by Aribo's reference to William of Hirsau: William was named abbot by Count Adalbert II of Calw, the proprietary overlord of Hirsau, in 1069. Yet William only received abbatial benediction at Ascensiontide 1071. The reason for the delay is uncertain, but may owe something to reservations about Adalbert's deposition of Abbot Frederick, who seems to have been removed for being too contemplative rather than for any spiritual or moral faults. It is possible to interpret

Aribo's phrase "now venerable abbot elsewhere" as a discreet reference to the time between 1069 and 1071, when William had not yet taken up his abbatial duties. I have already suggested, however, that this might actually be a reference to the time when Aribo was writing as a monk of Hirsau, after having left Freising: he was referring to his own monastery in a humble manner entirely consistent with contemporary writing practice. *De musica*, therefore, would belong to the period 1071–78.

The Structure and Content of *De musica*

De musica is a lengthy and sophisticated treatise that in its two full manuscript copies occupies some thirty folios. Its structure is somewhat unique among the south German treatises: it has many short chapters whereas most of the others have fewer, longer chapters. All of the chapters, 102 in total, are provided with headings, which can confidently be assumed to be Aribo's. A short letter of dedication addressed to Ellenhard of Freising prefaces the treatise.

In beginning *De musica* with a letter of dedication, Aribo was following well-established convention, which routinely saw the casting of scholarly works in letter form. The influential papal reformer Peter Damian (d. 1072), whose works were widely admired and imitated in Germany, had popularized this practice.[44] Aribo's illustrious predecessor, Abbot Bern of Reichenau, had written his own scholarly works on liturgy and music in letter form: his first, short, music treatise (the *Epistola de tonis*) was addressed to the teachers in the monastic school at Reichenau, while his longer *Prologus in tonarium* and accompanying *Tonarius* were addressed as a letter to Archbishop Pilgrim of Cologne (1021–36).[45] Similarly, the theologian Bernard of Hildesheim (formerly master of the cathedral school at Constance) addressed his *Liber canonum* to Archbishop Hartwig of Magdeburg (1079–1102).[46]

In the dedicatory letter Aribo addresses Ellenhard as his lord, and shortly afterwards—in the first chapter—alludes to the excellence of the singing at the cathedral of Freising. This is a strong indication that Aribo was at one time a member of the cathedral chapter, complementing the evidence of the twelfth-century Admont codex and the author of *De scriptoribus ecclesiasticis*.[47] The dedicatory letter is also notable for its extensive use of the *colores rhetorici* that were beloved of eleventh-century German clerks in the salutations and conclusions of their works.[48]

The first theme of *De musica*—and according to Aribo its principal theme—is a diagram of the monochord called the "quadripartite figure of the moderns" (quadripartita modernorum figura). According to Aribo this diagram purports to show the workings of the monochord; however, he exposes its flaws and in its place offers his own alternative, which he calls "Aribo's goat" or "roe" (caprea Aribonis). Aribo devotes Chapters 2–15 to this subject and returns to it in chapter 102, the final chapter of *De musica*. The treatise in fact ends with the decisive statement: "By no means does nature speak of one thing and my caprea of another" (Numquam aliud natura, aliud mea caprea dicit).[49] Aribo envisages Ellenhard as a judge in the contest between the quadripartite figure and *caprea*. Significantly, he uses the recondite word *palemon*—which in both full recensions is glossed "id est iudex" (that is, a judge)—to describe the role he wishes Ellenhard to play. Aribo must have expected Ellenhard to understand this learned reference to Virgil's *Eclogues*, in which the shepherd Palemon judges the singing contest between Dameta and Menalca.[50] Like Palemon, Bishop Ellenhard was the shepherd of his flock.

Aribo's discussion of the quadripartite figure and his *caprea* reveals the importance of the monochord to his contemporaries. The monochord—a single-stringed instrument with movable bridge—was used to pick out and verify melodies.[51] It was a laborious process, and one that so infuriated the famous eleventh-century Italian theorist Guido of Arezzo that he sought to popularize a method of sight singing, which would eventually evolve into the notation system of Western music.[52] Nevertheless, the monochord was seen as a physical manifestation of the harmonies and proportions that regulated music. For this reason it was important and, consequently, Bern of Reichenau, Herman of Reichenau, William of Hirsau, Frutolf of Michelsberg, and Theoger of Metz each began his music treatise with a discussion of the monochord. Aribo, although introducing an element of originality through the quadripartite figure and *caprea*, was nevertheless following his contemporaries. He tells us that in his day there were very few monochords without the quadripartite figure, probably an indication that it was often drawn on monochords as an aid. After finishing with his discussion of the quadripartite figure and his own *caprea*, he describes the range of the monochord in chapters 16 and 17: the monochord should have a range of two octaves, one being too restrictive and three being impossible because the sounds produced in the highest octave would be unintelligible. In chapter 18 Aribo prescribes that the two octaves of the monochord are to be divided into a series of four-note groups. These four tetrachords (.A.B.C.D., .D.E.F.G., .a.b.c.d., and .d.e.f.g., or the *graves*, *finales*, *superiores*, and *excellentes*) had been the basis of the musical system in Germany since Herman of Reichenau had codified them around the middle of the eleventh century.[53] They were chosen because they were symmetrical and allowed for the self-evident musical phenomenon of octave repetition.

From this point Aribo moves away from the monochord, only occasionally returning to it again (chaps. 21 and 61). He next discusses the tetrachords and the species of fourth, fifth, and octave (*diatessaron*, *diapente*, and *diapason*), which work together to constitute the modes. There is not always a clear order to the topics he discusses, with many of the individual topics seeming to arise as he thought of them. This part of *De musica* continues until chapter 61. Among its noteworthy features is the set of diagrams that Aribo devised to illustrate the overlap of the authentic and plagal modes or, as he analogized them, the male and female choirs (continuing the metaphor of authoritative and subjugate or master and servant popular among his contemporaries). He also compares the tetrachords to aspects of Christ: the tetrachord of the *graves* represents Christ's humanity, that of the *finales* his passion and death, the *superiores* his resurrection, and the *excellentes* his ascension. In Aribo's mind the progression from the lowest of the tetrachords (the *graves*) to the highest (the *excellentes*) parallels God's return to divinity from the baseness of human form. But we should not make the mistake here of believing that Aribo was engaging in "speculative" theory. His theory, like that of his German contemporaries, was rigorously practical. Music was the science of singing correctly, and the things he discussed—the tetrachords, species, and modes—were the things he and his contemporaries found useful for understanding music. His erudite analogies were designed both to illustrate practical concepts and, like the earlier allusion to Palemon, to please the intellect of his dedicatee.

Chapters 62–77 are devoted to the modes and represent a culmination of the previous subject matter. Aribo explains that in antiquity there were only four modes, but that each of these had been since divided in two, producing eight tones. He is particularly anxious to show that certain modes have both authentic and plagal properties. In particular, the notes .D. and .d. can be authentic or plagal because they are "double functioned" (.D. is simultaneously the fourth of the *graves* and the first of the *finales*, while .d. an octave above is the fourth of the *superiores* and the first of the *excellentes*). This was a point of particular importance for German theorists: William of Hirsau had stressed it in his treatise and criticized Guido of Arezzo with some severity for ignoring the double nature of these notes.[54] In order to prove the point, Aribo—also aware of Guido's position—turned to the resources of the *ars logica* and exploited the powerful weapon of dialectic. A number of chapters teem with the language of dialectic: Aribo speaks of being constrained in argument by an opponent, of proofs, maximal propositions, and predication. He drew this language from the textbooks of the *ars logica* he would have known from his duties as *scholasticus*: Porphyry's *Isagoge* (in Boethius's translation), as well as Boethius's *Commentarius in topica Ciceronis*, *De differentiis topicis*, and *De divisione*.[55]

Aribo devotes chapters 78–86 to measurement. Directions for measuring the monochord, organ pipes, and bells are a recurring feature of contemporary music theory manuscripts.[56] These directions were generally not concerned with the physical manufacture of instruments but were designed to show the mathematical processes of their tuning. They gave relative and not absolute measurements. There were many different methods of arriving at the correct measurements, and Aribo provides a number of these. He gives one for bells, which he describes as a "simple" method that can also be applied to the monochord. He also provides an alternative monochord measurement and three for organ pipes: an "old" method, the method favored by his colleague William of Hirsau, and his own, which he coyly describes as "little Aribo's method."

Chapters 87 and 88 are the two chapters of *De musica* in which Aribo addresses the wider issues of music, its value, and being a musician. In chapter 87 he contrasts the instinctive or untrained musician (*naturalis*) with the trained or skilled one (*artificialis*). This distinction owed its origin to Boethius, for whom the intellectual who understood harmonics was of greater value than the mere practitioner. It was subtly modified by Herman of Reichenau, who defined the skilled musician as the person who knows how to compose chants correctly, to judge them by rule, and to perform them fittingly.[57] Chapter 88—"Concerning the moral art of music"—continues this theme. The benefits of music are evident to all, even to those who have no training in it, just as morality is present in people, even though they may be uneducated and ignorant of it. But the educated perceive the different aspects of music just as they do of morality. They know, for example, that the tritone (the augmented fourth between .F. and .b.) is an abomination to be avoided, a point that Aribo expresses with an allusion to the futile singing efforts of Corydon from Virgil's *Eclogues*.[58]

The final part of *De musica* (chapters 89–101) sees Aribo turn to melody. This represents an application of the theory of tetrachords, species, and modes that occupies much of the preceding part of the treatise. The lengthy chapter 89—the longest chapter in *De musica*—discusses in detail the theory of melody put forward by Guido of Arezzo in the fifteenth chapter of his *Micrologus*. Guido's works of music theory were extremely popular and highly influential. They had reached Germany by Herman of Reichenau's time, but were not received uncritically there; German theorists, who had continued and developed the theoretical tradition of their Carolingian predecessors, viewed Guido through the critical lens of their own theory.[59] This is the context of Aribo's commentary on Guido in chapter 89. In chapters 90–93 Aribo continues his discussion of certain melodic categories derived from Guido.

For these chapters he relied upon a work known today as *Commentarius anonymus in Micrologum Guidonis Aretini*.[60] This treatise seems to have begun life as a set of glosses on *Micrologus* that was subsequently developed into a continuous commentary.[61] It was probably produced in the third quarter of the eleventh century and is another example of how German clerks interpreted Guido according to their own theoretical tradition. Chapters 94–101 of *De musica* see Aribo discuss melody from the perspective of the "consonances" (or intervals) and species, emphasizing the modal implications of the varieties of *diatessaron* and *diapente*.

Chapter 102 is a recapitulation. It is entitled "Concerning the repetition of *caprea*'s commendation" (De caprea repeticio commendationis) and returns to the theme of the suitability of *caprea* as a diagram for understanding the monochord and, consequently, the whole musical system. In this recapitulation Aribo again indulges in extensive use of the *colores rhetorici*, thus following the practice of his German contemporaries, who routinely laced the introductions and conclusions of their works with extravagant rhetorical devices. His practice in this regard points to the need for studying music treatises of the time within the broader context of contemporary intellectual and compositional practices.

Aribo's *Sententiae*

Chapter 102 is the concluding chapter of *De musica*. Nevertheless, in both of the full manuscript copies, as well as one of the fragmentary copies, chapter 102 is followed by two extra chapters, which have long puzzled modern scholars. The two extra chapters discuss Guido of Arezzo's teaching on types of melodic movement, a theme that Aribo had already discussed in chapter 89 of *De musica*. Joseph Smits van Waesberghe, who published the first modern edition of *De musica* in 1951, saw these chapters as the result of an argument between Aribo and the author of *Commentarius anonymus in Micrologum Guidonis Aretini*.[62] Chapter 89, in Smits van Waesberghe's view, caused the argument and the extra chapters represented Aribo's revised opinion.

Smits van Waesberghe's unwieldy argument remains unconvincing.[63] Although he perceived a change in Aribo's position between chapter 89 and the extra chapters, study of what Aribo actually wrote shows no such conflict: chapter 89 and the extra chapters are concerned with different aspects of Guido's melodic theory.[64] There were, therefore, no grounds for an argument between Aribo and the author of the commentary. Important internal evidence from *De musica*, overlooked by Smits van Waesberghe, makes the supposed argument not only unnecessary but also highly improbable. The text of *De musica* from the final section of chapter 89 until the end of chapter

93 (excepting the heading for chapter 92), as well as for most of the first extra chapter, is taken directly from the anonymous commentary.[65] Aribo, therefore, had access to the commentary while he was writing *De musica*. The evidence implies that he simply used the commentary as a source, not that he was engaged in a hypothetical debate with the anonymous author.

The two extra chapters are what historians classify as *sententiae*. *Sententiae*, or "sentences," are short teaching texts that take a saying (*sententia*) from an authority (*auctor*) and discuss its meaning. They were frequently used in theological scholarship, as the surviving sentence collections from the late eleventh- and early twelfth-century school of Laon demonstrate.[66] It is no surprise that a schoolmaster such as Aribo should also use this early scholastic technique for music. Indeed, the headings in the manuscripts from Admont and St. Peter's in Salzburg describe the chapters as *sententiae*.[67]

Aribo probably added the two *sententiae* to *De musica* in response to comments from a colleague who had read the treatise. One piece of evidence suggests that this could well have been Bishop Ellenhard himself. Most of *sententia* 1 is quoted from the anonymous commentary on Guido's *Micrologus*. Towards the end of the *sententia*, however, Aribo's own pen returns with the words "Quod nobis inuidet commodum detestabilis intercapedo locorum" ("That which is detestable to us grudges a convenient place of pause"—a phrase employing the literary device of *cursus planus* that is unmistakably Aribonian). The next line is a short quotation from *Micrologus* 17 (Aribo is no longer depending on the commentary at this stage), which is followed by the words "You ought to recall, my most dear lord, what the venerable Guido has said" (Recordari debetis, domine mihi dilectissime uenerabilem Guidonem dixisse).[68] The comment "my most dear lord" can only have been addressed to Aribo's lord, Ellenhard of Freising, and suggests that that *sententiae* were provided in response to questions that Ellenhard himself had asked.

This point also has important implications for our understanding of the writing process of *De musica*. It implies that Aribo worked on a preliminary version of the treatise to which he later added the *sententiae*. The *sententiae* were probably included in the dedicatory copy presented to Ellenhard of Freising. We can thus be confident that the form of the treatise transmitted by the two full recensions is its definitive form.

Sources

The primary musical influence on Aribo was the theoretical tradition of his eleventh-century German counterparts.[69] This tradition owed its origins to Abbot Bern of Reichenau who in his *Prologus in tonarium* and *Tonarius* had attempted to codify the Carolingian theory known to him. Bern's efforts were continued by his brilliant pupil Herman of Reichenau, who modified his teacher's arrangement of the species in order to make the tetrachords, species, and modes work together in one neatly-ordered system. One result of this was the addition of short commentaries and glosses to Bern's *Prologus in tonarium*, as scribes sought to update him in light of Herman's modifications. This soon led to an interpolated version of Bern's treatise.[70]

De musica shows that Aribo fully understood and practiced this theory. His discussion of the quadripartite figure at the beginning of *De musica* parallels the discussions of the monochord with which Bern, Herman, and William of Hirsau opened their treatises, albeit in a very individual way. Yet Aribo's direct textual indebtedness to Bern and Herman is minimal: there are no direct quotations from either author, and only in chapters 51 and 56—which discuss the species of *diatessaron* and *diapente*—is it possible to perceive the explicit influence of Herman.

William of Hirsau was an important influence on Aribo. William wrote his music treatise before 1069, while he was still a monk of St. Emmeram in Regensburg; it was here that he built up his reputation as a formidable scholar.[71] As Aribo tells us, he was William's correspondent and friend: one of the organ-pipe measurements he gives was communicated to him by William. In addition, Aribo's stress on the double function of the notes .D. and .d. was probably inspired by William's *Musica*.[72] William devoted a number of chapters to this point, in which he expressly criticized Boethius and Guido of Arezzo for failing to notice this point.[73] Although it is likely that Aribo knew William's treatise, as he probably knew Bern's and Herman's, he did not work passages of it into *De musica*. His own discussion of the double function of .D. and .d. took William's arguments in a new direction, using the sophisticated tool of dialectic to bolster the empirical proofs of his colleague.[74]

William of Hirsau features in a less obvious way through Aribo's presentation of the quadripartite figure. Among the early manuscripts of *De musica*, only one gives a diagram of the quadripartite figure: Darmstadt, Universitäts- und Hochschulbibliothek, Cod. 1988, fol. 171r. Besides this, the only surviving contemporary reference to the quadripartite figure is in an early twelfth-century manuscript from Benediktbeuern: Munich, Bayerische Staatsbibliothek, Clm 4622, fol. 178v, which describes the steps to be taken in measuring the quadripartite figure but gives no diagram.[75] This source attributes the figure to a monk named Otker: "a certain monk of Regensburg, Otker by name, devised this quadripartite measurement and named it the paradigm of the modes (theorema troporum), which we can call the riddle of the monochord (cribrum monochordi)."[76] The Benediktbeuern manuscript appears to have been copied after the publication of Aribo's *De musica*, because on fol. 178v it also transmits a set of measurement directions "according to Aribo." (That attribution, however, is false because two other manuscripts, one earlier and one contemporary, contain this text without attribution to Aribo.[77]) Clm 4622, therefore, is of limited usefulness for determining the origins of the quadripartite figure.

A diagram that does fit the description of the quadripartite figure, however, is found in William of Hirsau's *Musica*. William first calls it "the figure of the monochord" (*figura monochordi*) but later refers to it as the "riddle of the monochord" (*cribrum monochordi*) and the "paradigm of the modes" (*theorema troporum*), words identical to the description of the quadripartite figure in Clm 4622.[78] Whether William or Otker was the figure's inventor cannot be known, but it is probable that Aribo knew it from William's *Musica*. This explains why Aribo refers to it only as the quadripartite figure and never in the terms William used—Aribo was conscious that he was finding fault with the work of a renowned scholar who was also his friend. Any mentions of William or of the origins of the diagram are carefully avoided: Aribo merely says that he has encountered it on many monochords. His evasion parallels that of Herman of Reichenau, who referred to Abbot Bern as "that theorist" when he exposed the flaws in Bern's arrangement of the species.[79] Herman was disagreeing with his abbot, a thing he could have done neither lightly nor publicly in view of the teaching of the Rule of St. Benedict on obedience and humility. If William was now Aribo's abbot at Hirsau, then the requirements of the Rule would have made Aribo even more circumspect about connecting the quadripartite figure with William.

Figure 8. William of Hirsau's *cribrum monochordi* (Vienna, Österreichische Nationalbibliothek, Cod. 51, fol. 1v)

Domni Willehelmi abbatis monochordum

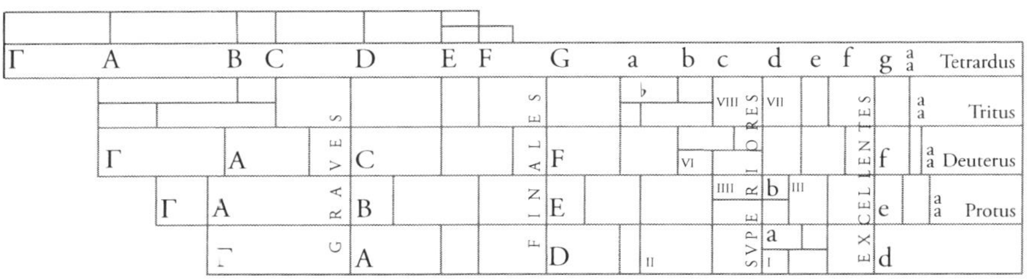

Figure 9. The quadripartite figure (Darmstadt, Universitäts- und Hochschulbibliothek, Cod. 1988, fol. 171r)

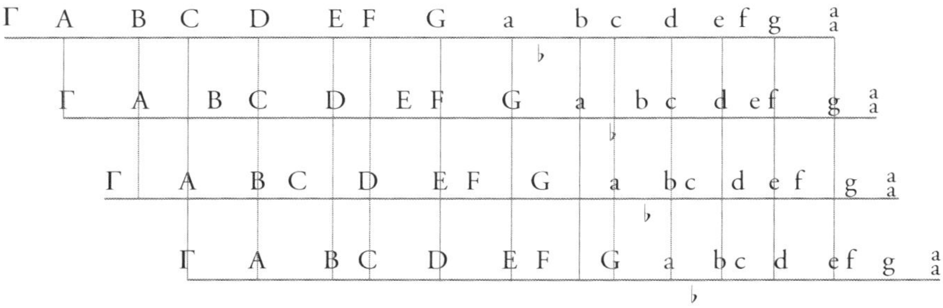

Guido of Arezzo's theory functions unlike any of the other sources for *De musica*: in the treatise his works are the subject of commentary and interpretation. Aribo, who is only interested in Guido's melodic theory, openly announces that his purpose is not only to comment on Guido but also to make him more intelligible: "Having set forth the useful ideas relating to melody that we share with lord Guido, not only have we expounded his own words but also proposed more convenient types of movement about which he has kept thoroughly quiet."[80]

Aribo's discussion of Guido, however, is bound up with his use of *Commentarius anonymus in Micrologum Guidonis Aretini*. The textual variants show that many of Aribo's extensive quotations from Guido come not from Guido at first hand, but from Guido as quoted in the commentary. Only the quotations from the beginning of chapter 89 to the words "in syllabas ut *Christi pugna*" in the same chapter, from chapter 94, and from the latter part of *sententia* 1 ("Quod nobis inuidet commodum . . . ") to the conclusion of *sententia* 2 are taken at first hand from Guido's works.[81] The Guidonian quotations from the last section of chapter 89 to end of chapter 93, and from the beginning of *sententia* 1 until the words "...quam absentibus scribendo" are all taken from *Commentarius anonymus*.[82]

Classical sources for music theory exert only a peripheral influence upon *De musica*. Aribo mentions Boethius by name only in chapter 26, where he delineates the tetrachords of the *graves*, *finales*, *superiores*, and *excellentes*. Here he outlines the tetrachords using the modern letter names for the notes ("according to Guido") and the old-fashioned Greek names ("according to Boethius"). In other places, Boethius's *De institutione musica* is perhaps the source for occasional comments, such as "the familiar is friendly and the unfamiliar is hostile" (chapter 87). In these cases, however, one suspects that Aribo was merely recalling his memory of the work, rather than deliberately quoting from Boethius. The peripherality of authors such as Boethius is standard in the south German music treatises. The theory of Aribo and his contemporaries was practical in orientation: it was concerned with singing Gregorian chant. Boethius did not really discuss singing at all and, as Guido of Arezzo had commented, Boethius was useful to philosophers but not to singers.[83] That is not to say that Boethius was ignored. Far from it; his *De institutione musica* and *De institutione arithmetica* were widely available in German libraries and elicited an important tradition of glossing.[84] Much of the technical vocabulary used by Aribo and his contemporaries was rooted in Boethius. By the eleventh century, however, Boethius had been well incorporated into Western theory and so the direct application of his musical works was limited.

As with the classical sources for music theory, so too was the direct application of Carolingian sources limited. *De musica* contains little obvious trace of Carolingian theory. A similar state of affairs obtains in contemporary treatises by William of Hirsau, Frutolf of Michelsberg, and Theoger of Metz. This is in large part due to Bern of Reichenau, who had synthesized the most important aspects of Carolingian theory in his *Prologus in tonarium*. Although Carolingian authors were available in German libraries, their influence on eleventh-century theorists usually came indirectly through Abbot Bern. This trend is also apparent in eleventh- and twelfth-century music textbooks: the scribes who compiled them largely eschewed Carolingian sources, preferring the "modern" treatises of the south German circle and Guido of Arezzo.[85]

The nonmusical sources of *De musica* are as important as its musical ones. The variety of these shows the breadth of Aribo's learning and serves as a salutary reminder that the members of the south German circle were scholars who applied the depth of their divine and secular learning to whichever subject they wrote about. The Latin Bible permeates *De musica*, as it did most contemporary literature. Aribo's decision to name his alternative to the quadripartite figure *caprea* is rooted in the story of the appropriation of Esau's birthright by Jacob (Gen. 27). The ease with which the monochord can be understood using *caprea* is expressed with a direct quotation from Genesis 27:20—"Voluntas enim Dei fuit ut cito mihi occurreret quod uolebam"—while the presentation of the diagram to Ellenhard parallels Jacob's offering to his father Isaac: a new offering that superseded the older or "firstborn" quadripartite figure.[86] In chapters 40–44 Aribo compares the tetrachords of the *graves*, *finales*, *superiores*, and *excellentes* to Christ's incarnation, passion, resurrection, ascension, and divinity, as only a cleric intimately acquainted with the Bible could. Yet here we get an informative glimpse that Aribo and his contemporaries—who so skillfully interlaced their works with biblical allusions—were working from the internalized memory built up through constant participation in the liturgy. In chapter 40 Aribo alludes to the story of Christ sitting and thirsting above the well, citing the Gospel of Matthew; but he uses the word *puteum* for well, which occurs only in John's version of the story.[87]

Unsurprisingly, Aribo knew and used the standard reference works of Cassiodorus and Isidore: he took the story of Orpheus from Cassiodorus's *Institutiones*, while relying on Isidore's *Etymologies* for his description of the sirens.[88] Nevertheless, Aribo was also aware of more recent literature on the subject: his comment that "the pleasant and flattering sirens of this world . . . similarly draw our souls into the most dangerous shipwreck" he owed to the influential eleventh-century papal reformer Peter Damian.[89] Of the church fathers, Gregory the Great and St. Ambrose are mentioned by name, but their works are not used. St. Augustine appears once, and there is an echo from an Epiphany sermon by Pope Leo the Great (440–61).[90]

Turning to secular literature, we see that Aribo was well acquainted with the classical poets, Cicero's rhetorical works, Plato's *Timaeus* (in the translation by Calcidius), and Macrobius's *Commentarius in Somnium Scipionis*, as well as the dialectical works of Porphyry and Boethius. There are explicit references and allusions to Virgil's *Eclogues*, *Georgics*, and *Aeneid* (although the phrase quoted from the *Aeneid* was a commonplace in music treatises, and was probably so because Isidore had quoted it);[91] quotations from Horace's *Ars poetica*, *Odes*, and *Satires*; an allusion to Ovid's *Fasti*; quotations from Cicero's *De natura deorum libri tres*, *De inventione*, and *Laelius de amicitia*, as well as the pseudo-Ciceronian *Rhetorica ad Herennium*; explicit references to Plato and Macrobius; as well as quotations from Boethius's *Commentarius in topica Ciceronis*. But the extent of Aribo's learning does not stop here, for a close study of *De musica* shows a deeper understanding and use of these sources. Plato's *Timaeus*, as filtered through Macrobius, exerted a profound influence on Aribo, as it did on his south German colleagues. Porphyry's *Isagoge* and Boethius's *De divisione* inform his dialectical approach to the division of the gamut at a fundamental level, while Boethius's *De differentiis topicis* and *Commentarius in topica Ciceronis* provided Aribo with the technical vocabulary for the most dialectically sophisticated parts of *De musica*.[92] As *scholasticus*, Aribo would have taught the subjects of the trivium and the quadrivium. His breadth of experience in both is reflected in *De musica*.

Neoplatonic Influences

Aribo mentions Plato by name three times in the course of *De musica*. The influence of Plato, however, runs much deeper in *De musica*, as it does in the treatises of Aribo's south German colleagues.[93] Plato's *Timaeus*, which was widely available in the partial translation by Calcidius,[94] provided the south German circle with a plan according to which the world was fashioned. This plan, which was based upon number and proportion, stressed the special importance of the number four. It is no coincidence that early in *De musica* Aribo draws a firm connection between the four elements that remained "after the bending of the primitive disorder" and the four modes—*protus*, *deuterus*, *tritus*, and *tetrardus*.[95] Music, being part of nature, must be consonant with her. For Aribo and his colleagues the system of tetrachords, species, and modes was a just and proper reflection of natural order, which concurred not only with the insights that had been granted to Plato but with the Christian belief that God had ordered the universe "in number and weight and measure."[96]

It was for precisely this reason that Aribo disapproved of the quadripartite figure. Whereas the quadripartite figure sets out the notes in an arrangement that is "against the nature of the monochord," Aribo's *caprea* represents them in their "true and natural position."[97] In his discussion of this topic Aribo repeatedly uses metaphors of birth and generation to juxtapose the unnaturalness of the quadripartite figure with the naturalness of *caprea*. Metaphors of generation feature prominently in the work of Plato's late antique interpreter Macrobius, who influenced not only Bern and Herman of Reichenau but also William of Hirsau and Theoger of Metz.[98] The late antique authors Macrobius, Boethius, and Martianus Capella—far more than Carolingian commentators such as John Scottus Eriugena—were the decisive influence in transmitting Plato to the south German circle.

Latin Style

Aribo's Latin style is far from straightforward. In some places he is complex to the point of being convoluted, but in others he writes exquisitely beautiful and subtle Latin. His syntax, which is often labyrinthine, sees him routinely divide agreeing noun-adjective clauses in favor of complex parallel constructions. Perhaps Aribo deliberately chose this frequently obtuse style to delight his dedicatee, Bishop Ellenhard of Freising. The dedicatory nature of *De musica* was certainly the justification for Aribo's most notable stylistic feature: lavish exploitation of the *ars dictandi* and the *colores rhetorici*.[99]

The *ars dictandi* was the art of writing persuasively using rhetorical figures, or *colores rhetorici*, as they were called by Aribo and his contemporaries. It was a medieval response to the classical models of rhetoric and was taught as a school discipline in the eleventh century. It was one of the three linguistic arts—grammar, rhetoric, and dialectic—that formed the trivium in the medieval curriculum of the seven liberal arts, which Aribo would have taught in his position as *scholasticus*. The sources used for the study of rhetoric included both classical and medieval works. The principles outlined in Cicero's *De inventione* and the pseudo-Circeronian *Rhetorica ad Herennium* were applied to the practical business of letter writing by popular eleventh-century manuals such as Alberic of Monte Cassino's *Flores rhetorici* or Master Onulf of Speyer's *Colores rhetorici*, a work designed to help a monastic schoolmaster instruct his pupils.[100] Such resources were supplemented by model letters, which were frequently copied into collections by clerks on the lookout for examples worthy of imitation. Perhaps the most famous example of this phenomenon is the *Codex Udalrici*, which was copied by Udalric of Bamberg ca. 1125.[101] Some of the items in Udalric's collection are polemics from the 1080s; they were copied not for their content but for their style.

As letter collections such as the *Codex Udalrici* suggest, the *artes dictandi* were beloved of Aribo's German contemporaries. I. S. Robinson has observed how the writers of eleventh-century polemical literature often strove to outdo each other with extravagant *colores* in the salutations and conclusions of their works.[102] This is also true of *De musica*. The opening and closing sections are replete with devices such as repetition (*repetitio* and *traductio*), isocolon (*conpar*), internal rhyme through similar endings (*similiter cadens*), prose rhyme (the various types of *cursus*), juxtaposition of contraries (*contentio*), and closely packed groups of words embracing a complete thought (*continuatio*). Elsewhere, too, Aribo employs these *colores* and others such as rhetorical questioning (*interrogatio*), brevity (*epistolaris brevitas*), and amplification through repetition (*conduplicatio*). By contrast, the passages Aribo took from *Commentarius anonymus* have a perceptively different and less sophisticated style about them. Indeed, the return of the *colores rhetorici* towards the end of *sententia* 1 heralds the return of Aribo's own pen and offers decisive stylistic proof that the preceding passages were written by another author.[103]

Aribo's exploitation of the *colores rhetorici* is consistent with the epistolary and dedicatory nature of *De musica*. Parts of the treatise seek to convince Ellenhard of the quadripartite figure's defects and of *caprea*'s advantages, and it is in those sections that the *colores rhetorici* are most evident. The result is an intricate and ambitious rhetorical collage that stems from Aribo's familiarity with the *artes dictandi*.

Influence

Scholars sometimes assume that the survival of a work in a limited number of manuscripts implies an equally limited dissemination. Herman of Reichenau's *Musica*, for example, which survives in only two full recensions, has long been regarded as a work of limited influence. However, this view is hard to reconcile with eleventh-century estimations of Herman's reputation.

Similarly, a study of the south German circle reveals the extent to which his teaching shaped the theoretical outlook of succeeding generations. This would not have been possible had his *Musica* enjoyed only a limited dissemination. To a lesser extent this is also true of Aribo: the survival of only two full recensions is misleading.

De musica was known to Frutolf of Michelsberg, who used it in his *Breviarium de musica*. Some of Frutolf's diagrams are derived from *De musica*, while he also copied the organ-pipe measurements that Aribo received from William of Hirsau.[104] In the early twelfth century the anonymous author or compiler of *Quaestiones in musica* made extensive use of *De musica*.[105] The first part of *Quaestiones* is cast as a set of questions and resolutions (an early example of the *quaestio* technique that would become standard in the scholastic texts of the so-called twelfth-century renaissance). Many of these resolutions incorporate extended passages from *De musica*. Other theorists were also acquainted with parts of *De musica*. The early twelfth-century theorist John, who may have written in the vicinity of St. Gallen, incorporated Aribo's interlocking circle diagrams into his own treatise.[106] These diagrams were one of the most enduringly popular aspects of *De musica*: they also survive in a short treatise extant in the late thirteenth-century manuscript Basel, Universitätsbibliothek, F. IX. 54, fols. 1r–4v, as well as a number of other late medieval sources.

NOTES

1. On the south German circle see McCarthy, *Music, Scholasticism and Reform*, pp. 11–53.

2. The standard work on the Gorze reform is Hallinger, *Gorze-Kluny*, yet Hallinger's study has been criticized for being too monolithic. For more recent literature on the Gorze movement, see Nightingale, *Monasteries and Patrons in the Gorze Reform*.

3. On Gorze and the liturgy see Mayr-Harting, *Ottonian Book Illumination*, 1:83–88, 2:126–7; Donnat, "Vie et coutume monastique," pp. 159–82; and Angenendt, "Die Liturgie in der Vita des Johannes von Gorze," pp. 193–211.

4. Henry II's appointments were not always welcomed; see Nightingale, *Monasteries and Patrons in the Gorze Reform*, pp. 19–20; Hauck, *Kirchengeschichte Deutschlands*, vol. 3, pp. 315, 508–10, 867–68.

5. McCarthy, *Music, Scholasticism and Reform*, pp. 27–28.

6. On Hirsau, see Jakobs, *Die Hirsauer*, pp. 36–71; Cowdrey, *Cluniacs and the Gregorian Reform*, pp. 196–213; Schreiner, "Hirsau und die Hirsauer Reform," pp. 59–84.

7. On William of Hirsau, see Pfaff, "Abt Wilhelm von Hirsau," 83–94; Wisenbach, "Wilhelm von Hirsau: Astrolab und Astronomie"; McCarthy, *Music, Scholasticism and Reform*, pp. 31–33.

8. For an introduction to papal reform, see I. S. Robinson, *Papal Reform of the Eleventh Century*, pp. 3–17; McCarthy, *Chronicles of the Investiture Contest*, pp. 1–14.

9. See I. S. Robinson, *Authority and Resistance in the Investiture Contest*, pp. 7–11.

10. See below, pp. xxvi–xxix.

11. For an introduction to Gregorian chant and the liturgy, see Hiley, *Western Plainchant*, pp. 1–46.

12. For discussions of medieval music theory, its origins, and its sources, see Bernhard, "Überlieferung und Fortleben"; Bernhard, "Das musikalische Fachschrifttum"; Huglo, "Grundlagen und Ansätze, der mittelalterlichen Musiktheorie."

13. Aurelian of Réôme, *Musica disciplina* 2, pp. 62–64.

14. The anonymous author of *Alia musica* (tenth century) adopted Boethius's table of octave species to furnish names for the modal octaves, in the process inverting Boethius's layout, while Hucbald of St. Amand (ca. 850–930) used Boethius's note names, tetrachords, and species. See *Alia musica* 15–20, pp. 107–11; Hucbald of St. Amand, *Musica* 29–30, 49–51, ed. Chartier, pp. 168, 200–202.

15. Pseudo-Odo of Cluny, *Dialogus de musica*, in Huglo, "Der Prolog des Odo zugeschriebenen 'Dialogus de Musica,'" p. 139: "Rarissime tamen et in prolixioribus cantibus voces ad alium tonum pertinentes, id est superfluas elevationes vel depositiones contra regulam invenimus. Sed quia illos cantus omnium usus unanimiter defendebat, emendare non praesumpsimus. Sane per singulos notavimus, ne veritatem regulae quaerentes dubios redderemus."

16. McCarthy, *Music, Scholasticism and Reform*, p. 22.

17. Frutolf of Michelsberg, *Breviarium de musica* 1, p. 26: "Musica est bene modulandi scientia per diutinam meditationem frequenti percepta experientia. Bene autem modulari est rata tonorum et intervallorum dispositione per legitimos excursus apta modulatione suaves cantus formare eosque post debitos ascensus et descensus congruo et legitimo fini aptare."

18. See I. S. Robinson, *Eleventh-Century Germany*, pp. 1–3.

19. Ibid., p. 8.

20. McCarthy, "Identity of Master Henry of Augsburg," pp. 154–55.

21. Guido of Arezzo, *Epistola ad Michahelem*, pp. 464–72.

22. Herman of Reichenau, *Musica* 4, p. 26; for Aribo, see below, *De musica* 19, p. 14.

23. For a wider discussion of modal terminology, see Atkinson, "'Harmonia,'" pp. 485–500.

24. For a guide to the extensive literature on Aribo's identity, see especially McCarthy, "Aribo's *De musica* and Abbot William of Hirsau," pp. 62–82.

25. See below pp. xxxv–xxxvi.

26. [Wolfger of Prüfening], *De scriptoribus ecclesiasticis*, ed. E. Ettlinger, *Der sogenannte Anonymus Mellicensis De scriptoribus ecclesiasticis*. On the identity of its author see Fichtenau, "Wolfger von Prüfening"; Bischoff, "Wolfger."

27. Contrary to Smits van Waesberghe's assertion; see *Aribonis De musica*, p. xxv. Cf. below, *De musica* 4, p. 4.

28. [Wolfger of Prüfening], *De scriptoribus ecclesiasticis* 106, p. 103.

29. Donizo of Canossa, *Vita Mathildis*, pp. 348–49, 351.

30. On Bernold, see I. S. Robinson, *Eleventh-Century Germany*, pp. 41–49. On Henry of Augsburg, see McCarthy "Identity of Master Henry of Augsburg," pp. 140–57.

31. A contemporary depiction of Ellenhard is found in an eleventh-century Freising sacramentary: Bamberg, Staatsbibliothek, Msc. Lit. 2, fol. 2v. See Leitshuh and Fischer, *Katalog der Handschriften der Königlichen Bibliothek zu Bamberg*, pp. 138–39. I am grateful to Dr. Adam Cohen for this reference.

32. *Chronicon Benedictoburanum*, p. 234.42–47.

33. Gawlik, *Intervenienten und Zeugen in den Diplomen Kaiser Heinrichs IV*, pp. 52–53.

34. See below, *De musica* 83, pp. 66–68.

35. McGuire, *Friendship and Community*, pp. 181–82, 194–95, 196–203, 210–21. See also I. S. Robinson, "Friendship Circle of Bernold of Constance," pp. 185–98.

36. See below, *De musica* 83, p. 66.

37. Wipo, *Gesta Chonradi II imperatoris*, pp. 24–25, 53. Bernold, *Chronicon*, p. 488. Bernold was referring to his own *De sacramentis excommunicatorum*, which he sent to his former teacher Bernhard of Hildesheim, who was, according to Bernold, "led by excessive zeal" to overstep orthodox theology in his dismissal of the sacramentality of schismatics.

38. Engelbert of Admont, *De musica* 1.2, p. 170.

39. I. S. Robinson, "Zur Arbeitsweise Bernolds von Konstanz," p. 52; Cowdrey, *Pope Gregory VII*, pp. 255–57; *Historia Hirsaugiensis monasterii*, p. 255.42; Schmid, "Sankt Aurelius in Hirsau"; and Klüppel, "Der heilige Aurelius in Hirsau."

40. Ernstbrunner, *Der Musiktraktat des Engelbert von Admont*, pp. 187, 296–97.

41. See below, pp. l–li, lii–liii, lxxii–lxxiv.

42. *Notae necrologicae ecclesiae maioris Frisingensis*, p. 83; McCarthy, "Aribo's *De musica* and Abbot William of Hirsau," p. 79.

43. Ibid., p. 82.

44. I. S. Robinson, "'Colores rhetorici,'" p. 231; McCarthy, "Literary Practice," p. 192.

45. Rausch, *Die Musiktraktate des Abtes Bern von Reichenau*, pp. 12–16, 31–68, 75–115. Two of Bern's liturgical works are cast as letters addressed to Archbishop Aribo of Mainz (1021–36): *Qualiter quatuor temporum ieiunia per sua sabbata sint observanda*, PL 142:1085–88; and *Qualiter adventus Domini celebretur*, ed. Schmale, pp. 39–46.

46. Bernard of Hildesheim (of Constance), *Liber canonum contra Heinricum IV*. Bernard's former pupil Bernold of St. Blasien (of Constance) comments in his chronicle for 1091 on the dedication to Archbishop Hartwig: Bernold, *Chronicon*, pp. 486–87.

47. See above, pp. xxvi–xxvii.

48. See below, pp. xli–xlii.

49. See below, *De musica* 102, p. 100.

50. Virgil, *Eclogues* 3.49–59.

51. On the monochord, see Adkins, "Technique of the Monochord," and Adkins, "Theory and Practice of the Monochord."

52. Guido of Arezzo, *Prologus in antiphonarium*, pp. 405–35. His response to the problem was to use the letters of the monochord and position them on or between color-coded lines as a visual projection of the up-and-down progress of the melody.

53. McCarthy, *Music, Scholasticism and Reform*, pp. 62–72.

54. William of Hirsau, *Musica* 15, 16, pp. 41–42.

55. Porphyry, *Isagoge: Translatio Boethii*, ed. Minio-Paluello; trans. Warren as *Porphyry the Phoenician: Isagoge*; Boethius, *In Topica Ciceronis commentariorum libri sex*; Boethius, *De differentiis topicis*, trans. Stump as *On topical differentiae*; Boethius, *De divisione*, ed. and trans. Magee as *Anicii Manlii Severini Boethii De divisione liber*.

56. For organ-pipe measurements, see Sachs, *Mensura fistularum*. For bell measurements, see Smits van Waesberghe, *Cymbala*. For studies of monochord measurements, see Markovits, *Das Tonsystem der abendländischen Musik in frühen Mittelalter*, pp. 29–52; Meyer, *Mensura monochordi*.

57. Herman of Reichenau, *Musica* 15, p. 47: "Oportet autem nos scire, quod omnis musicae rationis ad hoc spectat intentio, ut cantilenae rationabiliter componendae, regulariter iudicandae, decenter modulandae scientia comparetur."

58. Virgil, *Eclogues* 2.

59. See McCarthy, *Music, Scholasticism and Reform*, pp. 80–93.

60. There are two editions of *Commentarius anonymus in Micrologum Guidonis Aretini*: Vivell, "Commentarius anonymus in Micrologum Guidonis Aretini" (edited from one manuscript: Vienna, Österreichische Nationalbibliothek, Cod. 2502); and Smits van Waesberghe, *Expositiones in Micrologum Guidonis Aretini* (edited from three manuscripts: Vienna, Cod. 2502; Munich, Bayerische Staatsbibliothek, Clm 14663; and Florence, Biblioteca Medicea Laurenziana, Acq. e doni 33). See also Vivell, "Ein anonymer Kommentar."

61. McCarthy, "Origins of *Commentarius anonymus*." See below, *De musica* 89–93, pp. 80–84.

62. See above, p. xxxiv.

63. For a full discussion, see McCarthy, "Aribo's *De musica*, *Commentarius anonymus in Micrologum Guidonis Aretini* and Guido of Arezzo."

64. Ibid., pp. 144–51.

65. See below, *De musica* 89–93, pp. 80–84; *sententia* 1, pp. 100–104.

66. Lottin, *Problèmes d'historie littéraire*.

67. See below, *sententiae* 1 and 2, pp. 100, 106.

68. See below, *sententia* 1, p. 104.

69. For a wider view of south German theory in a broader European context, see Bower, "Transmission of Ancient Music Theory"; Gushee, "Questions of Genre."

70. McCarthy, *Music, Scholasticism and Reform*, pp. 72–80; also Rausch, *Die Musiktraktate des Abtes Bern von Reichenau*, pp. 24–25, 124.

71. For contemporary estimations of William's scholarly fame, see Haimo of Hirsau, *Vita Willihelmi Abbatis Hirsaugiensis*, p. 225; and Bernold of St. Blasien, *Chronicon* 1091, p. 486; translated in I. S. Robinson, *Eleventh-Century Germany*, pp. 301–2.

72. See below, *De musica* 62–71, pp. 46–52.

73. William of Hirsau, *Musica* 15–18, pp. 40–49.

74. See below, *De musica* 67–71, pp. 50–52; McCarthy, *Music, Scholasticism and Reform*, pp. 138–45.

75. Munich, Bayerische Staatsbibliothek, Clm 4622 binds together seven once-independent manuscripts dating from the late eleventh century to the middle of the thirteenth. The seventh manuscript (fols. 168r–179v), which contains these measurements, dates from the early twelfth century; see Glauche, *Katalog der lateinischen Handschriften*, pp. 219–26. See below, pp. lxxv–lxxvi.

76. Munich, Bayerische Staatsbibliothek, Clm 4622, fol. 178v: "Mensura quadripertite figurae. Quidam ratisponensis monachus nomine Otkerus adinuenit hanc mensuram quadripertitam et nominauit eam theorema troporum quod dicere possumus cribrum monochordi."

77. The eleventh-century Munich, Bayerische Staatsbiblithek, Clm 18914, fol. 41r, and a lost twelfth-century manuscript from the monastery of St. Blasien.

78. William of Hirsau, *Musica* 14, 40, 41, pp. 37–40, 70–75.

79. Herman of Reichenau, *Musica* 5, p. 28.

80. See below, *De musica* 95, p. 86.

81. See below, *De musica* 89, 94, pp. 76–80, 84; *sententiae* 1–2, pp. 104–108. Aribo's first set of quotations is taken from Guido of Arezzo, *Micrologus* 15, pp. 164–69. The final set comes from two different works of Guido: those in the last part of *sententia* 1 ("In sola enim . . . finalis debet esse") are from *Micrologus* 17, pp. 188–93, while the quotation that is the basis of *sententia* 2 is from *Prologus in antiphonarium*, lines 108–13, p. 432.

82. See below, pp. 80–84, 100–104.

83. Guido of Arezzo, *Epistola ad Michahelem*, p. 530.

84. See Teeuwen, *Harmony and the Music of the Spheres*, pp. 156–83; *Glossa maior in institutionem musicam Boethii*, ed. Bernhard and Bower.

85. McCarthy, *Music, Scholasticism and Reform*, pp. 208–9.

86. McCarthy, "Literary Practice," 197.

87. See below, *De musica* 40, p. 34.

88. Cassiodorus, *Institutiones* 2.5.9; Isidore, *Etymologiae* 11.3.

89. Peter Damian, *Letters* 31, 66, 112; vol. 1, pp. 303.21–304.2; vol. 2, pp. 266.20–22; vol. 3, pp. 278.18–279.1. Peter Damian's letters were widely disseminated and imitated in Germany. See below, *De musica* 77, p. 58.

90. See below, *De musica* 9, p. 6.

91. See below, *De musica* 60, p. 44.

92. See below, *De musica* 67–71, pp. 50–52.

93. For a fuller discussion of Neoplatonic influences on the south German circle, see McCarthy, *Music, Scholasticism and Reform*, pp. 147–74.

94. Ibid., pp. 148–50.

95. See below, *De musica* 2, p. 2.

96. Wisdom 11:21.

97. See below, *De musica* 10, 102, pp. 6, 98–100.

98. Macrobius, *Commentarius in Somnium Scipionis* 1.5.16, 1.6.1; Bern of Reichenau, *Prologus in tonarium* 4, pp. 39, 40; Herman of Reichenau, *Musica* 1, 2, 5, pp. 18–19, 22, 27; William of Hirsau, *Musica* 5, 7, pp. 19, 22–3; Theoger of Metz, *Musica* 14, p. 22.

99. On Aribo and the *colores rhetorici* see McCarthy, "Literary Practice," 191–208; Ilnitchi (*Play of Meanings*, pp. 109–13, 118) provides an alternative perspective.

100. Alberic of Monte Cassino, *Flores rhetorici*, pp. 131–61. Onulf of Speyer, *Colores rhetorici*, ed. Linde, pp. 356–81.

101. Udalric of Bamberg, *Codex Udalrici*, ed. Jaffé, pp. 17–469. On Udalric see Worstbrock, "Ulrich von Bamberg"; also Worstbrock, Klaes, and Lütten, *Repertorium der Artes dictandi des Mittelalters*, pp. 112–13.

102. I. S. Robinson, "'Colores rhetorici,'" 231.

103. See below, *sententia* 1, pp. 102–104. Aribo's pen returns with "Quod nobis inuidet commodum . . . ."

104. McCarthy, *Music, Scholasticism and Reform*, pp. 103–5.

105. See below, pp. lxxxi–lxxxiii.

106. John, *De musica*, ed. Smits van Waesberghe, p. 94.

Manuscripts

Introduction

De musica survives wholly or partly in some fifteen manuscripts dating from the late eleventh or early twelfth century to the fifteenth. Only two of these preserve the full version of the treatise; all others contain only parts.

The survival of *De musica* in this fashion reflects the popularity of the "textbook" (*Handbuch* in German) in the eleventh and twelfth centuries. At its most basic, the textbook was a manuscript that brought together different texts, or excerpts thereof, to form a convenient handbook for a particular subject. Some textbooks were the work of individual scribes, some were collaborative efforts by a team of scribes working in one scriptorium, some saw new material added to previously existing manuscripts, and yet others brought together independent manuscripts containing related material. Examples of such textbooks abound from eleventh- and twelfth-century Germany: the manuals of canonical and patristic *sententiae* compiled by Bernold of St. Blasien at the cathedral library of Constance[1]; a late eleventh-century textbook that brings together in one volume works on dialectic and rhetoric by Porphyry, Boethius, Cicero, and Marius Victorinus (now Oxford, Bodleian Library, Laud Lat. 49)[2]; or a compilation of computistical and astronomical texts by two twelfth-century scribes from the diocese of Augsburg (now Rome, Vatican Library, Pal. Lat. 1356, fols. 18–26 and 90–116).[3] The compilation of materials, often to a deliberate plan, was an integral part of the method of scholarship in the central middle ages, a method that applied to music as much as it did to any other subject.[4]

Many of the music treatises written by Aribo and his colleagues survive in textbook codices. These codices are only beginning to be studied by historians, but initial research shows that the monks and secular clerks who compiled textbooks did not hesitate to select the portions of the treatises they found most useful.[5] These clerks—one often suspects among them the activities of a teacher—freely combined sections of different texts and frequently arranged them in a thematic manner to suit their own needs. They did not always cite the *auctor* whose work they copied and where they were copying an already freestanding excerpt, they may not have known his identity. This was often the case with Aribo's *De musica*. A study of its manuscript tradition and textual variants shows that it circulated in a number of standard excerpts, which continued to be copied and modified independently of the full text.[6]

Full Recensions

R Rochester, New York, Sibley Music Library of the Eastman School of Music, ML 92/1200 (Admont, mid-twelfth century)

This manuscript formerly belonged to the monastery of Admont on the River Enns.[7] Admont was founded in 1074 by the staunch Gregorian Archbishop Gebhard of Salzburg (1060–88), with monks from the monastery of St. Peter in Salzburg (the home of the only other full recension of *De musica*).[8] In 1115 Admont was reformed by monks from Hirsau's daughter house of St. Georgen.[9] It was, therefore, a monastery linked with the Gregorian reform from its very foundation.

R is a collection of music treatises, measurement texts, and mnemonics: it contains pseudo-Odo of Cluny's *Dialogus de musica* (fols. 1r–11r); Aribo's *De musica* (fols. 11r–42r); Guido of Arezzo's *Micrologus*, *Regule rithmice*, *Prologus in antiphonarium*, and *Epistola ad Michahelem* (fols. 42r–73v); two texts on the measurement of organ pipes and one on the measurement of bells (fols. 74v–76r); Bern of Reichenau's *Prologus in tonarium* and *Tonarius* (fols. 76r–91r); Herman of Reichenau's mnemonic verses *E uoces unisonas* and *Ter terni sunt modi*—with diastemmatic neumes and not Herman's peculiar notational system that they were originally designed to illustrate (fols. 91v–92v); and a drawing of a "Guidonian hand" (fol. 93v).

All the texts in *R* have been copied across the quires, indicating that it was a planned codex. The greater part of *R* was copied by a single scribe, although he was helped by at least eight others, many of whose hands reappear throughout. Similarly, the hands of a number of rubricators—at least two of whom were also responsible for copying parts of the text—recur throughout the codex. *R* was therefore the result of collaboration in one scriptorium: it was intended as a music textbook that brought together some of the best modern treatises, a tonary, and a selection of measurement texts and mnemonic verses.

The main scribe of *R* also copied most of *De musica*. He wrote in a clear and functional Caroline minuscule with a tendency towards roundness in his characters. It is also noticeable that as he wrote his script tended to become cramped and more squat. Frequently he stopped copying just a few lines from the bottom of a folio and returned again at the first word on the next folio, the intervening text having been copied by one of his colleagues. He supplied some of the chapter titles for *De musica*, though the majority of these were added by another scribe, who wrote in a distinctive and flourishing script. (*R*, unlike *S*, transmits chapter headings throughout.) The main text scribe copied only one of the diagrams (that of the chant *Linguam refrenans* on fol. 41v), leaving the others for a scribe who wrote in a very slender and precise script.

Perhaps the most peculiar feature of *R* is its misordering of Aribo's text. On fol. 23v line 16 the words "Ab argumento precedenti" (chap. 67) are followed by "uel iambicum, appositus scandat per tonum" (chap. 91). Similar shifts take place on fol. 29v line 23, where "tres, quia li duas" (*sententia* 1) is followed by "possumus colligere" (chap. 67), and on fol. 40r line 14, where "per trocheicum semitonium" (chap. 91) is followed by "habet uoces in pedata neuma" (*sententia* 1). Two blocks of text, therefore, have been switched: the first from chapter 91 to *sententia* 1, and the second from chapters 67 to 91. This cannot have been the result of a binding error in *R*, because each of these shifts occurs in the middle of a line. The explanation is that this misordering preserves a similar misordering in the exemplar from which *R* was copied. It is certainly possible that in the intermediate manuscript the misordering was the result of a binding error. Each of the shifts in *R* took place while the main scribe of *De musica* was copying. He seems not to have noticed the disjunctions on fols. 23v and 29v, but one line after the final shift on fol. 40r he stopped copying, and the rest of the folio was completed by another scribe, perhaps older, who wrote in a more elegant and upright Caroline minuscule. It is tempting to speculate that the main scribe was finally confused and sought the help of a colleague. No alteration was made, however, and so *R* retains this idiosyncratic order.

R also transmits marginal glosses in a later hand, probably dating to the late thirteenth or early fourteenth century. These glosses, which appear throughout the codex, indicate that *R* continued to be used as a textbook by later generations of Admont monks.

Provenance. *R* was probably copied at Admont, judging from its style of production. Abbot Engelbert of Admont's references to Aribo suggest that Engelbert used *R* as a source for his own music treatise, written between 1276 and 1321.[10] The first definite reference to *R* is in a late fourteenth-century library catalog of Admont.[11] *R* was among ten manuscripts sold by Admont during a period of financial difficulty in the 1930s.

S Salzburg, Stiftsbibliothek St. Peter, Cod. a. V. 2, fols. 114–145 (St. Peter's in Salzburg, end of the eleventh century or beginning of the twelfth)

S is the earliest surviving full recension of *De musica*. It survives in the third of three once-independent manuscripts that comprise Salzburg, Stiftsbibliothek St. Peter, Cod. a. V. 2, a codex that was bound in its present form in the fifteenth century at the earliest. The first manuscript (fols. 1r–34v) contains the *Expositio moralis in Psalmum 12* by Abbot Erhard of St. Peter (d. 1436) and dates from the fifteenth century (the date 1435 is written on fol. 1v). The second (fols. 35r–113v), which is written in four different hands from the mid-twelfth century, contains a collection of extracts from works by Adelard of Bath, Boethius, Bernard of Clairvaux, Peter Abelard, and others.[12]

The third manuscript (fols. 114r–145v) comprises four regular quires of four bifolia. *De musica*, which occupies fols. 114v–145r, was copied by four different scribes.[13] The writing on fol. 114v, lines 1–14 (ending at the line change *re*|) is by Scribe A, and that on fol. 114v, lines 15–32 (beginning with the new line at |*gulis*) is by Scribe B. Lines 15 to 17, and perhaps part of line 18, have been erased by scraping and pouncing, which explains why Scribe B began copying in the middle of the word *regulis*. It is likely that the portion of erased text was originally copied by Scribe A. Scribe B was a contemporary of Scribe A, but his hand is spikier and he held his pen at more of an angle to the page. He also differs in his capital *S* and in always using a straight-backed *d* in preference to an uncial one. Scribe A returned to copy fol. 115r, line 1 (*discernendi*) to fol. 116v line 3 (*opposita*). Fol. 116v line 3 (*Sed*) to line 10 (*cito*) was then supplied by Scribe C. He was followed by Scribe A again, who copied from fol. 116v line 11 (*mihi*) to fol. 122v line 10 (*quartam*).

Fols. 122v (after line 10) to 123r are occupied by the interlocking circle diagrams that show the connection of the authentic and plagal versions of the four modes.[14] The circles are drawn in orange over the text inside them; the gamut and lettering outside the circles are in faded brown ink. Scribe A copied the first of the four circle diagrams, Scribe D the remaining three. The diagram drawn by Scribe A is distinguished from those drawn by Scribe D by its style of execution and content. This diagram presents the version of the circle diagrams transmitted by *D1* and other witnesses connected to it, whereas the other three diagrams present the incomplete version transmitted by *R*.[15] This suggests that *S* was copied from more than one source. The fact that this change in the style of diagram coincides with a change in scribes may also be significant. Scribe D, who began his copying with the second circle diagram, is responsible for the rest of the text and the remaining diagrams in the treatise. His hand is smaller than that of Scribe A; it is very neat and fine, and his letter strokes are not as thick.

The chapter headings and initial capitals throughout were supplied by Scribe A in ink that is now orange. Many of the chapter headings, however, were never supplied even though space was left for them. It is, perhaps, not a coincidence that the chapter headings stop only two chapters after Scribe D took over the copying of the text.

De musica ends at the end of fol. 145r, line 3, and is followed on line 7 by the beginning of pseudo-Odo of Cluny's *Dialogus de musica*, in the hand of Scribe D.[16] The initial capital *Q* was supplied by Scribe A, in exactly the same shade of ink used for Aribo's *De musica*, while a rubricated incipit must have been intended to fill the three-line gap between the end of *De musica* and the beginning of *Dialogus de musica*. The brown text ink of *Dialogus de musica* is more faded than that of the preceding text, but this merely reflects the varying intensity of the ink throughout the manuscript. Scribe D copied fol. 145r, lines 7 to 14 ("Quid est musica . . . in modum cythare |").

The incomplete beginning of *Dialogus de musica* is followed immediately at the start of line 15 by the anonymous satirical poem *Advertite omnes populi*, which is continued until its ending half way down fol. 145v.[17] The poem is written in a different shade of ink from *Dialogus de musica* and is the work of a later hand (perhaps dating to the second quarter or middle of the twelfth century). This evidence suggests that the original plan was to copy pseudo-Odo after Aribo. But that plan was never completed and a later scribe, returning to the manuscript, added the poem in the empty space.[18] It is possible, though not certain, that fols. 114r–145v circulated as an independent booklet: fols. 114r and 145v are somewhat faded, suggesting that they could have been de facto covers for the booklet. Nevertheless, they are not the only folios faded in this manner: fols. 116r, 122r, and 142r are in an almost identical state, which makes the argument for the booklet having been independent inconclusive.[19]

Provenance. S may well have been copied at St. Peter's.[20] It was there by at least 1435, when it was bound with the other two manuscripts into its present form.[21]

Partial Recensions

B Brussels, Bibliothèque Royale, MS 10162/66, fols. 81r–84r (93r–96r) (St. Laurence in Liège, fifteenth century)[22]

Sections transmitted. Chapters 2–15, 27–38, and the circle diagrams.

B is the first of two independent manuscripts that today constitute Brussels, Bibliothèque Royale, MS 10162/66. *B* belonged to the monastery of St. Laurence in Liège and dates from the fifteenth century.[23] Much of *B* was copied from *D*, which belonged to the neighboring monastery of St. James in Liège. *B* transmits *De musica* chapters 2–15, 27–38, and the intersecting circle diagrams on fols. 93r–96r. This excerpt was copied from *D* (specifically from *D1* and *D5*): not only is it identical in content but the variants are the same, and the presence or absence of chapter headings parallels *D1D5*.

Provenance. *B* originated at the monastery of St. Laurence in Liège (the ex libris "Sanctii Laurentii Liber" is written on the inside binding of the front cover).

D Darmstadt, Universitäts- und Hochschulbibliothek, Cod. 1988, fols. 147r–189v (St. James in Liège, early twelfth century)

Sections transmitted. *D1*: chapters 6–15, 27–38, and the circle diagrams; *D2*: chapters 45–58; *D3*: chapters 78, 81, 85; *D4*: two diagrams of melodic movement by the *diatessaron* and *diapente*; *D5*: chapters 2–5 and the diagram of the quadripartite figure; *D6*: chapters 16–26; *D7*: chapters 58–62.

This codex consists of three separate manuscripts: the first, fols. 1r–67r, dates from the fourteenth century and contains texts on alchemy, while both the second and third—fols. 68r–146v and 147r–189v, respectively—date from the early twelfth century and contain works of music theory. The manuscripts were bound together at the start of the fifteenth century.

The third manuscript (hereafter *D*) contains Bern of Reichenau's *Prologus in tonarium* and *Tonarius*, fifty-seven chapters from Aribo's *De musica* in seven distinct extracts, several short texts, and the Wolf Anonymous treatise.[24] A study of this manuscript's origins holds the key to understanding the complex way in which it transmits Aribo's text.

In its current state *D* consists of five quires: two quires of four bifolia (fols. 147r–154v and 155r–162v), a quire of six bifolia (fols. 163r–174v), a quire of a singleton plus three bifolia (fols. 175r–181v; fol. 175rv is the singleton), and a quire of four bifolia (fols. 182r–189v). The first four quires were copied by a group of scribes working in the same scriptorium during the early twelfth century. Although none of the individual hands are entirely consistent, they share certain common traits such as the mixing of three forms of uppercase *Q*, varying use of the *ct* ligature, the mixing of uncial and straight-backed *d*, varying use of lowercase *r* and uppercase *E*, and the tendency for the second stroke of the lowercase *x* to flourish below the line. The recurrence of the different hands throughout the manuscript, coupled with the fact that many of the works go across the quires, indicates that these four quires were—initially, at least—a planned collaboration. The fifth and last quire of *D* was copied by a single scribe whose handwriting obviously differs from that of his contemporaries who worked on the first four. This quire may originally have been independent: it contains the treatise known today as the Wolf Anonymous, a work dating probably from ca. 1060.[25] As this quire has no bearing on the state of Aribo's text, it can be ignored here.

The copying of first four quires of *D* was a three-stage process. The purpose of the first stage seems to have been to produce a music textbook containing Bern of Reichenau's treatise and tonary, followed by excerpts from Aribo. This was undertaken by four scribes: A, B, C, and D. Scribes A and B copied Bern's *Prologus in tonarium*, with A doing most of the work. This treatise occupies the entire first quire and four-and-a-half leaves of the second (today fols. 147r–157r, line 24). Bern's tonary was copied next, taking up the rest of the second quire and eight-and-a-half leaves of the third. Today it occupies fols. 157r, line 25–167r, line 15. As we shall see, however, fols. 167r–170v were a subsequent addition to *D*, so the tonary originally ended half way down the folio facing fol. 166v (today fol. 171r, line 18).[26] Scribe B did not play any part in copying the tonary. Instead, Scribe A was joined by Scribe C, who supplied the rubricated topic sentences and section headings until the end of fol. 161v. Scribe A then took over his own rubrication.

Scribe C filled the remainder of the third quire (today fols. 171v–174v) with an excerpt from *De musica*: the *caprea* diagram, chapters 6–15, 27–38, and the intersecting circle diagrams (*D1*). He wrote a clear and stylish little minuscule in ink that has now faded brown. The excerpt contains chapter headings in bright red ink; it looks as if Scribe B wrote the first four or five of these, with Scribe C taking over from there.

The fourth quire was originally a quire of three bifolia (today fols. 176r–181v; fol. 175rv is a subsequent addition). Here a new scribe, Scribe D, began copying another excerpt from *De musica* (*D2*, chapters 45–58) on fol. 176r. There appears to have been some confusion, however, for seven lines from the bottom of the page the text was erased and recopied by Scribe B, who then completed the excerpt, finishing it at fol. 177r, line 7. Unlike *D1*, *D2* contains neither chapter headings nor even spaces for them, suggesting that its exemplar may have lacked chapter headings. Scribe B continued adding material from *De musica*, copying a variant of chapter 78,[27] as well as chapters 81 and 85 (*D3*) from fol. 177r, line 8 to fol. 177v, line 14. *D3* does not transmit chapter headings, although space has been left for them. In fact, it is possible to make out just the imprint of an erased heading before chapter 81, at the top of fol. 177v. The conclusion to draw is that although the exemplar probably had chapter headings, in the end they were not copied. Finally, Scribe B followed *D3* with two diagrams of melodic movement by *diatessaron* and *diapente* on fols. 177v–178r (*D4*).[28] We cannot be certain of what happened next, or whether or not it was planned to fill the rest of the quire with other excerpts from Aribo. The fact that all the other hands in the quire differ from those of Scribes A, B, C, or D, and probably date from slightly later, suggests that the copying process was interrupted, and that at the end of the first stage the rest of the quire remained empty.

Scribe E seems to have been largely responsible for the second stage of the copying process. He is easily distinguishable from the Scribes A–D, as he wrote with a much more spiky script, used ink that is much blacker, and did his own rubrication. Yet he cannot have been working too long after the first stage, for one of his physical additions to *D*—fol. 175rv—contains both his own writing and the writing of a scribe who, if not actually Scribe B, is virtually indistinguishable from him.

At this stage Scribe E also inserted two bifolia (fols. 167r–170v) into the center of the third quire, making it a quire of twelve. The main reason for this addition seems to have been to supply *D5* (*De musica* chaps. 2–5 and the diagram of the quadripartite figure) before *D1*. The insertion, however, necessitated the repositioning of the concluding half a folio's worth of Abbot Bern's *Tonarius* so that this text retained its internal order.[29] Consequently, Scribe E erased what of Bern's text had been on fol. 171r and recopied it in his own distinctive minuscule on fol. 167r; both the erasure and the repositioned conclusion are clearly visible today.

Scribe E now had eight and a half blank leaves before the beginning of *D1* on fol. 171v. Working backwards he copied *De musica* chapters 2–5 from fol. 170v, line 16 to fol. 171r, line 12 (the portion on fol. 171v over the previously erased conclusion of Bern's *Tonarius*). The fact that he began *D5* halfway down fol. 170v perhaps suggests that the planned to fill the top half with the dedicatory letter and first chapter of *De musica*, which are just about the appropriate length for that space. On the remaining empty portion of fol. 171v he drew a diagram of the quadripartite figure that features so prominently in Aribo's treatise—the only diagram of it in the early manuscript tradition of *De musica*. Its rather amateurish and sketchy nature—especially when compared with the extremely elegant rendering of Aribo's *caprea* that already existed overleaf—suggests that Scribe E did not have a model in his source. Perhaps he deduced the nature of the diagram from the text or reproduced one drawn on a monochord, something that, as Aribo himself tells us, was a common occurrence.[30]

Scribe E supplied a second excerpt from *De musica* on the singleton fol. 175rv, which he added at the beginning of the fourth quire (*D6*). It contains chapters 16–26, without headings, although space has been left for them. Although Scribe E copied most of the excerpt, it was actually finished by a scribe whose hand looks remarkably similar to that of Scribe B. If this is Scribe

Figure 10. The first stage of the copying of the first four quires of *D*

Folios	*Quiring*	*Scribe*	*Foliation*	*Contents*
147r–154v	IV	AB	147r–157r	Bern of Reichenau, *Prologus in tonarium*
155v–162r	IV	AC	157r–166v	Bern of Reichenau, *Tonarius*
163r–174v	IV		+ 171r	
(omitting 167r– 170v)				
		C(B)	171v–174v	*D1* (*De musica* 6–15, 27–38, circle diagrams)
(omitting 175rv)				
176r–181v	III	DB	176r–177r	*D2* (*De musica* 45–58)
		B	177rv	*D3* (*De musica* 78, 81, 85)
		B	177v–178r	*D4* (*De musica*, diagrams)
			178v–181v	Empty

B, it suggests that the second phase of copying took place relatively shortly after the first; perhaps Scribe E was a younger contemporary of Scribe B.

Finally, Scribe E copied *De musica* chapters 58–61 and the first few words of chapter 62 on fol. 179r (*D7*). Three pieces of evidence indicate that this excerpt was intended to be longer. First, it breaks off mid-sentence after the fifth word of chapter 62. Secondly, the handwriting deteriorates markedly as it approaches the bottom of the folio, indicating that Scribe E was rushing to complete his task. Thirdly, the following three leaves (fols. 179v–180v) are occupied by a computus table, which must have been a later addition on blank folios. Had the table already existed when Scribe E was copying, he would never have attempted this excerpt here, for there was not the slightest chance of completing chapter 62 on fol. 179r. *D7* also lacks chapter headings, although space has been left for them.

At the end of the second stage, fols. 167r–170v, 178v, and 179v–181v remained empty. It is tempting to speculate that Scribe E was trying to execute Scribe B's original plan for more Aribo material, leaving empty spaces such as fol. 178v for the subsequent addition of diagrams or other material from *De musica*. Nevertheless, the copying process was again interrupted and that plan was never realized. Scribe E did no more work on the additional folios, for neither of the two texts currently between the new ending of Bern's tonary and *D5* was copied by him.

By the end of the second stage the first four quires of *D* were already in their current physical state. Although it is not possible to deduce the exact chronology of what happened next, the third stage essentially saw the addition of texts in the blank spaces (fols. 167r–170v, 178v, 179v–181v) by Scribes F and G. Their handwriting is closer to Scribe E's than to that of Scribes A–D. Scribe F, who wrote quite a large and bold hand, was the first to add material. He copied a text on the widely debated topic of the division of the semitone on fols. 167r–169v. He began this text, entitled "De ratione proportione et diuisione semitonii," two lines after Scribe E's repositioned conclusion to Bern's tonary and ended it three lines from the bottom of fol. 169v. On fols. 179v–180v he copied a computus table for the entire year, beginning in April and ending in March.

At some stage Scribe G completed the copying process by inserting short texts in the remaining spaces. His first addition, which occupies fols. 169v–170v, provides a brief overview of music's rudiments.[31] The format of its ending is unusual: it is copied continuously until the end of fol. 170v, line 15, where there is a sign directing the reader to the left-hand margin just below for its continuation and conclusion. This is because *D5* already occupied this folio from line 16 onwards. Scribe G's other additions are two chapters from Boethius on fol. 178v,[32] and two texts on fol. 181rv.[33]

Figure 11. The second stage of the copying of the first four quires of *D*

Folios	*Quiring*	*Scribe*	*Foliation*	*Contents*
147r–154v	IV	AB	147r–157r	Bern of Reichenau, *Prologus in tonarium*
155v–162r	IV	AC	157r–166v	Bern of Reichenau, *Tonarius*
163r–174v	VI	E	167r	Bern of Reichenau, new conclusion of *Tonarius*
			167r–170v	Empty
		E	170v–171r	*D5* (*De musica* 2–5, quadripartite figure)
		C(B)	171v–174v	*D1* (*De musica* 6–15, 27–38, circle diagrams)
175rv	I	EB?	175rv	*D6* (*De musica* 16–26)
176r–181v	III	DB	176r–177r	*D2* (*De musica* 45–58)
		B	177rv	*D3* (*De musica* 78, 81, 85)
		B	177v–178r	*D4* (*De musica*, diagrams)
			178v	Empty
		E	179r	*D7* (*De musica* 58–62, incomplete)
			179v–181v	Empty

Figure 12. The third stage of the copying of the first four quires of *D*

<table>
<tr><th>Folios</th><th>Quiring</th><th>Scribe</th><th>Foliation</th><th>Contents</th></tr>
<tr><td>147r–154v</td><td>IV</td><td>AB</td><td>147r–157r</td><td>Bern of Reichenau, Prologus in tonarium</td></tr>
<tr><td>155v–162r</td><td>IV</td><td>AC</td><td>157r–166v</td><td>Bern of Reichenau, Tonarius</td></tr>
<tr><td>163r–174v</td><td>VI</td><td>E</td><td>167r</td><td>Bern of Reichenau, new conclusion of Tonarius</td></tr>
<tr><td></td><td></td><td>F</td><td>167r–169v</td><td>'De ratione proportione et diuisione semitonii'</td></tr>
<tr><td></td><td></td><td>G</td><td>169v–170v</td><td>'| Cum quatuor sint…autem diatonicum |'</td></tr>
<tr><td></td><td></td><td>E</td><td>170v–171r</td><td>D5 (De musica 2–5, quadripartite figure)</td></tr>
<tr><td></td><td></td><td>C(B)</td><td>171v–174v</td><td>D1 (De musica 6–15, 27–38, circle diagrams)</td></tr>
<tr><td>175rv</td><td>I</td><td>EB?</td><td>175rv</td><td>D6 (De musica 16–26)</td></tr>
<tr><td>176r–181v</td><td>III</td><td>DB</td><td>176r–177r</td><td>D2 (De musica 45–58)</td></tr>
<tr><td></td><td></td><td>B</td><td>177rv</td><td>D3 (De musica 78, 81, 85)</td></tr>
<tr><td></td><td></td><td>B</td><td>177v–178r</td><td>D4 (De musica, diagrams)</td></tr>
<tr><td></td><td></td><td>G</td><td>178v</td><td>Boethius, De institutione musica 2.2.3</td></tr>
<tr><td></td><td></td><td>E</td><td>179r</td><td>D7 (De musica 58–61, incomplete)</td></tr>
<tr><td></td><td></td><td>F</td><td>179v–180v</td><td>Computus table</td></tr>
<tr><td></td><td></td><td>G</td><td>181rv</td><td>'|| Musica est motus uocum…et florebit |'</td></tr>
<tr><td></td><td></td><td>G</td><td>181v</td><td>'| Rursus hę positiones…sempiternus es filius ||'</td></tr>
</table>

D thus transmits seven separate excerpts from *De musica*. *D1* is virtually identical to M_2 and the later *Lz1*;[34] *W1* also transmits a reduced version of the excerpt.[35] This excerpt's appearance in four different sources suggests that it already existed independently by the time *D* was being copied and that Scribe C's archetype for *D1* was an independent excerpt and not a full copy of *De musica*.[36] But other versions of *De musica* must also have been in the scriptorium, for Scribes B and E added more excerpts. Whether the other *De musica* excerpts in *D* shared a single exemplar or each possessed an independent exemplar is unclear. *D6* was added to *D1* by Scribe E. The fact that he added material to complement *D1* by filling the gaps in Aribo's text indicates that he was well aware of the structure of *De musica* and must have had a relatively full copy.

Provenance. Each of the three manuscripts that comprise the Darmstadt codex carries a St. James ex libris in the hand of Philip of Othey, prior of the monastery in the early fifteenth century. Although it is not certain, *D* may well have been copied in the scriptorium of St. James.

F Frankfurt, Stadt- und Universitätsbibliothek, Fragm. lat. IX 75 (undetermined German origin, second half of the twelfth century)

Fragments of *De musica* are preserved on a number of stubs (*lagenfalze*) used to reinforce the binding of incunabulum Ohly-Sack, no. 1067. These reinforcing stubs occur at the centers of fols. 5/6, 25/26, 72/73, 89/90, 116/117, 148/149, and 156/157. It is possible to make out significant fragments of text only at fols. 5/6, 25/26, 72/73, and 89/90 because of the tightness of the binding and the fact that the stubs are so deeply recessed. Text from *De musica* survives only at fols. 5/6. The readable text on other stubs includes fragments of the contemporary treatise *Commentarius anonymus in Micrologum Guidonis Aretini* (fols. 5/6 and 89/90), various unidentified texts on music (fols. 5/6, 25/26, 72/73 and 89/90), and a text on baptism (25/26). All of the texts on music come from the same original manuscript. They are written in black ink that has faded brown, with occasional red decoration. The hand is a small, upright, and angular minuscule, dating perhaps from the second half of the twelfth century. The text on baptism is from a different but contemporary manuscript.

The fragments of *De musica* visible on the stub at fols. 5/6 comprise the end of chapter 8 ("<monochord>di potest quiuis etiam mediocriter his imbutus facillime contemplari"), most of chapter 9 ("De Aribunculi ammiratione. Hęc cum . . . ut naturam quam in"), and parts of chapter 15 ("secundam tono . . . Qua in uestrę gratię").[37]

Provenance. The incunabulum that transmits *F* belonged to the Dominican priory in Frankfurt. Nothing can be ascertained about the origin of the scraps from *De musica*.[38]

K Kassel, Landesbibliothek und Murhardsche Bibliothek der Stadt Kassel, 4° MSS Math. 1 (undetermined German origin, second quarter of the twelfth century)

Sections transmitted. Chapters 36–38, with the interpolated circle diagrams.

This manuscript of forty-seven folios is entirely devoted to works of music theory.[39] The original ink has faded to dark brown, with headings, initial capitals, and rubrication in red. It is the work of a single scribe, perhaps working in the second quarter of the twelfth century, who compiled a textbook of his own from a variety of sources. *K* contains Guido of Arezzo's *Micrologus, Regule rithmice, Prologus in antiphonarium*, and *Epistola ad Michahelem* in full; excerpts from the treatises by Bern and Herman of Reichenau, Aribo, Frutolf of Michelsberg, Theoger of Metz, and the Carolingian author Regino of Prüm; and collections of short didactic and mnemonic texts, diagrams, and directions for the measurement of organ pipes, bells, and geometrical figures. The scribe of *K* did not hesitate to rearrange his sources as it suited him: a study of the manuscript's contents shows that he adopted a definite thematic plan to cover what he considered the most important aspects of music theory.

Chapters 36–38 of *De musica* and the four circle diagrams that illustrate the intersection of the authentic and plagal modes appear on fols. 32v–33v. As this excerpt from *De musica* appears in a section of *K* devoted to the modes, the scribe altered each of the three existing chapter titles to suit his purpose: "De similitudine diuitum et pauperum ad tropos utrosque" (chapter 36) became "De concordia troporum ex similitudine divitum et pauperum," "De similitudine uirilis femineique chori ad authentos et plagas" (chapter 37) was changed to "Item de eadem re," while "De differentia autentorum et plagarum iuxta Horatium Flaccum" was rendered by the scribe simply as "Quomodo differunt autenti a plagalibus." Each of the circle diagrams that follows contains interpolated text not present in Aribo's original. The interpolated text, which contextualizes Aribo's diagrams, is taken from various parts of Bern of Reichenau's *Tonarius*. With some variations, this excerpt from *De musica* is also transmitted by *LM_1*.[40] The interpolated diagrams, but not chapters 36–38, are also transmitted by *Lz2V3*.[41]

Provenance. It is not known where *K* was copied, but its style and contents indicate a German origin. Severely damaged during World War II, *K* was restored in Berlin in 1981.

L Leiden, Rijksuniversiteit Bibliotheek, BPL 194 (St. James in Liège?, early twelfth century)

Sections transmitted. Chapters 37–38 with the interpolated circle diagrams.

L is a small book of forty-six folios. Like *K*, it is the work of a single scribe who set out to provide himself with a music textbook. Chapters 37 and 38 of *De musica* are copied on fols. 39v–40r, while the interpolated circle diagrams occupy fols. 40v–41r. The text of the interpolation for the first diagram appears twice: the scribe first copied just the text on the last seven lines of fol. 40r (immediately after chapter 38) before copying it with the diagram (in which form it usually appears) at the very top of fol. 40v. This excerpt is closely related to the Aribo excerpts transmitted by KM_1.[42] The other texts in *L* include Guido of Arezzo's *Micrologus*, pseudo-Odo of Cluny's *Dialogus de musica*, diagrams, and various mnemonic and didactic verses.

Provenance. L belonged to the monastery of St. James in Liège and may have been copied there. It entered the collection of the Bibliotheca Publica Latina in Leiden from the library of the scholar Franciscus Nansius (d. 1595).

Lz Leipzig, Universitätsbibliothek, Cod. 431, fols. 140r–161v (Pegau, early thirteenth century)

Sections transmitted. Lz1: Chapters 6–15 and 27–38; *Lz2*: interpolated circle diagrams.

This codex, which is a binding of five manuscripts dating from the eleventh century to the thirteenth, contains a mixture of theological, computistical, and musical texts.[43] All of the musical material, which was copied by one scribe in the early thirteenth century, is on fols. 140r–161v. This portion of *Lz* begins in the middle of chapter 16 of Guido of Arezzo's *Micrologus* ("<appo>||situs id est cum in eadem uoce . . . "), which suggests that a quire or quires containing some or all of the earlier parts of *Micrologus* once preceded fol. 140r. This interpretation is supported by the evidence of a thirteenth-century book inventory from Pegau, which records the presence there of "Guido on music."[44]

Lz1 transmits chapters 6–15 and 27–38 of *De musica* on fols. 157r–160v, while *Lz2* transmits the interpolated circle diagrams on fols. 160v–161r. *Lz1* is related to the earlier *D1D5*. Not only does *Lz1* transmit the same chapters as *D1* in the same order but also the diagram of Aribo's *caprea*. The variants show that of the other manuscripts transmitting this excerpt in full or in part ($D1M_2W1B$), *Lz1* is most closely related to *D1*. In addition, *Lz1* is the only manuscript besides *D5* to transmit a diagram of the quadripartite figure: this appears at the beginning of the excerpt on fol. 157r, thereby copying the layout of *D5*, in which the quadripartite figure immediately precedes the text of *D1* on fol. 171r of the Darmstadt manuscript.

Lz1 introduces a good many errors into the text of the *D1* excerpt. It also transmits two unique headings. The first, at the very beginning of the excerpt on fol. 157r, links Aribo with a *scholasticus* named Stephen:

> Aridbo ad stephanum scolasticum in suggillacione sequentis figure a quodam inperito musico male composite et constitucio alterius ab ipso edite iuxta privilegium musice.
>
> (Aribo to Stephan the schoolmaster disparaging the following figure, badly composed by a certain unskilled musician, and offering another devised by himself according to the law of music.)

The second heading, which appears at the bottom of fol. 158r, marks the end of the first part of the excerpt (chaps. 6–15) before continuing with the second (chaps. 27–38). It confuses Aribo and Stephen by attributing Aribo's discussion of the quadripartite figure in *De musica* to Stephen: "Dicta stephani scolastici de dispositione monochordi" (The teaching of Stephen the schoolmaster concerning the disposition of the monochord).

The reason for the scribe's confusion is unknown, as are the exact date and manner in which the mysterious Stephen was introduced into the history of this excerpt.[45] The conclusion must be that *Lz1* is a lineal descendent of *D1*(*D5*) that was influenced by an intervening manuscript or manuscripts.

Lz2 (fols. 160v–161r) transmits the interpolated circle diagrams, which combine Aribo's original diagrams with text from Bern of Reichenau's *Tonarius*. The reason for the combination of this excerpt with the excerpt deriving from *D1*—which contains Aribo's original circle diagrams—is unclear. It must reflect a manuscript or manuscripts between *D1*(*D5*) and *Lz* that drew from the excerpt containing the interpolated circle diagrams (represented by *KLM*$_1$), perhaps the same manuscript that was responsible for introducing the two confusing headings discussed above. Thus either the scribe of *Lz* decided to combine the *Lz1* and *Lz2* excerpts from the sources available to him, or the combination had been made by an earlier scribe.

Provenance. *Lz* may have been copied at the monastery of St. James in Pegau. It is listed in the thirteenth-century book inventory of Pegau.[46]

M$_1$ Munich, Bayerische Staatsbibliothek, Clm 14663, fols. 1r–33v (St. Emmeram in Regensburg, second half of the twelfth century)

Sections transmitted. Chapters 36–37 and the interpolated circle diagrams.

This codex of fifty-one folios, from the monastery of St. Emmeram in Regensburg, binds together two once independent manuscripts: fols. 1r–33v, containing works of music theory, and fols. 34r–51v, transmitting Calcidius's translation of and commentary on Plato's *Timaeus*. The first manuscript contains all four of Guido of Arezzo's music treatises, the anonymous treatise *Quomodo de arithmetica procedit musica*, an abridged excerpt from *Commentarius anonymus in Micrologum Guidonis Aretini*, a partial recension of pseudo-Odo of Cluny's *Dialogus de musica*, one excerpt from *De musica*, and the interpolated version of Abbot Bern of Reichenau's *Prologus in tonarium*.

M_1 probably dates from the second half of the twelfth century. It was copied by two scribes working in collaboration.[47] Scribe A, who was perhaps the elder of the two, copied fols. 1r–14v, the half-folio flyleaf that is fol. 27rv, and fol. 28r, line 18 to fol. 33v. Scribe B, whose hand can be distinguished from that of Scribe A by his slightly broader pen strokes, smaller aspect, distinctive uncial *d*, and lower-case *y*, copied fols. 17r–28r, line 17. The recension of Bern's *Prologus in tonarium* is incomplete: it breaks off mid-sentence ("cum omnis autenticus a suo ||") at the end of fol. 33v. It is likely that the text continued at the beginning of the first folio of the next quire, which is now missing. This manuscript, therefore, originally contained more material. Fols. 15rv and 16rv are singletons that have been inserted into M_1 from another manuscript. The handwriting on these folios (Scribe C) is contemporary with, if not slightly earlier than, that of Scribes A and B.[48]

Chapters 36–37 and the interpolated version of the circle diagrams are copied on fols. 28r–29r. This excerpt is closely related to the Aribo excerpt transmitted by *KL*.[49] The text on fol. 15rv of M_1, which has been attributed to Aribo, was copied from *Commentarius anonymus in Micrologum Guidonis Aretini* and not from *De musica*.[50]

Provenance. M_1 belonged to the monastery of St. Emmeram in Regensburg and was probably copied there. It is listed in the library catalog compiled by Dionysius Menger (1465–1530), the librarian and archivist of St. Emmeram.[51]

M_2 Munich, Bayerische Staatsbibliothek, Clm 14965a (undetermined German origin, first half of the twelfth century)

Sections transmitted. Circle diagrams, chapters 6–15 and 27–35.

M_2 was copied by five different scribes. It consists of four regular quires of four bifolia (fols. 1r–8v, 9r–16v, 17r–24v, and 25r–32v) and a fifth quire of three bifolia plus a singleton (fols. 33r–38v; fol. 39rv being the singleton). The first quire, all in the hand of Scribe A, transmits a diagram illustrating the mathematical proportions of the intervals (fol. 1r), a collection of notated didactic verses (fols. 1v–8v), and the diagrams of the four intersecting circles from *De musica* (fols. 7v–8r). The second and third quires and first two folios of the fourth (fols. 9r–26v) contain Guido of Arezzo's four treatises. These are in the hand of Scribe B, although some of the diagrams and notated examples (those on fols. 23v, 24r, and 25r, for example) were executed by Scribe A. Fols. 27r–30v, all in the hand of Scribe C, contain an extract from Bern of Reichenau's *Prologus in tonarium*, texts on the measurement of organ pipes, an extract from Macrobius's *Commentarius in somnium Scipionis*, and a text on the modes. Fols. 31r–32v complete the fourth quire, with chapters 2–15 and 27–35 of *De musica* in the hand of Scribe D. The fifth and final quire contains pseudo-Odo of Cluny's *Dialogus de musica*, texts for the measurement of organ pipes and bells, the antiphon *Alma redemptoris mater* complete with notation, another diagram of the intervals, and an incomplete diagram showing the correspondence between the Greek note names and the modern gamut. Scribe E copied *Dialogus de musica* and the measurement texts, while Scribe A was again responsible for the notated antiphon and diagrams. The work of Scribe A, who seems to have specialized in diagrams and notated examples, indicates that M_2 was a planned and cooperative effort to produce a music textbook in a single scriptorium.

M_2 transmits virtually the same text as *D1*, to which it is closely related. The relationship manifests itself in almost identical mise-en-page: like *D1*, M_2 has a diagram of Aribo's *caprea* horizontal in the margin. M_2 also transmits the chapter headings and in its variants and spellings is virtually identical to *D1*. The most substantial differences between the two sources are as follows: M_2 lacks chapters 36–38; M_2 separates the circle diagrams from the text, whereas *D1* transmits them in one block; and M_2 transmits a different version of the circle diagrams from *D1*.

The first two differences are probably the result of a change in plan during the production of M_2. The circle diagrams appear on fols. 7v–8r, near the end of a quire otherwise devoted to notated didactic examples. The first set of intersecting circles occupies the bottom third of fol. 7v, and the remaining three occupy the entirety of fol. 8r facing. The strangeness of their appearance here is further underlined by the fact that Scribe A has filled in all sorts of notated examples around the diagrams. He ended the sequence of examples he had begun on fol. 2r (with the didactic chant *Primum querite regnum Dei*) halfway down fol. 7v with the incomplete chant title *Domine ne <longe>*. At the bottom of fol. 7v he copied the chant *Pulchrę sunt*—adding a hybrid of traditional adiastematic neumes and Herman of Reichenau's notation—and continued it in a single line right across the bottom of fols. 7v and 8r. In the right-hand margin of fol. 8r Scribe A copied more chants with hybrid notation, squeezing them into the openings between the circle diagrams and continuing them onto fol. 8v. If, however, all of this is ignored and the circle diagrams are compared closely with the diagrams of *D1*, an important correlation is obvious: the layout of the circle diagrams in M_2 corresponds exactly to that in *D1*. This suggests that the archetype for M_2 contained precisely the same excerpt as *D1*. It was planned to copy this excerpt and Scribe A, who had a particular flair for diagrams, executed the first part of the plan. He followed the same mise-en-page found in *D1* and left the preceding folios to be filled with *De musica* chapters 6–15 and 27–38, as they appear in *D1*. For some reason, however, this never happened. During the production of the rest of the codex, Scribe D decided to, or was directed to, copy the *De musica* excerpt on what are now fols. 31r–32v. But he ran out of space and stopped at the end of chapter 35, leaving the last third of fol. 32v empty because it could not accommodate chapters 36–38, which in any case only made sense along with the circle diagrams. In the end, chapters 36–38 were never copied into M_2, and Scribe A returned to add notated didactic chants to the first quire, fitting them ingeniously around the diagrams he had so carefully copied. In any case, these chants and the circle diagrams were concerned with the modes, so he could make a virtue out of necessity to a certain extent. Such mistakes were not unknown in scriptoria where collaborative work was being undertaken: a pertinent illustration is provided by the roughly contemporary music textbook Vienna, Österreichische Nationalbibliothek, Cod. 51, where one of the scribes began to copy Bern of Reichenau's *Tonarius* even though one of his colleagues had already done so. When that scribe realized his mistake he gave up his labor mid-sentence.[52]

Although the layout of the circle diagrams in M_2 replicates that of *D1*, the diagrams themselves are different: text contained within the diagrams of M_2 differs from *D1*. The collation of the circle diagrams from the different sources indicates that M_2 is an independent variation on the *D1* text and is not related to the version of the diagrams represented by *R* (and three quarters of *S*).

Provenance. M_2 belonged to the monastery of St. Emmeram in Regensburg from 1801, where its catalog number was Em. y. 2. A note on fol. 2r dated 1802 indicates that M_2 was bought the previous year by Abbot Celestin of St. Emmeram from the Nuremberg scholar Christopher Theophil von Murr (1733–1811). The bottom of fol. 1r contains the note 'me possidet C. T. de Murr, 1799'. M_2 and another contemporary music theory manuscript (now Munich, Bayerische Staatsbibliothek, Clm 14965b) were purchased by von Murr in Bamberg in 1799.[53]

M_3 Munich, Bayerische Staatsbibliothek, Clm 29770 Frag. 3 (undetermined south German origin, mid-twelfth century)

Sections transmitted. Chapters 47–52, 53 and 54, 55–59, 61, 75, 87–94, [95–102, *Sententiae* 1, 2]

This fragment consists of two separate folios, today numbered 1 and 2. Each was originally part of a bifolium: in addition to the body text, the rectos transmit line ends on their left-hand side while the versos transmit the beginnings of lines on their right-hand side. Each folio also preserves the holes from sewing and binding that were in the center of the original bifolium. The right-hand edge of both rectos is worn, indicating that these fragments were used as book bindings. The ink on fol. 1v has been badly damaged, possibly as a result of having been glued to form a pastedown for a cover. *M_3* is written, one column per folio, in a single and clear minuscule probably dating from the first half of the twelfth century. There are no headings, but the chapters are distinguished by paragraph marks and larger red initial capitals.

The body text on each folio is from *De musica*, beginning on fol. 1r with the final ten words of chapter 47. This is followed immediately by chapters 48–52, 55–59, and 61 in their entirety. Chapters 53 and 54 are replaced by a short text of two lines, unique in the manuscript tradition of *De musica*. Fol. 1v contains chapters 75, 87, and 88, which is continued and completed on fol. 2r. Fol. 2rv continues with chapters 89–94, complete and in their proper order. The lack of chapters 60, 62–74, and 76–86 is, therefore, not the result of binding, but was either a conscious decision by the scribe or the result of the exemplar he followed.

It is possible to reconstruct the fragmentary text on the right-hand edge of fol. 2v. This folio (originally a recto) began towards the end of Aribo's first *sententia* with the words "|| predictę tarditatis in hunc modum." It contained all the remaining text from this *sententia*, the diagram of the chant *Linguam refrenans* and the second *sententia*. There may, however, have been some internal reordering at the very end, as there are inconsistencies between the fragmentary text and the order as represented by the two full recensions. The fragmentary texts on the edges of the other folios, while concerned with music, are not from *De musica*.

The abrupt beginning of *M_3*, ten words from the end of chapter 47, suggests that this fragment was originally preceded by more text from *De musica*. How much, and whether it extended back to the beginning of the treatise, cannot be ascertained. The continuity of chapter 88 from fol.1v to fol. 2r indicates that fols. 1rv and 2rv were successive folios in a quire; the survival of the fragmentary text from the *sententiae* on the same bifolium as fol. 2rv indicates that another bifolium—which transmitted the text from chapter 95 to where the fragmentary text begins—once constituted the center of that quire.[54] The fact that the fragments on the edges of the other folios are from music theory texts suggests that *De musica* was followed on this quire by other theoretical texts, in the manner that was common at the time. M_3, therefore, may well be a surviving fragment of a much larger music textbook.

Provenance: M_3 is of undetermined south German origin. It was bound with Munich, Bayerische Staatsbibliothek, Clm 17459, a manuscript from the monastery of Scheyern (in the diocese of Freising), which contains a mixture of fourteenth- and fifteenth-century material.[55]

Sf St. Florian, Stiftsbibliothek, Cod. XI 35, fol. 1rv (undetermined south German origin, mid-twelfth century)

Sections transmitted. Chapters 89–91.

A portion of *De musica* is contained on the flyleaf of St. Florian, Stiftsbibliothek, Cod. XI 35 (fol. 1rv).[56] The fragment comprises most of chapter 89, all of chapter 90, and the first few lines of chapter 91 ("<Gui>do docet . . . motus honestior"). It is written in a clear twelfth-century minuscule, with reddish-orange initial capitals and chapter headings. The trimming of *Sf* to function as a flyleaf has resulted in the loss of approximately three lines from chapter 89 ("collationis iubilationem . . . alleluia, Vado"). In its variants, *Sf* is closely related to M_3, with the exception that it transmits interlinear neumes for the example chants cited in the text (these neumes are absent in M_3). *Sf*, like *RS*, transmits interlinear neumes for the chants cited in chapters 89 and 90. It is unique in transmitting interlinear neumes for the three chants cited in chapter 91 (*Ecce ego mitto vos*, *Et dicent gloria tibi Domine*, and *Benedic Domine*). Whether or not these neumes were present in Aribo's original is unclear;[57] *R* and *S* both transmit interlinear neumes a little later on for the chants cited in chapter 94.

Provenance. *Sf* is of undetermined south German origin. The manuscript in which it is bound, a twelfth- or thirteenth-century codex containing theological material, belongs to the Augustinian canonry of St. Florian near Linz and may have been copied there.[58]

V Vienna, Österreichische Nationalbibliothek, Cod. 787, fols. 47r–62v, 63r–70v (Baumgartenberg, third quarter of the twelfth century)

Sections transmitted. V1: chapters 82–86; *V2*: variant of chapter 78; *V3*: interpolated circle diagrams.

This codex, which binds together three originally separate manuscripts, belonged to the Cistercian monastery of Baumgartenberg in the diocese of Passau.[59] The first manuscript (fols. 1r–46v), which contains St. Ephraem's *De compunctione cordis*, was copied by a single scribe—Scribe A. The ink is black and the script, which looks more Caroline than proto-Gothic, probably dates to the first half of the twelfth century. The headings and rubrication were added in red ink by another scribe—Scribe B—whose hand is more proto-Gothic and who was, perhaps, younger. Fol. 46v contains a drawing of a "Guidonian hand." This drawing must date from the time when the three manuscripts were bound together or later; it represents the filling in of an empty folio with musical material relevant to the second and third manuscripts of the codex.

The second manuscript (fols. 47r–62v) was a collaborative effort on the part of three scribes: Scribes C, D, and E.[60] It contains portions of Theoger of Metz's *Musica* (fols. 47r–53v), didactic verses on the modes (fols. 53v–57v), the parts of Aribo's *De musica* dealing with organ pipe measurements (fols. 57v–59v), and a collection of notated didactic verses (fols. 59v–62v). The text and headings from fol. 47r to fol. 59v were copied by Scribe C. He wrote in a fine, clear minuscule that is transitional between Caroline and proto-Gothic. The text and notation of the musical examples were supplied by Scribe D. The neumatic notation is on four lines with the .F. line generally colored red (although sometimes faded). Some of the musical examples are incomplete: on fols. 53r–57v space has been left for diastematic notation that was never supplied (the staff letters .c., .a., .F., and .D. are written vertically, but there are no staff lines, neumes, or text). Scribe C finished on fol. 59v, having copied Aribo's directions for the measurement of organ pipes.

The final portion of the second manuscript (fols. 59v–62v) contains a collection of notated didactic verses in the hand of a third contemporary, Scribe E. The verses, which are concerned with the modes and musical intervals, are of the type frequently found in contemporary music-theory manuscripts; their relevance to the material that preceded them suggests that their addition was not merely filling in at the end of a quire but a conscious decision to supply complementary material, perhaps by Scribe C, who directed Scribe E to do the work. These points, coupled with the fact that all the texts go across the quires, indicate that this manuscript was a planned collection fitting the pattern of a music textbook.

The second manuscript should probably be dated to the middle of the twelfth century, both on the basis of Scribe C's handwriting and its connection with a manuscript from the nearby Cistercian monastery of Zwettl (now Zwettl, Stiftsbibliothek, Cod. 328).[61] Not only does the Zwettl manuscript transmit the portions of Theoger's *Musica*, the didactic verses on the modes, and some of the notated didactic verses found in *V*, but it also shares identical variant readings. This has led Fabian Lochner to suggest that both of these manuscripts were copied from an original that belonged to the monastery of Heiligenkreuz—of which Baumgartenberg and Zwettl were daughter houses, founded in 1142 and 1138, respectively.[62]

The third manuscript (fols. 63r–70v) contains parts of Guido of Arezzo's *Micrologus* on fols. 63r–70r and on fol. 70rv the interpolated version of Aribo's circle diagrams (as in *Lz2* and related to the excerpt transmitted in KLM_1).[63] The entirety of the third manuscript has been copied by Scribe F. His hand is smaller and far less elegant that that of Scribe C from the second manuscript, although it is probably contemporaneous. There are marginal and interlinear glosses in red ink in a contemporary—if not the same—hand and on fol. 64r a gloss in a larger hand that appears more Caroline and may be the work of an older scribe. Some of these glosses have been lost due to subsequent trimming of the pages. A different style of red initial capital further distinguishes this manuscript from the second. On the whole, it is a far less tidy and more amateur affair, especially the text and diagrams on fol. 70rv, which are copied in an unskillful and squashed manner, with a good deal of triangular decoration in yellow and red.

The date at which the three manuscripts were brought together can be deduced from two pieces of evidence. The terminus post quem is established by the front and back flyleaves, which contain in three columns writing that probably dates from the late twelfth century. The terminus ante quem is supplied by an early thirteenth-century library catalog from Baumgartenberg, which lists *V* in the form in which it survives today.[64] The present codex was constituted, therefore, around the turn of the thirteenth century.

V1 (fols. 57v–59r) consists of chapters 82–86 of *De musica*, the same excerpt as *W4*.[65] The variants show that *V1* is closest to *W4*, although *V1* introduces a good number of errors and transmits a much less clean text than *RSW4*. *V1* was not copied from *W4*, however, because it transmits a passage in chapter 83 that *W4* lacks ("quinta perficitur . . . cum medietate diametri"). It is inconsistent in its transmission of the chapter headings, having a unique heading for 82, none for 83, mangling the end of the heading for 84, and transmitting Aribo's headings for 85 and 86. The textual evidence suggests that *V1* stems from the archetype of *W4*, probably through an intermediate copy or copies.

V2 (fol. 59rv) follows *V1* in the manuscript. It transmits the varied recension of chapter 78,[66] and so is closely related to *D3W3*. Yet *V2* introduces many errors to the *D3W3* text. It cannot have been copied from *D3*, because as with *W3*, *V2* transmits the heading at the beginning of chapter

78 but not the second heading in *W3* before the variant ending. Neither can it have been copied from *W3*, because it transmits a portion of text lacking there ("segreges ac ex aliis tribus .e. conformes. Cui dimidium super"). *V2* probably goes back through intermediate copies to the archetype of *D3W3*.

V3 (fol. 70rv) consists of the intersecting circle diagrams that have been combined with text from Bern of Reichenau's *Tonarius*. This adapted excerpt is also transmitted in *KLLz2M*$_1$.[67]

Provenance. *V* belonged to the Cistercian monastery of Baumgartenberg in the diocese of Passau and was probably copied there. Its three constituent manuscripts were bound together in their present form by the early thirteenth-century.[68]

W Wolfenbüttel, Herzog-August Bibliothek, Gud. lat. 334 8° (SS. Ulrich and Afra in Augsburg, mid-twelfth century)

Sections transmitted. W1: chapters 6, 7, 9, 10, 27–29, 31–35; *W2*: chapter 81; *W3*: chapters 78–80; *W4*: chapters 82–86; *W5*: diamond-shaped diagram; *W6*: chapter 102.

This codex of 177 folios was copied at the monastery of SS. Ulrich and Afra in Augsburg in the mid-twelfth century.[69] It is a music textbook that contains Guido of Arezzo's four treatises; Theoger of Metz's *Musica*; extracts from Aribo's *De musica*; directions for the measurement of organ pipes, monochords, and bells; a tonary; and other didactic verses. It also has special local significance: the tonary it contains on fols. 139v–174v is the tonary by Udalschalk, abbot of SS. Ulrich and Afra from 1127 to 1151.

Three scribes—one illustrator and two text scribes—worked together on the production of *W*. On the first quire (fols. 1r–4v, an irregular quire), the *pictor* provided stylish illustrations in red, pale greens, and muted yellows that foreshadow the content of the textbook. We see Pope Gregory I notating his eponymous chant (fol. 1r), the scene of Pythagoras discovering the musical consonances while walking by a smithy (fols. 1v and 2r), a personified and matronly *Musica* sitting with a monochord on her lap (fol. 2v), Guido of Arezzo poised at his writing desk having written the opening words of his treatise *Regule rithmice* (fol. 4r), and a Guidonian hand (fol. 4v).[70] The *pictor* was followed by Scribe A, who copied fols. 5v–127v and 129r–139v, and Scribe B, who copied fols. 139v–174v. Fol. 128rv is a singleton insert in the hand of a third contemporary (Scribe C), while the end matter (fols. 175r–176v) is a fragment from a thirteenth-century missal that was added to *W* at a later date. Excepting the first quire containing the illustrations (fols. 1r–4v), the last quire of four bifolia (fols. 167r–174v), and two singleton inserts (fols.

77rv and 128rv), *W* is laid out uniformly in quires of five. Scribes A and B copied all the material across these quires.

Material from *De musica* appears in six separate parts of *W*. The variants of these excerpts indicate that they were not copied from a single archetype. *W1* transmits chapters 6, 7, 9, 10, 27–29, and 31–35 on fols. 57r–61r. The contour of *W1* implies that it is a reduced version of the *D1M*$_2$ excerpt.[71] This interpretation is corroborated by the textual variants and by the fact that like *D1M*$_2$, *W1* transmits the diagram of Aribo's *caprea* vertically in the margin. The possibility that *W1* is closer to *M*$_2$ than to *D1*—because *W1* lacks chapters 36–38 and the circle diagrams—does not find conclusive support in the variants and should probably be put down to the selective nature of the *W1* excerpt. *W1* also does not transmit the chapter headings of *D1M*$_2$: it has headings only for chapters 6 and 28, each of which is unique in the manuscript tradition of *De musica*. It is likely that Scribe A suppressed Aribo's headings and added two of his own. The fact that *W1* is a condensed version of *D1M*$_2$ indicates that he was quite willing to emend his source as it suited him.

W2, *W3*, and *W4* are found in the part of *W* that contains an extensive collection of measurement texts for organ pipes, bells, and monochords (fols. 90v–111r). *W2* (fol. 101v) consists of *De musica* chapter 81. It is closer in its variants to *SD2* than to *R*. Whereas neither *S* nor *D2* transmits a heading for chapter 81, the heading in *W2* ("Item alia ab acutis incipiens") is obviously derived from Aribo's original, known only from *R* ("Alia monochordi mensura ab acutis incipiens"). It is possible that the archetype of *W2* was not a copy of *De musica* at all but a collection of measurement texts that contained an already excerpted chapter 81. Nevertheless, that archetype still retained an echo of Aribo's original heading.

W3 (fols. 103r–104v) comprises chapters 78–80, with Aribo's chapter headings. Like *D3V2*, it transmits the variant second half of chapter 78.[72] *W3* cannot have been copied from *D3*, because *D3* transmits neither a heading for chapter 78 nor chapters 79 and 80. *W3* also has a unique heading before the variant second half of chapter 78, a heading not present in *D3V2* ("De ponderatione cymbalorum"). Consequently, *W3* and *D3* either share an archetype containing the three chapters in question with the variant second half of chapter 78, or stem from copies of this archetype. The variants for chapters 79 and 80 show that *W3* is closer to *S* than to *R*. Uniquely, however, *W3* is the only witness to transmit the line "qua circinus est uice quinta. Ex .A." from chapter 80, which implies that *W3* goes back independently on the *S* side to an early recension of *De musica*.

W4 comprises chapters 82–86 (fols. 106r–110v), with Aribo's chapter headings. The variants show that *W4* is equally balanced in terms of its relationship to *R* and *S*, although it contains an appreciable number of minor errors that do not significantly change the meaning of the text: "sua" for "sui," "sesqualtera" for "sesqualteraque," and "inter" for "in," for example.

W5 consists of the diamond-shaped diagram that precedes the final chapter of *De musica*. It was added by Scribe A to fill a blank side (fol. 127v) between the end of pseudo-Odo of Cluny's *Dialogus de musica* (fols. 112r–127r) and the beginning of a section of the manuscript devoted to notated didactic verses (fols. 129r–139r). Scribe A must have thought it provided an apt means of summing up the theoretical texts he had copied in an earlier part of *W*: he provided the diagram with the unique heading "Inter quas chordas et literas quemlibet sit consonantia."

W6 transmits the final chapter of *De musica* (chap. 102). It was not part of the original plan for *W*, but was added afterwards: fol. 128rv, on which it survives, is a singleton that has been inserted between fols. 127rv and 129rv. The writing by Scribe C is smaller than that of Scribes A or B, and differs markedly in style; it could be contemporary or perhaps even earlier in date. The variants show that *W6* was copied neither from *S* nor from *R*, but is closer to *S* than to *R*. Uniquely, however, *W6* transmits the correct reading *utique* instead of *utque* (*RS*), suggesting that it may derive from an early copy of *De musica*. The physical evidence gives the impression that *W6* is from an unfinished copy of *De musica* that was subsequently dissected: this excerpt transmits neither the heading—though space has been left for it—nor the final sentence of chapter 102, and is followed by a blank half folio (fol. 128v). The scribal differences between it and the rest of *W* suggests that the manuscript from which it came was not produced in the scriptorium of SS. Ulrich and Afra, but travelled there from another monastery. When this happened is unknown. The original manuscript may have arrived at Augsburg and been dissected in time for the insertion of *W6* between fols. 127rv and 129rv soon after *W* was produced or even during the original collation and binding. It is equally possible that that manuscript was dissected and inserted at a much later date, perhaps at the same time that the end material was added to *W*. In either case, the monk who inserted it was familiar with *De musica* and thought that the stray final chapter would find a good home with the diamond-shaped diagram (*W5*) that had been copied for a very different reason.

Provenance. *W* was copied at the monastery of SS. Ulrich and Afra in Augsburg. Sometime before 1651 it was bought by Bernard Rottendorf (d. 1686) and then passed to the archeologist and classical scholar Marquard Gude (1635–89). It was bought for the ducal library at Wolfenbüttel by G. W. Leibniz in 1710.

The Variant of Chapter 78 in *D3*, *V2*, and *W3*

A variant of the second half of chapter 78—in place of Aribo's text from "Reponderationes cerę" to "de tribus synemmenon conficias"—occurs in three manuscripts: *D3V2W3*. The variant itself comprises two separate measurement texts. The first text ("De reponderatione cerę primi cymbali . . . quę supersunt cymbalum statuas") is transmitted in a number of contemporary manuscripts in addition to *D3V2W3*. These include M_2, fol. 38r; Munich, Bayerische Staatsbibliothek, Clm 19421, fol. 27rv (a late eleventh-century manuscript from the monastery of Tegernsee); and Vienna, Österreichische Nationalbibliothek, Cod. 51, fol. 55vb (a textbook codex of undetermined south German origin dating from first half of the twelfth century). The second text ("Dimidium .G. sibi iungas . . . de quo residuo synemenon habeas") is found only in *D3V2W3*.[73]

Erroneous Attributions

Under this heading are listed a number of manuscripts that have previously been cited as sources for *De musica*, but which collation has shown to be false attributions.

Brussels, Bibliothèque Royale, MS 10162/66, fols. 54r–79v (66r–91v).[74] Joseph Smits van Waesberghe listed this portion of the Brussels manuscript as a source for *De musica* in his 1951 edition, although he did not subsequently use it in his critical apparatus.[75] It is actually a fifteenth-century copy of the copy of the treatise *Quaestiones in musica* transmitted in Darmstadt, Universitäts- und Hochschulbibliothek, Cod. 1988, fols. 110v–143v.

Brussels, Bibliothèque Royale, MS 10162/66, fol. 96rv (108rv) ("<E>t alie uoces . . . Vve sesqualterarum"). This excerpt was cited in Smits van Waesberghe's edition as a partial source for *sententia* 1.[76] Although it appears both in *Commentarius anonymus in Micrologum Guidonis Aretini* and *sententia* 1, the variants show that it was copied from the anonymous commentary and not from *De musica*. The confusion arises because the text of the Brussels excerpt is contained within the long passage that Aribo quoted from the commentary.

Munich, Bayerische Staatsbibliothek, Clm 4622, fol. 178v.[77] This codex from the monastery of Benediktbeuern combines seven manuscripts dating from the late eleventh century to the middle of the thirteenth.[78] Its seventh constituent manuscript, dating from the early twelfth century, transmits a set of organ-pipe measurements entitled "Organica dispositio secundum Aribonem." What the scribe incorrectly attributed to Aribo was actually copied from a short anonymous treatise on the measurement of the monochord found in two other contemporary manuscripts without attribution to Aribo: the eleventh-century Tegernsee manuscript Munich, Bayerische Staatsbibliothek, Clm 18914, fol. 42r, and a lost twelfth-century manuscript from St. Blasien.[79]

Munich, Bayerische Staatsbibliothek, Clm 14663, fol. 15rv ("Et alię uoces . . . Miserere mei fili Dauid"). Like Brussels, Bibliothèque Royale, MS 10162/66, fol. 96rv (108rv), this excerpt was also cited in Smits van Waesberghe's edition as a partial source for the first *sententia*.[80] The reason for the confusion is the same: the excerpt in question appears both in the anonymous commentary and Aribo's *sententia*. The textual variants of fol. 15rv show clearly that it is more closely related to the other surviving manuscripts of *Commentarius anonymus* than to *R* and *S*, which transmit the extract from the commentary as it appears in Aribo's *sententia*. Furthermore, the evidence of the variants is supported by contextual evidence from M_1, which contains all four of Guido of Arezzo's music treatises. *Micrologus* (fols. 1r–11r), however, is detached from the other three, which have been copied together (fols. 17r–24v). The intervening section contains three texts: the anonymous *Quomodo de arithmetica procedit musica* (fols. 11r–14v), the excerpt in question (fol. 15rv) and another extract from *Commentarius anonymus* (fols. 15v–16v). Fols. 15rv and 16rv are singletons, inserted between the second and third quires (fols. 9r–14v and 17r–24v) because they complemented the other material in the manuscript. As both folios are in one hand—different from but contemporary to the main hands of M_1—it is more plausible that the text is an abridged extract from *Commentarius anonymus*, rather than two separate items (one from Aribo's *sententia* and the other from the *Commentarius anonymus*). Consequently, this part of M_1 should not be considered a source for *De musica*.

Munich, Bayerische Staatsbibliothek, Clm 18914, fol. 42r. Listed in Smits van Waesberghe's edition, this set of monochord measurements ("Organalis mensura hoc exigit . . . et finita est mensura") from an eleventh-century Tegernsee manuscript is not part of *De musica*.[81]

Copenhagen, Det Kongelige Bibliothek, S. 73 8°, fols. 1v–37r. This twelfth-century manuscript was cited in Smits van Waesberghe's edition as a source for *De musica*.[82] Nevertheless, it is a source for *Quaestiones in musica*, not Aribo's treatise.

Vienna, Österreichische Nationalbibliothek, Cod. 2502, fols. 1r–19r. This twelfth-century manuscript transmits the treatise *Commentarius anonymus in Micrologum Guidonis Aretini*, which was used by Aribo both in *De musica* and *sententia* 1.[83] Smits van Waesberghe treated it as if it were a source for *De musica*, using it in some of the instances where Aribo quoted from the commentary but not in others.[84]

Florence, Biblioteca Medicea Laurenziana, Acq. e doni 33, fols. 2v–51r. This twelfth-century manuscript of German origin is also a source for *Commentarius anonymus in Micrologum Guidonis Aretini*. It is, presumably, the *F* that appears mysteriously in Smits van Waesberghe's critical apparatus.[85] But there is no mention of it among Smits van Waesberghe's sigla or in the manuscript descriptions that precede his edition.[86]

Manuscript Circulation of the Diagrams

Aribo's diagrams are integral to his treatise. They are remarkably consistent in their transmission across the manuscripts, but in some instances variants of the diagrams offer important clues to manuscript filiations.

Caprea

The only manuscripts to transmit *caprea* are the manuscripts of the excerpt preserved by *D1Lz1M$_2$W1*. The three twelfth-century witnesses—*D1M$_2$W1*—are remarkably consistent in their transmission of *caprea*: in each of the three it appears vertically in the margins. *Lz1*, dating from the thirteenth century, transmits *caprea* horizontally. *Caprea* is not transmitted by either of the full recensions, *RS*.

The Quadripartite Figure

There are good reasons for believing that the diagram of the quadripartite figure was not part of Aribo's original. The figure was so well known that a diagram of it was not necessary: Aribo says that there were "very few monochords without it."[87] Aribo's language also makes clear that he is describing something that he had not represented visually. This was not the case with *caprea*, since Aribo comments on specific aspects of the diagram that presuppose the existence of a visual representation in his treatise (he describes the "red-colored tetrachordal lines," for example).[88]

D5 is the only early source to transmit the quadripartite figure, apart from the later *Lz1*, which is a lineal descendant of *D*.[89] The diagram as it appears in *D* (fol. 171r) is very rudimentary and amateurish, especially when compared with William of Hirsau's *theorema troporum*, which is, in fact, the real quadripartite figure.[90] This suggests that the diagram of the quadripartite figure in *D* could have been a gloss from another source: it might have already been in the exemplar of *D5* or have been added independently by the scribe when *D1* was supplemented with *D5*. As it appears in *D*, therefore, it looks very much as an afterthought. For these reasons,

I do not believe that the diagram of the quadripartite figure was part of Aribo's original treatise.

The Circle Diagrams

Aribo's intersecting circles diagrams were one of the most popular parts of *De musica*: in addition to being transmitted by *BD1M$_2$RS*, they formed the basis of the excerpt represented by *KLLz2M$_1$V3* and were used by subsequent theorists, such as John in the early twelfth century.[91] These diagrams consist of four sets of two intersecting circles. Each circle circumscribes the ambit of an octave. When intersected, the two circles span the ambit of an octave and a fourth, or in other words, the combined authentic and plagal range of each of the modes.

There are, however, two main branches to the tradition of these diagrams. They have the intersection of the circles and the span of an octave and a fourth in common but differ in the accompanying text that describes this arrangement. The first branch is represented at its earliest stage by *D1*; the second by *R*. *R*, however, is incomplete, with only the first of the four sets having been finished. The *D1* version forms the basis of the interpolated version of the diagrams found in *KLLz2M$_1$V3*, although some of the detail in *D1* has been omitted in these manuscripts. *M$_2$* contains a unique version.[92] Collation with the other sources, however, shows that the *M$_2$* version derives from the *D1* version and not from *R*; the changes in *M$_2$* were perhaps the individual contribution of its scribe. Finally, *S* combines the two traditions: its first set of circles is identical to *D1*, while its second, third, and fourth are the same as the incomplete second, third, and fourth sets from *R*. Interestingly, the transition from the first to the second circle in *S* coincides with a change of scribe.[93] The implication of this is that *S* was copied from two sources; one on the *D* side of the manuscript tradition, the other on the *R* side. The incomplete nature of the second version in *R* and *S* indicates that the exemplar for this version was never completed. This still leaves the intriguing question: if the circle diagrams in *S* were copied from two sources, why prefer an incomplete version (represented by *R*) over a complete and detailed version (represented by *D*)?

It is possible only to speculate that two versions of the circle diagrams may go back to different drafts of *De musica* by Aribo. Other evidence, such as the addition of the *sententiae*, suggests that Aribo wrote a preliminary version of *De musica* before the final version that he presented to Ellenhard of Freising. If so, then perhaps the circles transmitted by *R* (and three quarters of those by *S*) stem from the initial and unfinished version, in which case the more detailed circles of *D* (and a quarter of those in *S*) stem from the final version. The version of the second, third, and fourth sets of circles in Smits van Waesberghe's edition conflates the two traditions.[94]

The Synemmenon Diagram

This little diagram ends chapter 74.[95] It occurs only in *RS*, as these are the only sources for this chapter. Although the positioning of the notes .a. and .c. in these sources differs, both agree on the positioning of .b. above the line and .♭. below. The version of the diagram in Smits van Waesberghe's edition is inaccurate.[96]

The Organ Pipe Diagrams

RSV1W4 are the sources for these two diagrams, which occur in chapter 83.[97] The first is a drawing of an organ pipe, showing the length and the position of the lip. The second shows the division of the pipe's diameter by a third and a half. Smits van Waesberghe did not print the first diagram.[98]

Melodic and Intervallic Diagrams

RS transmit a sequence of five diagrams between chapters 101 and 102.[99] Two of these diagrams are also transmitted by *D4*, while one is transmitted by *W5*.

The first diagram (transmitted by *RS*) illustrates melodic movement by the leap (*saltatrix*), step (*spissa*), fourth (*quaternaria*), and third (*ternaria*). The second diagram (transmitted by *D4RS*) is more complex. It illustrates how the four types of melodic movement over the ambit of a *diapente* correspond to the four versions of the metrical foot called the epitrite. The third diagram (also transmitted by *D4RS*) continues this theme but deals with the ambit of a *diatessaron*: it illustrates how the four types of movement correspond to the meter of *insule*, and the *bachian*, *antibachian*, and *amphymacrus*. The fourth diagram (only transmitted by *RS*) shows the division of the gamut into double-*diapason*, *diapason*, *diapente*, *diatessaron*, and tone. Diagrams of this type appear quite frequently in contemporary music theory manuscripts and owe something to the Boethian tradition of harmonics. This fourth diagram, however, is Aribo's own version and would later influence Frutolf of Michelsberg. These four diagrams are not edited properly in Smits van Waesberghe's edition but are only presented in a number of unclear plates from *RS*.[100]

The fifth and final diagram is a diamond-shaped one that is designed as a key for finding the notes that produce the different intervals. It is transmitted by *RSW5*. The diamond is in two halves: the bottom triangle is a matrix of notes, and the top triangle is the key to this matrix. By starting from the top and running his finger across to the opposing note of a row, a reader can find each of the intervals described in the text of the top triangle. The diamond is surrounded by text explaining the purpose of the figure. Smits van Waesberghe's edition omits the surrounding text and skews the diamond by forty-five degrees, robbing the figure of its meaning.[101]

The Vowel Diagram

This diagram, which belongs to *sententia* 1, is transmitted by *RS* (it is also present in M_3 but most of it has been lost due to the later trimming of this source).[102] The diagram is originally from *Micrologus* 16, from which Aribo was quoting at that point.[103]

The Linguam refrenans Diagram

The diagram of the chant *Linguam refrenans* (transmitted by *RS*) is from the end of *sententia* 1 and provides a visual graph of Aribo's discussion of this chant.[104] It is likely that Aribo was inspired by *Micrologus*, which he was using at this point, because Guido has a similar diagram using the chant *Sancte Iohannes meritorum tuorum*.[105]

Chants and Notation

Aribo's chant citations occur in chapters 31, 65, 74, 77, 89–91, 94, 98, *sententia* 1, and *sententia* 2. Some of these citations are accompanied by adiastematic or unheighted neumes. The first chant cited in chapter 31 is *Alliga domine in vinculis*; of the three sources *D1RS*, only *D1* has neumes, and those only on the word *Alliga*. For the remaining four chants in this chapter—*Ecce nomen Domini*, *Ecce in nubibus caeli*, *Ecce ueniet Deus et homo*, and *Leua Hierusalem*—each of the three sources transmits interlinear neumes, although there are some differences, caused partially by the abbreviation of the chant title in *D1S*. In chapters 65, 74, and 77 neither *R* nor *S* transmits neumes. In chapters 89–91, where the sources are *RS*M_3*Sf*, there is no uniform practice: *RS* transmit neumes for certain chants but not for others, M_3 consistently lacks neumes for the portion of text it covers, and *Sf* consistently transmits neumes for the section it covers. In these chapters, therefore, *Sf* is sometimes the only source transmitting neumes. *RS* transmit neumes for the chant citations in chapter 94 but not for those in chapter 98. In the *sententiae* the situation is again inconsistent: some chants are notated only in *R*, others only in *S*, and yet others in neither.

The lack of consistency in the sources makes it difficult to determine whether or not Aribo provided neumes for his chant citations. He would certainly not have needed to do so and could reasonably have expected his clerical audience to be familiar with the examples he cited. The neumes that appear inconsistently in the sources may well have been added by intermediate scribes.

Quaestiones in musica and the Transmission of *De musica*

The treatise entitled *Quaestiones in musica* survives in three manuscripts: Darmstadt, Universitäts- und Hochschulbibliothek, Cod. 1988, fols. 110v–143v, and Copenhagen, Det Kongelige Bibliothek, S. 73 8°, fols. 1v–37r, both dating from the twelfth century; and Brussels, Bibliothèque Royale, MS 10162/66, fols. 54r–79v (66r–91v), dating from the fifteenth. The Brussels recension was copied from Darmstadt, which is the earliest of the three.

Quaestiones in musica is in two parts. The first part, which deals with the usual topics of German music theory, is divided into twenty-seven chapters or "questions," as the rubric in the Darmstadt manuscript indicates. The resolution to these questions is provided by the text of each chapter in a manner that prefigures the *quaestio* technique usually associated with the twelfth-century schools of northern France. Much of this first part is a deft collage of quotation, with lengthy passages from pseudo-Odo, Guido, Bern and Herman of Reichenau, the Wolf Anonymous, and Aribo being adapted and abridged as necessary, or linked with material supplied by the compiler. The second part focuses on musical proportions and harmonics; much of it was copied directly from the Carolingian treatise *Scolica enchiriadis.*

Cölestin Vivell suggested that *Quaestiones in musica* was written by Franco of Liège (1047–ca. 1093), while Rudolph Steglich argued for the authorship of Rudolf of St. Trond (ca. 1070–1138). There is, however, no evidence to support either of these attributions.[106] A more accurate impression of the origins of *Quaestiones in musica* is provided by palaeographical and textual analysis, which links its earliest source with *D*, the copy of Aribo's *De musica* that belonged to the monastery of St. James in Liège.

A number of points suggest that the second manuscript in the Darmstadt codex originated in the same scriptorium as its companion third manuscript (*D*). Both belonged to the monastery of St. James in Liège. Both are more or less contemporary, and similar in their size, text blocking, ruling pattern, and style of minuscule. The physical evidence is supported by the textual evidence: the variants of the Aribo quotations in the Darmstadt copy of *Quaestiones in musica* are almost identical to those of the Aribo excerpts in *D*.

The first part of *Quaestiones in musica* incorporates all or part of twenty-two chapters from *De musica* (chapters 16–18, 21, 26, 31, 32, 53, 54, 60, 64, 67, 70, 71, 73–75, 78, 82, 84, 86, and 89). Like other contemporary German treatises, *Quaestiones in musica* begins with the monochord.

Its compiler/author depended heavily on Aribo for this topic: he selected chapters 16–18, 21, and 26 of *De musica* (all dealing with the monochord) and copied them together on fol. 112r–113r of Darmstadt, MS 1988. The headings he supplied himself. He combined chapters 31 and 32 into one unit on fols. 118v–119r and did the same with chapters 53 and 54 on fols. 124v–125v, including Aribo's diagrams as well, although changing them slightly. Chapters 73 and 74 appear along with chapter 60 in the middle of the answer to *quaestio* 9 on fols. 113v–114r. Chapter 75, sometimes abbreviated and paraphrased, forms most of the answer to *quaestio* 12 on fol. 115rv. An abridged version of chapter 64, all of chapter 67, the end of chapter 70, and all of chapter 71 constitute the answer to *quaestio* 13 on fols. 115v–116r. A short passage from chapter 89 is split into two parts on fols. 126v and 127r, respectively. Chapter 78 occupies most of fol. 129rv. Significantly, the second half of this chapter is the variant version transmitted by *D3V2W3*.[107] But here again the scribe followed his own design, for he transitioned seamlessly into another text before the end of the variant second half. An excerpt from chapter 82, and chapters 84 and 86 are combined in one unit on fols. 129v–130v.

Although the variants of the Aribo passages show that the second manuscript of the Darmstadt codex is closely related to *D*, they also indicate that it was not copied from *D*. Perhaps the most telling example is found at the end of chapter 26 of *De musica*. The text of the chapter's last two lines reads: "Idem est Boetii mese, paramese, trite diezeugmenon, paranete diezeugmenon. Tetrachordum excellentium est .d.e.f.g. secundum Guidonem, iuxta Boetium autem paranete diezeugmenon, nete diezeugmenon, trite hyperboleon, paranete hyperboleon." *D* renders this passage "Idem est Boetii mese, paramese, trite diezeugmenon, Paranetediezeugmenon, Netediezeu|gmenon, Tritehyperboleon, Paraneteyperboleon" with the added comment "et excellentium" in the margin. *Quaestiones in musica* renders it "Identidem iuxta boetium nete diezeugmenon, trite yperboleon, Peranete yperboleon || nete yperboleon." The confusion apparent in both sources indicates the presence of a shared exemplar in which the passage was corrupt. Furthermore, *Quaestiones in musica* includes some chapters from *De musica* that are not found in the various excerpts of *D*. The existence of these extra chapters corroborates the theory of a shared exemplar and reinforces the suggestion that one of the exemplars of *D* was a relatively full version of *De musica*.

Quaestiones in musica, therefore, seems to have been compiled from the same sources as *D*. The closeness of the two manuscripts, coupled with the codicological and palaeographical evidence, suggests that they were produced in the same scriptorium. Thus the Darmstadt copy of *Quaestiones in musica* may well be the original of the treatise. If that is so, its author was neither

Franco of Liège nor Rudolf of St. Trond, but an anonymous scribe working in the scriptorium that produced *D*, quite possibly the scriptorium of St. James's monastery in Liège.

The Relationship of the Manuscripts

Full Versions

The surviving manuscripts indicate that *De musica* circulated in a number of versions. The full version is represented by *RS*. Neither was copied from the archetype of *De musica*. The variants show that *RS* are not related and represent different sides of the manuscript tradition. Nevertheless, the conflation of the two versions of the circle diagrams in *S* suggests that it was influenced by a second manuscript that belonged to the *R* side of that tradition.

Excerpted Versions

The division of *De musica* into many chapters made it a favorite choice for scribes in search of excerpts for their music textbooks. Consequently, most of the surviving sources transmit only portions of the treatise. Collation of the manuscripts shows that excerpts were made early in the history of *De musica* and that these excerpts circulated independently, being copied in turn by later generations of scribes. The excerpts can be divided into three distinct groups (designated ε1, ε2, and ε3 in the stemma).

The first excerpt (chapters 6–15, 27–38, and the intersecting circle diagrams) is represented at its earliest stage by $D1M_2$. These witnesses ultimately derive from the same archetype, which must have been excerpted during the late eleventh century or at the very beginning of the twelfth (ε1 in the stemma). $D1M_2$ are virtually identical except that M_2 omits chapters 36–38, separates the circle diagrams from the text, and transmits an independent variation of those diagrams derived from the version witnessed by *D1*.[108] *W1* is a reduced version of the first excerpt, transmitting only chapters 6, 7, 9, 10, 27–29, and 31–35.

D1 was the direct or indirect archetype for *Lz1* in the thirteenth century. *Lz1* was also influenced by another, unknown source, which was responsible for introducing the confusing and contradictory headings about the *scholasticus* Stephen.[109] The circle diagrams at the end of *Lz1* (designated *Lz2* here) stem not from ε1 but from ε3. Perhaps this excerpt was the source that introduced the headings into *Lz1*.

D1, along with *D5*, was the direct archetype for *B* in the fifteenth century. By the time the scribe of *B* copied the material from *De musica*, the third manuscript of the Darmstadt codex was already in its present form, containing the *D5D1* sequence on fols. 170v–174v. This explains why *B* comprises chapters 2–15 and 27–38, along with the circle diagrams.

The second excerpt (ε2 in the stemma) centers on the chapters of *De musica* devoted to measurement texts (chaps. 78–86). Measurement texts were an important constituent of music theory textbooks and Aribo's nine chapters on the subject were a popular quarry for scribes. Collation of the manuscripts has uncovered a very complicated dissemination for these chapters, represented by *D3V1V2W2W3W4*. The exact origins of these excerpts are probably unrecoverable, but the following contours can be made out. The scribe of the *W* was the only one to copy all nine of these chapters. He did not copy them in numerical or physical sequence, however, with the result that there are three separate groupings scattered throughout his textbook: *W2* (chap. 81, fol. 101v), *W3* (chaps. 78–80, fols. 103r–104v), and *W4* (chaps. 82–86, fols. 106r–110v). The separation of these excerpts, as well as their variants, suggests that they derive from different sources. *D3* contains only chapters 78, 81, and 85, which were obviously copied together by the same scribe. It is impossible to tell whether he decided to excerpt these chapters or whether his source already had them in excerpted form. *V1* (chapters 82–86) and *V2* (chapter 78) were also copied contiguously by a single scribe, again leaving open the possibilities of an archetype where this reordering had already been made, a selection by that scribe from a single fuller archetype or a combination of two sources by that scribe.

From these possibilities the following can be deduced: *D3V2W3* are connected by the variant of chapter 78, which only they transmit. This variant probably entered the tradition of *De musica* early because, although it is not present in either of the full recensions, *W3* seems to go back to an early copy of *De musica* independent of the full recensions.[110] *W4* and *V1*, both of which transmit chapters 82–86, are obviously linked: they share an archetype. Finally, *W2* was not copied from *D3* and may stem from a collection of measurement texts that already contained the excerpt.

The third excerpt (ε3 in the stemma) consists of chapters 36–38 and the version of the circle diagrams that includes passages from Bern of Reichenau's *Tonarius*. This excerpt is represented in part or in full by *KLLz2*M_1*V3*. The existence of a single original version can be inferred from these witnesses. Although *L* is the earliest, it cannot have been the archetype because it omits chapter 37. *K*, which is the only one to transmit the entire excerpt, contains headings that are the individual contribution of its scribe and not Aribo's originals. M_1 omits chapter 38, while *V3* and *Lz2* contain only the interpolated circle diagrams. In the case of *Lz*, the interpolated circle diagrams have been substituted for Aribo's original diagrams at the end of ε1. This implies that the scribe of *Lz* or of its archetype had access to both the first and third excerpts. It is possible that he preferred the interpolated version because of its explanatory material.

The remaining excerpts are found in *D* and *W*. *D2* (chapters 45–58), *D4* (two of the melodic movement diagrams), *D5* (chapters 2–15), *D6* (chapters 16–26), and *D7* (chapters 58–61) suggest that more than one version of *De musica* was present in the scriptorium in which *D* was copied. *W5W6* are excerpts from the end of *De musica*. *W5* (the diamond-shaped diagram) was added to fill a blank side and may have been taken from a full version of *De musica*. *W6* is a singleton insert into the Wolfenbüttel codex that may have been part of an unfinished copy of *De musica*.

Fragmentary Versions

The fragmentary sources M_3*Sf* are not related to the three standard excerpts. M_3 transmits a substantial portion of *De musica*: chapters 47–52, an abbreviation in place of chapters 53 and 54, chapters 55–61, 75, 87–94, and, based upon reconstruction, chapters 95–102 with the two *sententiae*. M_3 is therefore unlikely to represent the perpetuation of an excerpt. M_3 was probably copied from a full version of *De musica* and may originally have transmitted more of the earlier part of the treatise. For the portions it does transmit the other witnesses are *RS*, supplemented by *D2D7* and *Sf*. The variants show it to be closer to *D2D7SSf* than to *R*.

The fragmentary *Sf* (chaps. 89–91) may well have once transmitted a much larger portion of *De musica*. For the portion it now transmits the only other witnesses are M_3*RS*. As it is, it transmits neumed chant examples not present in either of the full recensions. The variants show that it is closer to M_3*S* than to *R*.

The textual variants for the small legible portion of *F* show that it is closest to *D1*M_2*S*. Its exceptionally fragmentary nature makes it impossible to identify whether it was originally part of ε1, another unrelated excerpt, or a full version of *De musica*.

The Stemma

The stemma is designed to illustrate the complex dissemination of *De musica*. In order to provide a clearer overview of the manuscript tradition, the multiple excerpts in *DLzVW* have not been differentiated. Nevertheless, the dependence of these manuscripts on multiple sources is clearly evident. The place of *F* in the stemma is conjectural.

Figure 13. The stemma of *De musica*

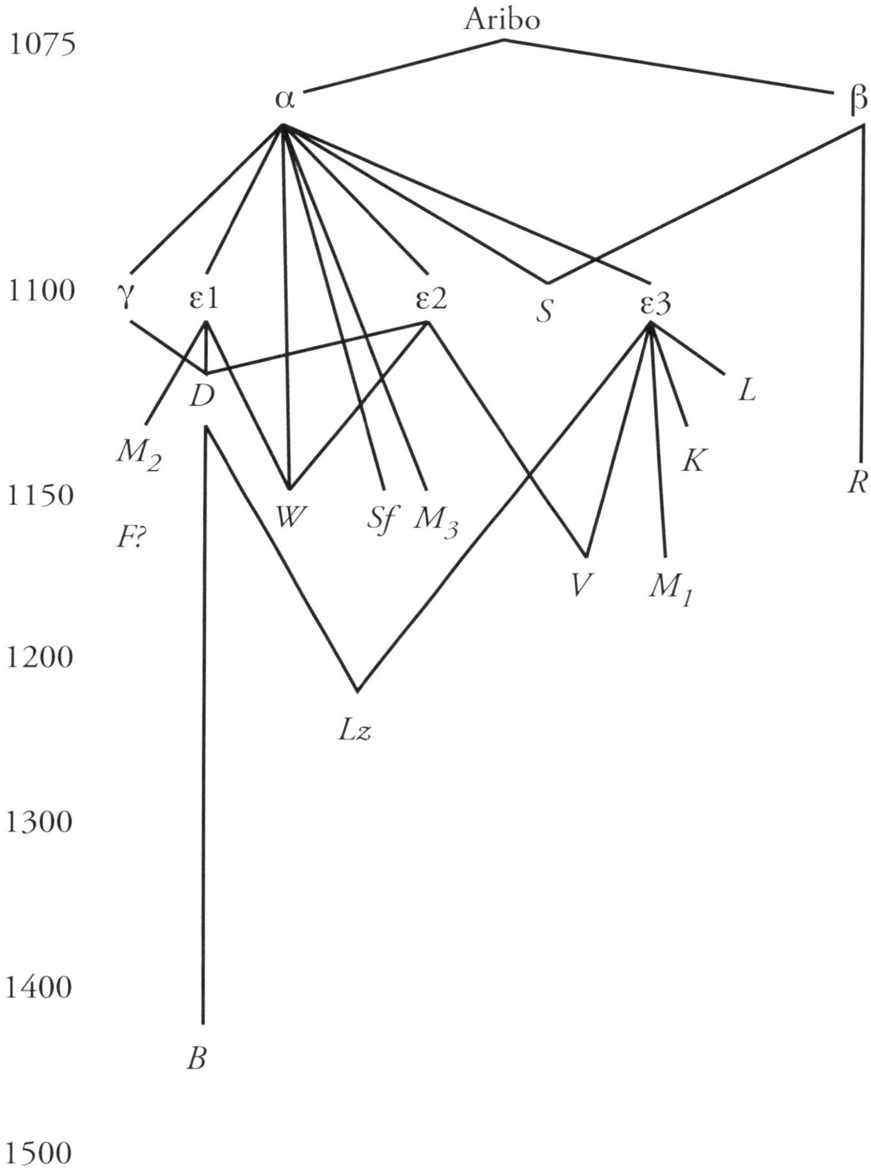

Conclusions

A number of full recensions of *De musica* are no longer extant. If, as I have suggested above, the *sententiae* are Aribo's response to questions Bishop Ellenhard asked after reading an early version of the treatise, then that preliminary version is among the lost manuscripts. Those lost manuscripts include the final version, which contained the *sententiae*. Furthermore, it is possible to infer the existence of the dedication copy that was presented to Bishop Ellenhard—the copy that the author of *De scriptoribus ecclesiasticis* seems to have seen in the twelfth century.[111] But the fact that none of the surviving manuscripts preserves the dedicatory verses quoted by Wolfger implies that these manuscripts stem from a version that lacked these verses. This version was probably Aribo's own copy, the final version mentioned above. It is certain that it was the final version, and not the hypothetical preliminary version, because it contains the two *sententiae*. It is witnessed by *RS*, as well as the abridged M_3.

At this point the tradition of *De musica* splits into two branches (represented by α and β in the stemma). All the surviving manuscripts derive from α except *R*, which derives from β. The internal misordering of *R* points to the existence of at least one manuscript between it and Aribo's autograph.

It is probable that other full versions once existed on the α side. *D* was influenced by at least two exemplars, one of which may have been a full copy (designated γ in the stemma).[112] *Sf* may be the sole surviving fragment of a relatively full copy, and *W5W6* probably go back to an early full copy or copies of the treatise.[113]

There were really only three excerpts of *De musica* in independent circulation: ε1 (chapters 6–15, 27–38, and the circle diagrams), ε2 (having its basis in the nine measurement chapters of *De musica*), and ε3 (chapters 36–38 and the interpolated version of the circle diagrams).

R and *S*, the two full recensions of *De musica*, stem from closely linked scriptoria. Admont, at which *R* was probably copied, was founded in 1074 by Archbishop Gebhard of Salzburg with monks from St. Peter's, at which *S* may well have been copied. This link was renewed when monks from Admont reformed St. Peter's according to the customs of Hirsau in 1116. It may explain how the circle diagrams of *S* were influenced by the *R* version. The earliest and most formative stages of the excerpted tradition of *De musica* can be traced to two scriptoria: the scriptorium were *D* was copied (possibly St. James in Liège) and SS. Ulrich and Afra in Augsburg, where *W* was copied. SS. Ulrich and Afra, like Admont, was reformed from St. Georgen, one of Hirsau's most important daughter houses. If Aribo ended his career as a monk of Hirsau, as I have suggested, then the Hirsau network holds the key to the early dissemination of *De musica*.

NOTES

1. On Bernold's compilations see especially Autenrieth, *Die Domschule von Konstanz*, pp. 30–115.

2. McCarthy, *Music, Scholasticism and Reform*, p. 182.

3. Schuba, *Die Quadriviums-Handschriften der Codices Palatini Latini*, p. 34.

4. See McCarthy, *Chronicles of the Investiture Contest*, pp. 24–25.

5. McCarthy, *Music, Scholasticism and Reform*, pp. 182–215.

6. A point first made by Ilnitchi, *Play of Meanings*, pp. 39–45. My research confirms Ilnitchi's idea in general, although it modifies the detail substantially.

7. Formerly Admont, Stiftsbibliothek, Cod. 494.

8. On Gebhard of Salzburg and reform, see Steinböck, *Erzbischof Gebhard von Salzburg*; Weinfurter, *Salzburger Bistumsreform und Bischofspolitik*.

9. Jakobs, *Die Hirsauer*, p. 60. See also Arnold, "Admont und die monastische Reform."

10. See Englebert of Admont, *De musica*, pp. 187, 296–97; Rusconi, "L'insegnamento del canto liturgico."

11. *MBÖ*, p. 62.

12. Burnett, "Omnibus convenit Platonicis," pp. 260–61.

13. Contrary to Ilnitchi, *Play of Meanings*, p. 28, and RISM B 3/6, p. 43, which state that *De musica* was copied by a single scribe.

14. See below, pp. 30–34.

15. See below, pp. 30, 121–22.

16. Pseudo-Odo of Cluny, *Dialogus de musica*, p. 252.

17. Von der Leyen, *Deutsches Mittelalter*, pp. 90–93.

18. Modifying Ilnitchi, *Play of Meanings*, who claims that the pseudo-Odo excerpt is a scribal exercise that has "no significance for our understanding of the original format or scope of the *libellus*" (p. 28).

19. Ibid., pp. 28, 34–35. The suggestion that *S* is representative of the early dissemination of *De musica* in booklet form is attractive, but must be approached with caution.

20. Ibid., p. 60n28, draws attention to the similar neumatic notation shared by *S* and contemporary manuscripts with a definite origin at St. Peter's.

21. See above, p. lii.

22. Two different foliation systems are in use for Brussels, Bibliothèque Royale, MS 10162/66. The foliation used by Smits van Waesberghe in *Aribonis De musica* and RISM B 3/1 is given first. The foliation in parentheses is that of Pesce, *Guido*, pp. 46–49, and Ilnitchi, *Play of Meanings*, pp. 19–20.

23. Pesce, *Guido*, pp. 46–49; RISM B 3/1, pp. 58–62; 3/6, pp. 118–19.

24. RISM B 3/1, pp. 40–41; 3/6, p. 278. Ilnitchi's description is sometimes inaccurate (*Play of Meanings*, pp. 20–22).

25. Wolf, "Ein anonymer Musiktraktat"; McCarthy, *Music, Scholasticism and Reform*, pp. 44–45.

26. See below, pp. lvi–lviii.

27. See below, p. lxxv.

28. See below, p. lxxix, pp. 94–96.

29. *D*, fol. 167r, lines 1–15 (originally fol. 171r, lines 1–18): "||ne dicam cantare liceat…preceptis obidere |"; Rausch, *Die Musiktraktate des Abtes Bern von Reichenau*, pp. 60–61.

30. See below, pp. lxxvii–lxxviii; *De musica* 2, pp. 2–4.

31. Smits van Waesberghe, "Relazione inedita di una lexione di Guido d'Arezzo," 42–45.

32. Boethius, *De institutione musica* 2.2–3, pp. 227–29.

33. Smits van Waesberghe, *Muziekgeschiedenis der Middeleeuwen*, pp. 154–70.

34. See below, pp. lxv–lxvii, lxiii–lxiv.

35. See below, p. lxxiii.

36. See below, pp. lxxxiii–lxxxiv.

37. The diagram of the *caprea* between *De musica* 8 and 9 is not transmitted. Some passages from *De musica* 15 cannot be made out because of the binding.

38. Powitz, *Mittelalterliche Handschriftenfragmente*, p. 136; RISM B 3/6, p. 298.

39. McCarthy, *Music, Scholasticism and Reform*, pp. 183–96.

40. See below, pp. lxiii, lxiv–lxv.

41. See below, p. lxiv, lxxii.

42. See above, p. lxii; below, pp. lxiv–lxv.

43. Pesce, *Guido*, pp. 105–9; RISM B 3/6, pp. 312–14.

44. Helssig, *Katalog der Handschriften*, p. 67.

45. McCarthy, "Aribo's *De musica* and Abbot William of Hirsau," pp. 64–65.

46. Helssig, *Katalog der Handschriften*, p. 67.

47. Correcting my comment in "Origins of *Commentarius anonymus*," 218n5.

48. McCarthy, *Music, Scholasticism and Reform*, pp. 201–2.

49. See above, pp. lxii–lxiii.

50. See below, p. lxxvi.

51. *MBDS* 4/1, p. 264.

52. The first copy of Bern's *Tonarius* is on fols. 56v–62r; the abandoned copy is on fols. 71r–72v.

53. Klemm, *Die romanischen Handschriften*, p. 22; RISM B 3/3, p. 124; 3/6, p. 339.

54. The size of the handwriting in *M3*, coupled with the length and nature of the intervening text, enables a confident estimate of one bifolium and not more.

55. RISM B 3/3, p. 165.

56. Czerny, *Die Handschriften der Stiftsbibliothek St. Florian*, p. 11; RISM B 3/1, pp. 37–39; 3/6, p. 51.

57. See below, pp. lxxx–lxxxi.

58. Holter, "Romanische Buchkunst," p. 558; "Bibliothek und Archiv," p. 62.

59. RISM B 3/1, pp. 37–9.

60. My examination of the manuscript has established that quire 7 (fols. 47–54) is a quire of one bifolium (fols. 47/54) and six singletons, contrary to Ilnitchi, *Play of Meanings*, who states that it consists of "eight separate leaves with their stubs folded as to form a gathering" (p. 29).

61. RISM B 3/1, pp. 48–49; 3/6, p. 66.

62. Theoger of Metz, *Musica*, p. 136.

63. Guido of Arezzo, *Micrologus*, pp. 80–214.

64. *MBÖ*, p. 18: "Effrem de compunctione et musica Widonis in uno."

65. See below, pp. lxxiii–lxxiv.

66. See below, p. lxxv.

67. See above, pp. lxii–lxv.

68. See above, pp. lxix–lxx.

69. Hörberg, *Libri sanctae Afrae.* pp. 87–88. See also RISM B 3/1, pp. 212–17; Pesce, *Guido*, pp. 209–15.

70. Fol. 3 transmits a notated text based upon the Advent *O antiphons* on the recto and is empty on the verso. It may originally have been part of another manuscript.

71. See above, pp. liv, lxi, lxv–lxvii.

72. See below, p. lxxv.

73. For editions of these texts, see Smits van Waesberghe, *Cymbala*, pp. 41–42, 54.

74. See above, note 22.

75. *Aribonis De musica*, p. iv.

76. Ibid., pp. iv, 65–69; RISM B 3/1, p. 62; Pesce, *Guido*, p. 49; Ilnitchi, *Play of Meanings*, pp. 20, 33, 41, 47.

77. *Aribonis De musica*, pp. viii, 45.

78. Glauche, *Katalog der lateinischen Handschriften*, pp. 219–26. See above, pp. xxxvi–xxxvii.

79. Martin Gerbert published these measurements based upon the St. Blasien copy: *Scriptores ecclesiastici* 1, p. 347a. See also McCarthy, "Literary Practice," p. 196.

80. *Aribonis De musica*, pp. vii, 65–70; RISM B 3/3, p. 118; Pesce, *Guido*, p. 136; Ilnitchi, *Play of Meanings*, pp. 25, 33, 47.

81. *Aribonis De musica*, pp. ix, 44.

82. Ibid., pp. iv, 7–8, 9, 11, 13–15, 25–26, 28, 40–41, 43–44, 45.

83. See above, pp. xxxiv, xxxviii, xlii.

84. *Aribonis De musica*, pp. xi, 51–53, 65–71.

85. Ibid., pp. 65–70.

86. Ibid., pp. i–xiii, xxix.

87. See below, p. 2.

88. See below, p. 6.

89. See above, p. lvi.

90. See above, pp. xxxvii–xxxviii.

91. John, *De musica*, p. 94.

92. See above, pp. lxvi–lxvii.

93. See above, p. lii.

94. *Aribonis De musica*, pp. 19–20.

95. See below, p. 54.

96. *Aribonis De musica*, p. 35.

97. See below, p. 68.

98. *Aribonis De musica*, p. 42.

99. See below, pp. 94–98.

100. *Aribonis De musica*, pp. 60–63.

101. Ibid., p. 59.

102. See below, p. 106.

103. Guido, *Micrologus*, pp. 184–85.

104. See below, p. 106.

105. Guido, *Micrologus*, pp. 184–85.

106. Vivell, "Die *Quaestiones in musica*," p. 70; Vivell, "Nachtrag zu den *Quaestiones in musica*," p. 51; Steglich, *Quaestiones in Musica*, pp. 1–11; McCarthy, *Music, Scholasticism and Reform*, pp. 51–52.

107. See above, p. lxxv.

108. See above, pp. lxvi–lxvii.

109. See above, p. lxiv.

110. See above, p. lxxiii.

111. See above, pp. xxvi–xxvii.

112. See above, p. lxi.

113. See above, p. lxxiv.

The Present Edition

Previous Editions

The first printed edition of *De musica* was published in 1784 by Dom Martin Gerbert (1720–93) in his *Scriptores ecclesiastici de musica sacra potissimum.*[1] Gerbert, a learned theologian and music historian, became abbot of the monastery of St. Blasien in the Black Forest in 1764, having previously been a monk there. Before becoming abbot, he traveled extensively throughout Europe, meeting distinguished scholars and searching libraries for medieval theological, liturgical, and musical sources. Although his scholarly efforts were hampered by the great fire that destroyed St. Blasien in July 1768, he managed to complete and publish a number of important works in the remaining years of his abbatiate. His last work was *Scriptores ecclesiastici de musica sacra potissimum*, a three-volume edition of over forty medieval music treatises that made available in print for the first time the writings of many members of the south German circle of music theorists.

For his edition of *De musica*, Gerbert used two manuscripts: *R* and M_1. As M_1 transmits only a small portion of *De musica*, Gerbert depended mainly on *R*. This made for an idiosyncratic and sometimes faulty text: he noted the internal misordering of the text in *R*, for example, but did not emend it. Gerbert's text was used by the nineteenth-century compilers of the *Patrologia Latina* (Paris, 1844–55) who in the process of copying introduced many more errors into the text.[2]

In 1951 the Dutch musicologist Joseph Smits van Waesberghe published a new edition of *De musica*. Drawing attention to the deficiences of Gerbert's edition, Smits van Waesberghe promised a "fresh text on critical lines."[3] Unlike Gerbert, he had the opportunity to collate a good number of other manuscripts, including *S*, the only full recension besides *R*. The identification of FM_3LzSf as sources for Aribo postdates Smits van Waesberghe's edition.

Unfortunately, Smits van Waesberghe's edition does not live up to his promise. His list of manuscripts includes a number that have only tangential connections with *De musica.* The critical apparatus is often confused and contains frequent errors: some readings are omitted, others incorrectly transcribed, and still more given that do not exist in the manuscripts at all. Smits van Waesberghe also seems to have printed passages of *De musica* that quote *Commentarius anonymus in Micrologus Guidonis Aretini* from the available printed edition of that treatise, rather than from the relevant manuscripts of *De musica.* Furthermore, his edition gives insufficient attention to the numerous diagrams in *De musica,* which are integral to the coherence of the treatise: the interlocking circle diagrams are misplaced, the diagrams of the melodic intervals and the proportions of the gamut are not edited (they are presented in a number of unclear photographic plates without reference to their order), while the important text that frames the diamond-shaped diagram is not printed.[4]

Establishing the text

Based upon collation of the manuscripts the following witnesses can be eliminated. The later manuscripts of ε1 (*BLz1*) are lineal descendants of *D* and offer no improvement upon the text transmitted by the earlier witnesses to ε1. (Although M_2 might well have been eliminated because of its closeness to *D1*, it has been thought worthwhile to record its variants on account of its relatively early date in the transmission of ε1.) *V1* and *V2*, which go back to ε2 but which introduce many errors and erratic readings, have also been eliminated. The manuscripts of ε3 (*KLLz2*M_1*V3*) transmit texts that offer few improvements on that of *D1RS*, while their diagrams reflect a later adaptation of Aribo's originals. Finally, the fragmentary *F* has been eliminated for besides one or two unique errors, it offers no revealing textual variants.

This critical elimination leaves seven manuscripts for the edition: *D*M_2M_3*RSSfW*. The full recensions, *R* and *S*, are the basis of this edition. On the whole, the readings of *S* have been preferred to those of *R*. Important exceptions to this practice will be found in some technical passages. For example, most of the manuscripts render *semiditonus* (the minor third) as *semitonus* (the semitone). The musical sense of these passages, however, requires *semiditonus.* This corruption must have entered the transmission of *De musica* early, for it is consistently transmitted in virtually all manuscripts except *R*. It is possible that the corruption was also in the archetype of *R*, but that its scribe used his musical sense to correct the error. *R* and *S* are supplemented by *D*M_2M_3*SfW* for the portions of Aribo's text these partial and fragmentary witnesses transmit. They demonstrate both the general accuracy of the text transmitted in *RS* and support the conclusion that *S* represents the main branch of the transmission of *De musica.* *Sf,* which adds little in the way of textual variants, has been included for the notated chant examples of which it is the sole witness. The variant second half of chapter 78 transmitted by *D2V2W3*, which is not original to Aribo, has not been edited here.[5]

The editing of diagrams presents unique difficulties. Whereas it is easy to present a list of variant readings for a passage of text, it is less satisfactory to do so for images. Fortunately, in most cases the transmission of the diagrams of *De musica* is very consistent in the sources. The most notable exceptions are the intersecting circle diagrams.[6] The *D* version of the circle diagrams has been preferred here over the incomplete *R* version on account of the early date of *D* and the accuracy of its text. The *D* version corresponds to the first of the circle diagrams in *S*, is the version used in *KL*, and is the basis of the version used in M_2 (although, as discussed above, M_2 transmits a unique adaptation in terms of its text). The incomplete *R* version (also represented by the second, third, and fourth diagrams of *S*) is given in appendix 1. The diagram of the quadripartite figure, which is probably an accretion to Aribo's original, has not been printed in the text, although it has been given according to *D* in appendix 2.[7]

The second manuscript of Darmstadt, Universitäts- und Hochschulbibliothek, Cod. 1988—which is a source for *Quaestiones in musica* and not Aribo's treatise per se—has not been used for this edition. While it would have been easy to use chapters from *De musica* that were copied with little alteration, it would have been more difficult, and in many cases nonsensical, to use passages that had been abridged and edited substantially by the compiler of *Quaestiones in musica*. Nevertheless, the derivation of its Aribo material from the same early sources as *D* made its collation imperative.[8] That collation has shown that the Darmstadt copy of *Quaestiones in musica* is very close to *D* for their shared portions of Aribo's text. For these portions it does not offer any improvements on the text transmitted by *D* or the other witnesses. For the Aribo material not transmitted in *D*, the Darmstadt copy of *Quaestiones* usually confirms the text transmitted on the *S* side. Like *D4RS*, it transmits the diagrams of melodic movement by *diatessaron* and *diapente* but places them with chapters 53 and 54 in its rearrangement of Aribo instead of before chapter 102, where they are in *RS*. Although there is a certain amount of logic to this placement, it was ultimately the decision of the scribe of *Quaestiones*, who was quite willing to rearrange his sources as it suited him.

The marginal glosses present in *R* are not included in this edition.[9] To have included them would give a false impression of Aribo's original text and of the glosses themselves. These glosses appear throughout *R* and not just its copy of *De musica*. They merit an individual study that addresses them in their proper codicological and intellectual contexts.

Editorial Practice

Spelling has been standardized, with variants noted only where they might affect interpretation. In choosing a standard for the non-technical Latin, I have generally been guided by the most usual spelling in *DRS*—for example, *tercia*, not *tertia*, is consistently used. There is some variation in the manuscripts regarding the use of *e* and *ę*, with no one witness being entirely consistent (*D* is perhaps the most consistent, *R* and *S* somewhat less so). Consequently, I have chosen to print *ę* where there is manuscript evidence for it. Punctuation has been standardized and modernized.

The chapter divisions follow *DRS* for the portions where *DS* have chapter headings, and *R* alone where it is the only source to transmit headings. The almost complete agreement among these sources for the headings they share indicates that *R* preserves the original headings.

Note names are printed with a point on either side (for example .A. and .a.). "Square-b" or "hard-b" is printed as .b.; "round-b" or "soft-b" as .♭.

Interlinear neumes are printed in the text only when they occur in both *R* and *S*. Where there is a discrepancy in the neumes transmitted, the variants are recorded in the critical apparatus. Where neumes are transmitted not by *R* and *S* but by some other manuscript(s), they have been recorded in the critical apparatus.

Translation

Aribo's Latin style is inconsistent. Sometimes it is elegant but other times it is convoluted to the point that his meaning can be difficult to ascertain. My aim has been to translate Aribo in a manner that accurately reflects his style, while at the same time seeking to make the English translation readable. In order to balance these demands, I have sometimes had to break up Aribo's long sentences and render active as passive, or vice versa. I have not hesitated to add words to the English translation when these are required by sense and, in order to avoid unnecessary pedantry, I have not sequestered these additions within square brackets. The availability of the Latin text on the facing page makes square brackets unnecessary and allows the Latinate reader to follow the translation process for himself or, in ambiguous passages, to arrive at another alternative.

I have tried, as far as possible, not to leave technical terms in Latin. Exceptions to this are *diatessaron*, *diapente*, and *diapason* (which are used throughout to avoid confusion about the meaning of "fourth" or "fifth"); *diezeugmenon* and *synemmenon* (for which there is no convenient English equivalent); the tetrachords of the *graves*, *finales*, *superiores*, and *excellentes*;

the descriptive modal names *protus*, *deuterus*, *tritus*, and *tetrardus*, as well as *dorius*, *hypodorius*, *lydius*, *hypolydius*, and so forth; and the ancient Greek note names (*meson*, *lichanos meson*, and so forth). The titles of the chants cited by Aribo have been retained in Latin.

Two terms that might well have been left in Latin but which I have chosen to render in English are *intensio* and *remissio*. Each has a complex meaning. *Intensio* generally refers to the melodic movement whereby a chant or a phrase starts or moves upwards from its beginning. The concept of *intensio* includes not only the interval covered but also the form of tones and semitones involved in this movement. *Remissio* is the reverse of this, as a chant returns whence it came. *Intensio* and *remissio* are related to the linguistic concepts of *arsis* and *thesis*, which were also used by Aribo and his contemporaries. My translation of *intensio* and *remissio* varies according to the context but is usually rendered by "extension" or "beginning" and "remission," "returning," or "ending."

The term *neuma* occurs repeatedly towards the end of *De musica* and in Aribo's *sententiae*. An important study by Karen Desmond has argued that *neuma* was part of a hierarchy of grammatical terms used to analyze melody in eleventh-century music treatises.[10] Although Desmond consistently translates *neuma* as "sub-phrase," I usually translate it as "melodic figure" or simply "figure."

NOTES

1. Gerbert, *Scriptores ecclesiastici* 2, pp. 197–230.
2. PL 150.1307–46.
3. *Aribonis De musica*, preface.
4. See above, pp. lxxix–lxxx.
5. See above, p. lxxv.
6. See above, pp. lxxviii–lxxix.
7. See above, pp. lxxvii–lxxviii; below, p. 125.
8. See above, pp. lxxxi–lxxxiii.
9. The glosses on *De musica* are transcribed—often faultily—in Smits van Waesberghe's edition (*Aribonis De musica*).
10. Desmond, "*Sicut in grammatica*."

De musica and *Sententiae*

[a]Incipit musica Aribonis scholastici.[a]

Domno[b] suo Ellenhardo presulum dignissimo, in uniuersa morum honestate preclaro, Aribo, quę preparauit "Deus diligentibus se." Litterarum mearum, pater et domine uenerabilis, presentię uestra queso presentetur dignatio, donec auribus misericordię percipiatis quid meus stilus pannosus uidelicet referat legatus. Qui licet "ueste nuptiali" non intret, prius tamen deprecor iterum atque iterum non abhorreatur quam suam legationem representet.

[1.] [a]Laus presulis de pericia musicę.[a]

Cum summe capacitatis in musicę monochordique sitis regulis, ut cantilenarum uestrarum obseruata diligentia affatim uobis perhibent[b] testimonia, presumpsi uos eligere palemonem[c] ad cuiusdam theorematis, id est, speculationis perceptionem. Post seriarum rerum laboriosam intensionem in istis aliquando quasi ludi blandientem habeatis remissionem.

[2.] [a]De quadripertita modernorum figura.[a]

Est quędam quadripertita figura modernis adeo uenerabilis ut paucissima sine ea sint monochorda. Quę ita construitur ut una series primi[b] insimul et secundi toni mensuram contineat, secunda tercii et quarti, tercia quinti et sexti, quarta septimi et octaui. Cuius dispositio[c] non ultimę [d]commoditati famulatur.[d] Nam sicut post abecedarii indiscretam generalemque seriem specialiter erant coadunandę uocales, semiuocales, mutę, ita post naturalem monochordi permixtionem specialius erant tropi cum suis subiugalibus discernendi, sicut etiam elementa lucidius apparuerunt discreta relicto sinu primitiuę confusionis. Dispositis separatim tropis euidentius intuemur qualiter protus cum suo subiugali constet prima grauium id est .A., prima finalium id est .D., [e]prima superiorum id est .a., prima excellentium id est .d.[e] Distinctius quoque uidemus quomodo deuterus cum suo plaga construatur secunda grauium, secunda finalium, secunda superiorum, secunda excellentium, id est .B.E.b.e.; quomodo tritus cum plagali constituatur omnibus terciis, id est .C.F.c.f.; qualiter tetrardus sibique plaga subiunctus[f] disponatur[g] ex omnibus

[a–a] Summi doctoris Tractatus, hic est Aribonis *S*
[b] <D>omno *R*
[1.] [a–a] *om. R*
[b] perhibet *S;* perhibet *corr.* perhibent *R*
[c] id est iudicem *R;* iudicem *S (interlinear gloss in text hand)*
[2.] [a–a] *om. D5*
[b] prima *S*
[c] dispositi[a>o] *S*
[d–d] famulatur commoditati *R;* commoditata famulatur *S*
[e–e] *om. R*
[f] subiectus *D5*
[g] disponantur *R*

Here begins the music treatise of Aribo the schoolmaster

To his lord the most worthy of bishops Ellenhard,[1] in everything honorable and distinguished in morals, from Aribo the things that God has prepared for "those that love Him."[2] May your honor deign to have presented to you the gift of my letters,[3] most venerable father and lord, so that you may perceive with a sympathetic ear what my ragged pen obviously conveys to you poorly. Though he who lacks a "wedding garment" may not enter,[4] nevertheless, I pray again and again that he should not be rejected before he presents his message.[5]

1. Praise of the bishop for his skill in music.

Since you are of supreme capacity in the rules of music and of the monochord, as the diligence observed in your singing provides ample testimony,[6] I have presumed to choose you as judge[7] of a certain theorem,[8] that is, to consider a speculation. After the laborious investigation of grave matters, you will not infrequently in this have a soothing remission as in a game.[9]

2. Concerning the quadripartite figure of the moderns.

There is a certain quadripartite figure so venerable to the moderns that there are very few monochords without it.[10] It is so constructed that its first row contains the measure of the first and second tones at the same time, its second row the third and fourth tones, its third row the fifth and sixth tones, and its fourth row the seventh and eighth tones. Its layout does not make for the greatest convenience. For while its careless and general lettering of the rows resulted particularly in a jumbling together of the vowels, semi-vowels, and mutes,[11] the natural mixing together of the monochord resulted in the discernment of each of the tropes with its own special subservient version—much as the discrete remaining elements appeared more clearly after the bending of the primitive disorder.[12] Discussing the tropes separately, we shall see more clearly how *protus* with its plagal constitutes the first note of the *graves* (that is, .A.), the first of the *finales* (that is, .D.), the first of the *superiores* (that is, .a.) and the first of the *excellentes* (that is, .d.). We shall also see more clearly how *deuterus* with its plagal is constructed from the second of the *graves*, the second note of the *finales*, the second of the *superiores*, and the second of the *excellentes* (that is, .B.E.b.e.); how *tritus* with its plagals is constructed from all the third notes (that is, .C.F.c.f.); how *tetrardus* of itself as well as the plagals joined to it is arrayed from all of the

quartis; quarta grauium, id est .D., quę est duplicis naturę, quia sicut est [h]quarta grauium,[h] ita est prima finalum. Quę omnia lucebunt in sequentibus cum de troporum tetrachordorum[i] principalium chordarum natura disseremus habundantius, quia presans tractatus principaliter est de quadripertita figura pretitulatus.[j]

[3.] [a]De uitio quadripertitę.[a]

Est tamen aliquid in eadem figura quod[b] mihi, ut minus sapiens dico, non uidetur usque ad fundum penitus esse limpidum.

[4.] [a]Attentum facit presulem.[a]

Huc pater auriculas conuerte benignius[b] ambas,
Has presul "nugas meditans" sis "totus[c] in illis."

[5.] [a]Homines reprehendere degenerantes.[a]

Solent[b] homines admodum improbare cum uident aliquem de parentum uirtute degenerare. Scimus autem et istam et omnem musicam figuram natiuitatis suę primordium sumpsisse de primitiua regularis monochordi dispositione. Cum autem hic uideamus collecta quę ibi sunt dispersa, hic dispersa quę ibi sunt collecta, nonne [c]ista degenerat figura[c] a sua genitrice monochordi uidelicet mensura?

[6.] [a]De peruersa tetrachordum collectione.[a]

In ista figura collectę sunt in unum locum [b]omnes graues,[b] in unum locum omnes finales, similiter in unum omnes superiores, omnes etiam excellentes. Quod penitus non concedit monochordi natura quę cuilibet tetrachordorum quatuor diuersa partitur[c] loca.

[7.] [a]De peruersa diezeuxi, id est disiunctione.[a]

In ista figura disiunctę sunt quarta grauium, prima[b] finalium,

[h–h] grauium quarta *trans.* quarta grauium *R* (*indicated by interlinear* a *and* b)
[i] tetracordarum *D5*
[j] pretitulandus *R*
[3.] [a–a] *om. D5;* Quadripertę *R*
[b] quid *corr.* quod *R*
[4.] [a–a] *om. D5;* Adtentum *R*
[b] benignus *R*
[c] tutus *S*
[5.] [a–a] *om. D5*
[b] <S>olent *D5*

[c–c] degenerat ista figura *trans.* ista degenerat figura *R (indicated by interlinear* a *and* b*)*
[6.] [a–a] De peruersa tetracordorum collectionem M_2*;* Collectio figurarum grauium, superiorum, finalium, excellentium *W1*
[b–b] graues omnes *trans.* omnes graues *W1* (*indicated by interlinear* a *and* b)
[c] patitur $D1M_2$
[7.] [a–a] *om. W1*
[b] et prima *M2,* et *marked for deletion*

fourth notes. The fourth of the *graves*—that is, .D.—is naturally double-functioned, for just as it is the fourth of the *graves*, so too is it the first of the *finales*.[13] All these things will shine clearly in the following, when we will talk more abundantly about the nature of the tropes and the principal notes of the tetrachords, since this treatise is primarily about the quadripartite figure mentioned in the title.

3. Concerning the defect of the quadripartite figure.

There is something in this same figure that to me, though I speak less than wisely, does not really seem to be completely correct.

4. The bishop is made attentive.

Now, father, turn both of your ears most kindly
To this, bishop, that musing on trifles you may be wholly intent thereon.[14]

5. To reprove degenerate men.

Men are accustomed to indignancy whenever they see anyone degenerate from the virtue of his parent. We know indeed that each and every musical figure took the origin of its birth from the primitive disposition of the rule of the monochord. When, however, we see things here brought together that there are separated and here separated that there are brought together,[15] does not this figure degenerate from its parent,[16] namely the measure of the monochord?

6. Concerning its perverse bringing together of the tetrachords.

In this figure all of the *graves* and all of the *finales* are brought together in one place. Similarly with all of the *superiores* and even all of the *excellentes*. The nature of the monochord most definitely does not allow this, for each tetrachord is distributed over four different points.

7. Concerning its perverse *diezeuxi*, that is disjunction.

In this figure the fourth of the *graves* and the first of the *finales*, the

quarta superiorum, prima excellentium, quę in monochordi naturali structura unum et eundem obtinet locum, utpote in una et eadem littera.

[8.] De acumine non naturali proti et grauitate tetrardi non competenti.

In hac eadem quadripertita figura protus est acutissimus, tetrardus grauissimus. Quod quam contrarium sit naturę monochordi, potest quiuis etiam mediocriter his imbutus facillime[a] contemplari.

[9.] [a]De Aribunculi ammiratione.[a]

Hęc cum diutina mecum admiratione reuoluerem[b] et si [c]quid naturalius[c] occurreret indagarem,[d] inueni capream matri simillimam. Quę habet in uno loco quartam grauium, primam finalium, quartam superiorum, primam excellentium. Quę habet in [e]quatuor locis diuersis[e] graues, finales, superiores,[f] excellentes.[g] Quę habet protum grauissimum, tetrardum acutissimum, ut naturam quam in principali genitricis gremio possideant, in filię mansiunculis non amittant.

[10.] [a]De miniatis tetrachordorum lineis.[a]

Quatuor obliquę lineę quatuor tetrachordis, id est grauium, finalium, superiorum, excellentium, minio superinductę, quadripertitam[b] nostri tropici theorematis[c] ita penetrant[d] latitudinem, ut non solum[e] demonstrent unamquamque grauium, finalium, superiorum, excellentium in sui tropi interuallo, sed etiam in uero et naturali[f] loco, secundum protoplastę[g] conditionis quę est in monochordo testimonium.

[11.] [a]Quid bene quid male[a] quadripertita explicet.

Quadripertita modernorum figura bene exprimit unamquamque principalium litterarum seu chordarum suo[b] tropo contraditam, sed in hoc delinquit: quod eas in alio loco quam monochordum uelit constituit. Diuisiones troporum quod minus est bene condit. Grauitatis acuminisque legem quod

[8.] [a] difficillime *D1M₂*
[9.] [a–a] De dictatoris ammiratione *R; om. W1*
[b] reuoluerem et admiratione reuoluerem *R*
[c–c] quis naturalis *W1*
[d] *om. W1*
[e–e] loco quatuor diuersos *S*
[f] superiorum *M₂*
[g] *om. R*
[10.] [a–a] tetrachordarum *R; om. W1*
[b] quadripertita *S*
[c] theo reumatis *W1*
[d] Sycculatis | † †nis *S in right hand margin*
[e] *om. D1M₂W1*
[f] naturale *M₂*
[g] prothoplaste *D1M₂*
[11.] [a–a] Quid male quid bene *S*
[b] seu *M₂*

fourth of the *superiores* and the first of the *excellentes* are disjunct, although in the natural structure of the monochord they hold one and the same place, as indicated by one and the same letter.

8. Concerning the unnatural high position of *protus* and the inappropriate low position of *tetrardus*.

In this same quadripartite figure *protus* is in the highest position, *tetrardus* in the lowest; and how contrary this is to the nature of the monochord anyone can very easily contemplate, even if he is only imbued with a mediocre knowledge of these matters.

9. Admiration of little Aribo.

When I reflect upon these things in my own mind with constant wonder and consider what might occur more naturally, I have found *caprea* very like a mother. She has in the same place the fourth of the *graves*, the first of the *finales*, the fourth of the *superiores*, and the first of the *excellentes*.[17] She has in four different positions the *graves*, *finales*, *superiores*, and *excellentes*. She has *protus* in the lowest position and *tetrardus* in the highest, so that the nature they possess in the original bosom of the mother[18] is not lost when in the little house of the daughter.

10. Concerning the red-colored tetrachordal lines.

The four oblique lines drawn over the four tetrachords in red—that is, the tetrachords of the *graves*, *finales*, *superiores*, and *excellentes*—so intersect the quadripartite breath of our diagram of the tropes[19] that not only do they demonstrate each of the *graves*, *finales*, *superiores*, and *excellentes* within the bounds of its trope but also in its true and natural position according to its basic condition, the evidence of which is in the monochord.

11. What the quadripartite figure explains well and what it explains badly.

The quadripartite figure of the moderns explains well how each of the principal letters or notes is connected to its trope; but in this it goes astray: it puts them in a place other than what the monochord wishes. The divisions of the tropes, which are of lesser importance, it explains well; but the law of low

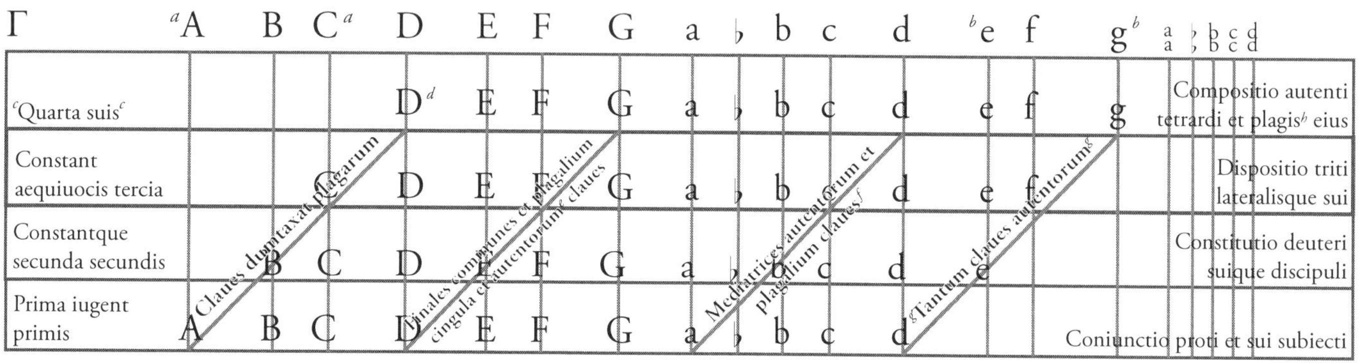

[**Diagram 1**]

[a–a] *W1 notates* .A., .B. *and* .C. *continuously to the bottom of the grid*

[b–b] *W1 notates* .e., .f. *and* .g. *continuously to the bottom of the grid*

[c–c] *om.* M_2

[d] M_2 *notates only the columns for* .D. *and* .G. *in the lower octave of the diagram*

[e] autenticorum W1

[f] *om.* M_2W1

[g–g] Claues tantum autenticorum *W1*

[h] plagalis *W1*

Diagram 1.

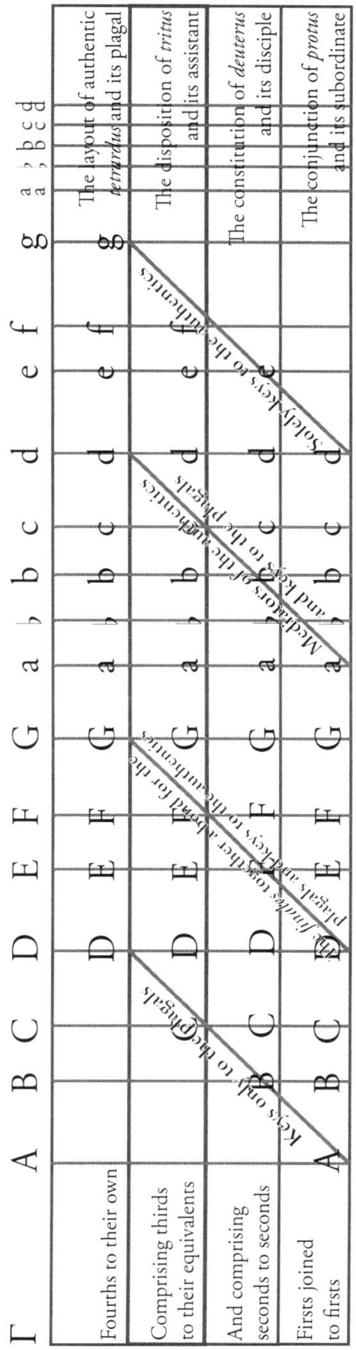
Γ A B C D E F G a ♭ b c d e f g a ♭ b c d
Fourths to their own
Comprising thirds to their equivalents
And comprising seconds to seconds
Firsts joined to firsts
The layout of authentic *tetrardus* and its plagal
The disposition of *tritus* and its assistant
The constitution of *deuterus* and its disciple
The conjunction of *protus* and its subordinate
Keys only to the plagals
The *finales* together abound for the plagals and keys to the authentics
Mediators of the authentics and keys to the plagals
Solely keys to the authentics

maius est non caute distribuit. Sed gratia lausque[c] [d]sit "patri luminum,"[d] a quo est "omne datum optimum et omne donum perfectum," nostra immo sua ut dicamus cum psalmista: Non nobis domine, non nobis sed nomini tuo da gloriam. Et bene diuisiones troporum constituit, et naturalem[e] secundum monochordorum grauitatis et acuminis eorum differentiam euidenter proponit.[f]

[12.] De naturali capreę ueritate et eiusdem mensurę magna facilitate.

Hęc cum tantam[a] habeat[b] naturę ueritatem secundum antiquissimam monochordi natiuitatem, potest eam et hoc commendare uberius quod simplex monochordi mensura fiat hac parum celerius. Omnis tonus, omne semitonium, omne etiam synemmenon, omnis denique quatuor troporum mensura est ęquissime sibimet opposita. Sed illius quę mihi causa fuit huius tanta est in metiendo[c] difficultas, tam inextricabilis perplexio, ut admodum dura sit eiusdem textura.

[13.] Quare caprea tali nomine censeatur et quid presuli offeratur.

Nostri theorematis nouitatem propter eius mensurę celeritatem nuncupaui capream et quia uelocius accurrebat[a] cum uenabar eam. "Voluntas" enim "Dei fuit ut cito [b]mihi occurreret[b] quod uolebam." Eandem pater reuerende[c] capream uobis offero degustandam cordis palato, ut siquid uobis [d]sapiat in ea[d] "benedicat mihi anima" uestra.

[14.] Quę sit in caprea commoditas.

Habetis in ea planam mensurandi facilitatem, naturę non redarguendam ueritatem, quę omnia monochordi representat legitima sicut decet. Nam de primitiuo monochordo deriuatiuam[a] aliter quam monochordum uelit componere figuram, hoc est iuxta pedem dextrum calceum formare sinistrum. Quod quomodo [b]in nostro theoremate[b] sit[c] deuitatum, uestro penitus sit iudicio reseruatum.

[15.] Quę [a]causa sit contrarietatis[a] inter monochordum et quadripertitam modernorum.[b]

[c] laus est *M_2*
[d–d] patri sit luminum *$D1M_2$*
[e] naturale *R*
[f] proposuit *$D1M_2$*
[12.] [a] tant[ę>a]m *D1*
[b] habebat *M_2*
[c] me sciendi *M_2*
[13.] [a] occurrebat *R*
[b–b] occurreret mihi *R*
[c] uenerande *R*
[d–d] in ea sapiat *R*
[14.] [a] diriuatiuam *$D1M_2$*
[b] theoremate in nostro *R*
[c] *om.* *M_2*
[15.] [a–a] sit contrietas *corr. above to* causa sit contrietatis *R*
[b] figuram modernorum *R*, figuram *added above*

and high position, which is of greater importance, it does not lay down carefully. But thanks and praise to the "Father of lights" from whom be "every best gift and every perfect gift"[20] for our or rather his diagram, that we may say with the psalmist "not unto us, O Lord, not unto us: but to thy name give glory."[21] It lays down the divisions of the tropes well and proposes clearly according to the monochord their natural difference of low and high position.

12. Concerning the natural truth of *caprea* and how easy it is to measure it.

It has so great a measure of natural truth according to the most ancient birth of the monochord, that it enables—and this commends it abundantly—the simple measurement of the monochord to be made a little more quickly. Every tone, every semitone, even every *synemmenon*, and lastly every measure of the four tropes, is positioned properly on it. But these, of which my cause has been, are so great in their measure of difficulty, so inextricably perplexing, that it has been difficult to write of their meaning.

13. Why *caprea* may be called by this name, and what is offered to the bishop.

Our new diagram, on account of the swiftness of its measurements, I have called *caprea* because it ran all the faster when I hunted it: "it was the will of God that what I sought came quickly in my way."[22] Reverend father, I present to your palate the same *caprea* tasting of the heart, that if you taste of these things, "your soul may bless me."[23]

14. What convenience is in *caprea*.

You possess in this a straightforward facility for measuring, which need not contradict the truth of nature that represents all the lawful aspects of monochord as it ought. For the quadripartite figure wishes to compose a figure derived from a monochord other than the original monochord itself, which is similar to putting the right shoe on the left foot. How this is derived in our diagram has been entirely reserved for your judgement.[24]

15. Why there may be contradiction between the monochord and the quadripartite figure of the moderns.

Causam autem contrarietatis inter illam quam moderni diligunt[c] figuram et monochordum arbitror esse, immo[d] scio, quod dispositiones troporum ita uarie incipiunt ut prima secundam tono, [e]secunda terciam tono, tercia quartam semitonio[e] precedat, cum potius in illis procurari deberet quatinus primę dispositionis[f] grauis, id est .A., secundę dispositionis grauem,[g] id est .B., tono precederet; secundę dispositionis grauis, [h]idem uidelicet .B.[h] tercię dispositionis grauem,[i] id est .C., semitonio preiret; tercię dispositionis grauis,[j] [k]idipsum scilicet .C.,[k] quartę dispositionis grauem,[l] id est .D., tono rursus preueniret. Quod facillimum esset si ab uno principio ipsas mensurarum integritates[m] inchoarent, aut a grauibus incipientes dictam diuersitatem inceptionis obseruarent. Sed hęc hactenus de caprea. Qua in uestrę gratię scrutinio derelicta, tendimus ad alia.

[16.] [a]Cur monochordo una diapason non sufficiat.[a]

Monochordum una diapason non esse contentum triplex esse causa[b] creditur. Vna quod simplicioribus curtum uideretur, qui irreflexibili uoce ad organalem ignorant reuerti grauitatem, sicut equus indocilis[c] rigidęque ceruicis non potest in arto circinari clypeo. Secunda quod uox acutior mulcet aures gratiosius, sicut etiam gracile corpus blanditur oculis iocundius. Tercia quod ipsa naturalis chordę ac uocis possibilitas ulteriores spontanea petit metas, sicut nonnumquam in amena loca uoluntate procedimus non necessitate.

[17.] [a]Cur diapason tres non sint in monochordo.[a]

Tribus diapason protensum esse monochordum non patitur altissimę fidis sonus gracillimus nulli subteriorum consonus. Sicut enim pueruli[b] tenellę uocis inmoderato acumine cantilenas edunt adeo inconsonas, ut easdem sciens[c] uir non intellegat [d]illas, ita et ęquo fidis acutior[e] non intellegitur[d] more [f]clangens parrę[f] recinentis et cicadę.

Est modus in rebus sunt certi denique fines.
Vltra quos citraque nequit consistere uerum.

[c] diligenter *M₂*
[d] i[***] *erasure in M₂;* inmo *R*
[e–e] secunda terciam semitonio, tercia quartam tono *D1M₂S*
[f] dispositi|nis *R*
[g] *om. M₂*
[h–h] idem .b. uidelicet .b. *S*
[i] graue *S*
[j] grauis grauis *D1*
[k–k] .c. *M₂;* idipsum .C. scilicet *S;*
[l] graue *S*
[m] integritates integritates *S*

[16.] [a–a] *om. D6;* De hoc quod monochordum nec in disiuncta nec in coniuncta diuiditur *R*
[b] *om. D6*
[c] indocibilis *D6*
[17.] [a–a] *om. D6*
[b] pueroli *S;* pueri *R*
[c] *om. R*
[d–d] *om. R*
[e] acutio *S*
[f–f] clangentis barrę *R*

The cause of the contradiction between the monochord and that figure which the moderns esteem I think—or, rather, I know—to be as follows: the layout of the tropes begins in so varied a fashion that the first precedes the second by a tone, the second precedes the third by a tone, and the third precedes the fourth by a semitone,[25] when it should have been arranged so that the first of the *graves*—that is, .A.—precedes the second of the *graves*—that is, .B.—by a tone, the second of the *graves*—namely, the same .B.—precedes the third of the *graves*—that is, .C.—by a semitone and the third of the *graves*—obviously the same .C.—precedes the fourth of the *graves*—that is, .D.—by a tone. This might have been easiest had the entirety of the measurements begun from one original, or if beginning from the *graves* they had observed the aforesaid diversity of the beginning. But enough about *caprea*. Leaving these things to the scrutiny of your grace, we turn to other matters.

16. Why one octave does not suffice for the monochord.

The monochord is not to be satisfied with one octave, the reason for which is believed to be threefold. First, because it might seem incomplete to the more simple, who with an unconstrained voice do not know how to limit themselves to the instrument's low range, just as the untamed and stiff-necked[26] horse cannot be led trotting in a narrow circle. Secondly, the higher voice delights the ears more graciously, as also the slender body flatters the eye joyously.[27] Thirdly, the very ability of the natural note and voice spontaneously seeks further measures, as sometimes we walk in a delightful place by choice and not by necessity.

17. Why there may not be three octaves in the monochord.

The monochord is not allowed to be extended into three octaves because of the most thin sound of the highest part of the string, consonant with none of the lower sounds. For as little boys of tender voice give forth singing so untuneful by reason of its immoderate shrillness that a man who knew the songs would not recognize them, so too the higher strings cannot be made out since they resound in the fashion of screeching owls[28] and tree-crickets.[29]

There is measure in all things. There are, in short, fixed bounds,
Beyond and short of which there can be no truth.[30]

[18.] [a]Cur monochordum in tetrachorda diuidatur.[a]

Diuisum esse monochordum in tetrachorda potius quam in[b] dichorda uel trichorda seu pentachorda hęc est ratio: quod post diapason in [c]nullo est tanta[c] ut in tetrachordis similitudo. Si enim in dichorda facta fuisset diuisio primum occurreret dissimilitudo, quia post tonum qui est ab .A. in .B. sequitur semitonium. Si autem in trichorda itidem diuersitas semitam obsideret. Nam post semiditonum[d] qui est ab .A. in .C. sequeretur ditonus a .C. in .E. At si diuisio fuisset per pentachorda[e] eadem dissimilitudinis obuiaret inportunitas. Quoniam quidem ab .A. in .E. est diapente, et ibi sequitur semitonium faciens dissimilitudinem.

[19.] [a]Tetrachorda [b]quedam esse[b] prime quedam secunde similitudinis.[a]

Tetrachordorum[c] ergo quędam primę quedam similitudinis sunt secundę. Primę: Grauium, Finalium, Superiorum, Excellentium, quia plena similitudine intenduntur[d] et remittuntur tono, semitonio, tono. Quędam [e]similitudinis sunt[e] secundę: Hyperboleon, Diezeugmenon, Meson, Hypaton. Quę quamuis inuicem comparata nihil differant intensa et remissa, quia unumquodque illorum[f] intenditur semitonio et ditono remittitur autem ditono et semitonio, ipsa tamen intensio et remissio dissimilis est. Quę in prioribus est simillima quia sicut tono, semitonio, tono intenduntur,[g] [h]ita et remittuntur.[h]

[20.] [a]De similitudine neumarum.[a]

Similitudo tetrachordorum[b] similitudini seruit neumarum, quia eadem neuma quę intenditur ab .A. in .D. intenditur a .D. in .G. Quę remittitur a .G. in .D. remittitur etiam a .D. in .A. Sic etiam in ceteris, ut facillime potest perpendere quiuis.

[21.] [a]De hoc quod monochordum nec[b] in disiuncta, nec in coniuncta diuiditur.[a]

Monochordum non esse diuisum uel in penitus coniuncta uel in penitus disiuncta tetrachorda[c] hęc est ratio: quod predicta tunc cessaret similitudo.

[18.] [a–a] *om. D6;* Cur in tetrachorda diuidatur *R*
[b] aut in *R*
[c–c] nulla est tanta *D6;* nullo tanta est *R*
[d] semitonium *D6S*
[e] pentacordum *D6*
[19.] [a–a] *om. D6*
[b–b] esse quedam *S*
[c] Tetracordarum *D6*
[d] et intenduntur *R*
[e] sunt similitudinis *R;* similitudines *corr.* similitudinis *S*
[f] eorum *D6*
[g] intenditur *D6*
[h–h] remittitur *D6; om. S*
[20.] [a–a] *om. D6*
[b] tetracordarum *S*
[21.] [a–a] *om. D6*
[b] nec nec *S*
[c] tetracordo *S*

18. Why the monochord is divided in tetrachords.

The monochord is to be divided in tetrachords rather than in dichords or trichords, or even in pentachords, for this reason: because after the octave there is nothing that is as similar to it as the tetrachord. For if it were divided in dichords the first thing to occur would be dissimilarity, since after the tone that is from .A. to .B. a semitone would follow. If, however, it were divided in trichords, an irregularity would again block our way, since after the one-and-a-half tones from .A. to .C. there would follow two tones from .C. to .E. And if the division had been made according to pentachords the same inconvenient dissimilarity would be encountered, since there is a fifth between .A. and .E. and there then follows a semitone, making for dissimilarity.

19. Certain tetrachords of a first type of similarity and certain of a second.

Certain of the tetrachords, therefore, are of a first type of similarity and certain are of a second.[31] The first: *graves*, *finales*, *superiores*, and *excellentes*, which are entirely similar, having an extension and remission of a tone, semitone, and tone. Those of the second type of similarity: *hyperbolean*, *diezeugmenon*, *meson*, and *hypaton*. In their comparison there is no difference between extension and remission since each of them goes up by a semitone and two tones and comes back down by the same two tones and semitone; yet of themselves extension and remission are different.[32] The former are similar since as their extension proceeds by tone, semitone, and tone, so too does their remission.

20. Concerning the similarity of musical phrases.[33]

The similarity of the tetrachords is paralleled by a similarity of the musical phrases, since the same phrase that extends from .A. to .D. extends from .D. to .G., and that which returns from .G. to .D. returns also from .D. to .A. This is also so with the others, as anyone at all can easily imagine.

21. Concerning the reason why the monochord is neither divided disjunctly nor conjunctly.

The monochord is to be divided neither completely by conjunct steps nor completely by disjunct ones for the reason that by such a division the aforementioned similarity ceases.

Si enim inciperet tetrachordum superiorum in .G. ubi desinit finalium similitudo deficeret, quia tetrachordum superiorum intenderetur ditono[d] et semitonio cum priora[e] tono, semitonio, tono. Item diuersitas occurreret[f] si penitus disiuncta fuissent tetrachorda. Quę omnia quia satis sunt manifesta non est opus dicere plenius.

[22.] [a]De diezeugmenon et synemmenon.[a]

Priori patet ratione quod tetrachorda diezeugmenon [b]et synemmenon[b] sint necessaria. Si enim aut coniunctio aut disiunctio tetrachordorum esset penitus et similitudo periret et creber in cantu defectus occurreret.

[23.] [a]De hoc quod quelibet chorda superius et inferius quartam et quintam uelint habere propter diatesseron et diapente que multum[b] dominantur in cantu.[a]

Propter diatesseron et diapente, quę in cantilenis pollent precipue, desiderat unaqueque chorda uel littera quartam quintamque supra uel infra habere. Quapropter .F. et .f. admodum indigent synemmenon, ut grauis supra quartam acuta infra habeat quintam ad se resultantem per diapente.

[24.] [a]De communione tetrachordorum.[a]

Eadem intensio et remissio [b]omnibus est[b] illis tetrachordis quę ascendunt, id est Grauium, Finalium, Superiorum, Excellentium. Omnibus autem descendentibus, id est Hyperboleon, Diezeugmenon, Meson, Hypaton eadem est intensio eadem quoque [c]est et[c] remissio, quamuis ascensus sit dissimilis et descensus, quia ascensus est semitonio ditono, descensus ditono semitonio.

[25.] [a]De differentia tetrachordorum ascendentium et descendentium.[a]

Qualiter autem eadem differant tetrachorda si uacat et placidi rationem admittis[b] edam. Differunt nomine quod est planum. Differunt qualitate quod debet explanari, quia latine nuncupata potius sunt constitutiua specierum trium symphoniarum diatesseron, diapente, diapason quam Grece uocata. Differunt specie quia hęc in medio illa semitonium habent in extremo.

[d] [t]ritono *erased* ritono *but not corr. D6*
[e] priore *D6*
[f] occurret *R*
[22.] [a–a] *om. D6*
[b–b] *om. D6*
[23.] [a–a] *om. D6*
[b] ualde *S*
[24.] [a–a] *om. D6*
[b–b] est omnibus *D6*
[c–c] *om. D6R*
[25.] [a–a] *om. D6*
[b] admittitis *D6S*

For if one begins the tetrachord of the *superiores* at .G. where that of the *finales* ends, similarity will be wanting since the tetrachord of the *superiores* rises by two tones and a semitone, while the former rises by tone, semitone, and tone. Diversity would again occur if the tetrachords were made completely disjunct. As all of this is plainly evident, it is not necessary to say more.[34]

22. Concerning *diezeugmenon* and *synemmenon*.

For the above reason the tetrachords of *diezeugmenon* and *synemmenon* are necessary.[35] For if the conjunction or the disjunction of the tetrachords was complete, their similarity would be lost and frequent errors would occur in singing.

23. Concerning the fact that certain notes may wish to have a fourth or a fifth above or below on account of the *diatessaron* and *diapente*, which dominate much in singing.

On account of the *diatessaron* and *diapente*, which are especially prominent in songs, each note or letter desires to have the interval of a fourth or fifth either above or below. Wherefore .F. and .f. particularly require *synemmenon*, so that the lower may have a fourth above and the higher a fifth below, returning to itself by way of a *diapente*.[36]

24. Concerning the communion of tetrachords.

Extension and remission are the same for all tetrachords of the ascending group—that is, *graves*, *finales*, *superiores*, and *excellentes*. All those of the descending group—that is, *hyperboleon*, *diezeugmenon*, *meson*, and *hypaton*—have the same extension and the same remission, however much ascent may be unlike descent, because the ascent is by a semitone and two tones and the descent by two tones and a semitone.[37]

25. Concerning the difference of the ascending and descending tetrachords.

I shall demonstrate, however, how the same tetrachords differ, "if you will allow me time and listen quietly to reason."[38] That the names differ is clear. That they differ in quality ought to be explained, because the ones named in Latin rather than in Greek are constitutive of the three species of symphony called the *diatessaron*, *diapente*, and *diapason*. They differ in species because the latter have the semitone in the middle, the former the semitone at the extremity.[39]

[26.] [a]De quibus litteris et chordis unumquodque tetrachordum consistat.[a]

Tetrachordum grauium secundum Guidonem constat .A.B.C.D., quod idem iuxta Boetium est proslambanomenos, hypate hypaton, parhypate hypaton, lichanos hypaton. Tetrachordum finalium [b]Guidonice est[b] .D.E.F.G., hoc ipsum est[c] in Boetio lichanos hypaton, hypate meson, parhypate meson, lichanos meson. Tetrachordum[d] superiorum iuxta modernos est .a.b.c.d.[e] Idem est Boetii mese, paramese, trite diezeugmenon, [f]paranete diezeugmenon. Tetrachordum excellentium est .d.e.f.g.[g] secundum Guidonem, iuxta Boetium autem paranete diezeugmenon, nete diezeugmenon, trite hyperboleon, paranete hyperboleon.[f]

[27.] [a]Qualiter tetrachorda species operentur.[a]

Nunc disputemus qualiter [b]ista tetrachorda[b] operentur constitutionem[c] specierum diatesseron et diapente. Tetrachordum grauium tetrachordo[d] finalium collatum omnes diatesseron[e] species quę quatuor sunt perficit hoc modo. Prima grauium primę iuncta[f] finalium parturit primam [g]diatesseron speciem.[g] [h]Sic secunda grauium cum secunda finalium secundam diatesseron[i] progenerat speciem.[h] Eodem modo [j]uice sunt[j] parentum tercia grauium, tercia finalium, [k]quarta grauium,[k] quarta finalium tercię et quartę speciei diatesseron. Eadem diatesseron specierum natiuitas[l] est in copulatione[m] superiorum et excellentium, et tam naturali ordine id est ut [n]prima de primis[n] secunda de secundis tercia et quarta de terciis ac[o] quartis procedat; et hoc necessario quia superiorum et excellentium collatio nihil est aliud quam collationis grauium et finalium repetitio. Vnde est necesse ut quicquid inter graues et finales idipsum fiat inter superiores et excellentes; quia sicut eędem superiores quę graues ita [p]sunt eedem[p] excellentes quę[q] finales.

[26.] [a–a] *om. D6*
[b] est Guidonice *R*
[c] *om. D6*
[d] et excellentium *in marg. D6*
[e] .D. *corr.* d *R*
[f–f] Paranetediezeugmenon, Netediezeu|gmenon, Tritehyperboleon, Paraneteyperboleon. || *D6*
[g] .D.E.F.G. *corr.* d e f g *R*
[27.] [a–a] *om. W1*
[b–b] tetracorda ista *M₂*; tetrachorda ista *W1*
[c] constitutiones *W1*
[d] tetracordum *M₂*
[e] dyapente *W1*
[f] iunct[ę>a] *W1*
[g–g] speciem dyatessaron *W1*
[h–h] *om. R*
[i] speciem dyatessaron *marked with superscript* a *and* b *for transposition W1*
[j–j] sunt uice *S*
[k–k] *om. W1*
[l] con|nexio uel natiuitas *W1*
[m] copulationem *W1*
[n–n] de primis prima *R*
[o] et *W1*
[p–p] ęedem sunt *D1M₂*; eedem sunt *W1*
[q] que *R*; atque *S*

26. Of which letters and notes each of the tetrachords consists.

The tetrachord of the *graves* according to Guido consists of .A.B.C.D., with the same in Boethius being *proslambanomenos*, *hypate hypaton*, *parhypate hypaton*, and *lichanos hypaton*.[40] The tetrachord of the *finales* for Guido is .D.E.F.G.; for Boethius *lichanos hypaton*, *hypate meson*, *parhypate meson*, and *lichanos meson*. The tetrachord of the *superiores* according to the moderns is .a.b.c.d. The same in Boethius is *mese*, *paramese*, *trite diezeugmenon*, and *paranete diezeugmenon*. The tetrachord of the *excellentes* is .d.e.f.g. according to Guido or, according to Boethius, *paranete*, *diezeugmenon*, *nete diezeugmenon*, *trite hyperboleon*, and *paranete hyperboleon*.

27. How the tetrachords determine the species.

Let us now discuss how the tetrachords determine the constitution of the species of *diatessaron* and *diapente*. The tetrachord of the *graves* in the company of the tetrachord of the *finales* accounts for all the species of *diatessaron*, of which there are four, in this manner. The first of the *graves* joined to the first of the *finales* produces the first species of *diatessaron*. So too the second of the *graves* with the second of the *finales* creates the second species of *diatessaron*. In the same manner the third of the *graves* and the third of the *finales*, and the fourth of the *graves* and the fourth of the *finales* stand in the place of parents to the third and fourth species of *diatessaron*. The same birth of the species of *diatessaron* occurs in the joining of the *superiores* and *excellentes*, and proceeds in such a natural order that the first proceeds from the first notes, the second from the second notes, the third and the fourth from the third and the fourth notes; and with necessity since the combination of the *superiores* and *excellentes* is nothing more than a repetition of the combination of the *graves* and *finales*.[41] Wherefore it is necessary that that which is done between the *graves* and the *finales* should be done similarly between the *superiores* and the *excellentes*, because just as the *superiores* are the same as the *graves*, so too the *excellentes* are the same as the *finales*.

[28.] [a]Quod diatesseron et diapente inter[b] diuersa constent tetrachorda.[a]

Omnes ergo quatuor diapente species ita[c] inter finales constant et superiores, sicut omnes diatesseron aut inter graues[d] et finales aut inter superiores consistunt et excellentes, eodemque ordine disponentis[e] naturę ut prima de primis et quęlibet species de sui nominis constet chordis ac litteris.

[29.] [a]Quod in[b] locis diatesseron diapente non inueniatur nec diatesseron in sedibus diapente.[a]

Admodum naturalem esse generationem specierum diatesseron[c] inter graues ac[d] finales et inter superiores ac[e] excellentes; diapente autem specierum inter finales et superiores naturalem esse ortum: ex hoc potest perpendi quod nec naturaliter inter graues et finales aut superiores et[f] excellentes diapente procedunt species ubi diatesseron naturales habent sedes, nec inter finales et superiores inueniuntur naturales diatesseron sedes sicut diapente [g]species sunt inibi[g] naturaliter procedentes. Naturales dico species ut prius dixi de sui nominis literis consistentes,[h] ut prima de primis et cętera.

[30.] De formalibus speciebus.[a]

De formalibus tempestiuum est dicere speciebus. Formales [b]dicendę sunt[b] species[c] quę formam[d] habent non naturam, sicut[e] a .D.[f] in .G., forma est primę speciei diatesseron habens semitonium in medio. Sed quia non inter duas constat primas, sed inter primam et quartam, dicenda est prima formalis non prima naturalis. Naturalis autem [g]est prima[g] quę non solum in medio habet semitonium, sed inter duas primas consistit, ut illa quę est inter .A. et .D., quarum altera [h]grauium altera est prima finalium.[h] Sic[i] species diapente inter .A. et .E.[j] prima est formalis[k] non naturalis, quia licet ut prima naturalis scandat

[28.] [a–a] Quomodo constent quatuor species dyapente *W1*
[b] in *D1M₂*
[c] *om. M₂W1*
[d] *om. W1*
[e] disponentes *corr.* disponentis *D1*
[29.] [a–a] *om. W1. The latter half of R reads* nec in sedibus diapente diatessaron *with superscript letters* a c d b, *indicating that diatessaron was ommitted by error and that the correct order is as in S.*
[b] inter *M₂*
[c] *om. R*
[d] et *W1*
[e] et *D1M₂W1*
[f] aut *W1*
[g–g] habet species inibi *W1*
[h] existentes *W1*
[30.] [a] speciebus quatuor *M₂;* litteris *S*
[b–b] sunt dicende *R*
[c] *om. R*
[d] forma *M₂*
[e] sicut est *R*
[f] .B. *M₂*
[g–g] prima est *S*
[h–h] prima est grauium altera finalium *R;* grauium altera prima est finalium *D1*
[i] Sicut *M₂*
[j] .G. *M₂*
[k] finalis *D1M₂*

28. That the *diatessaron* and the *diapente* exist between different tetrachords.

All four species of *diapente* thus exist between the *finales* and *superiores*, just as all the species of *diatessaron* exist between either the *graves* and *finales* or the *superiores* and *excellentes*; and they exist in the same order of natural distribution, for the first species exists between the first notes and each of the others between the notes or letters of its name.

29. That in the place of a *diatessaron* a *diapente* is not to be found, neither a *diatessaron* in the place of a *diapente*.

The generation of the species of *diatessaron* is exceedingly natural between the *graves* and *finales*, and between the *superiores* and *excellentes*. On the other hand, the species of *diapente* have a natural origin between the *finales* and *superiores*. From this it is possible to deduce that the species of *diapente* do not naturally proceed from the *graves* and *finales* or from the *superiores* and *excellentes* (where the species of *diatessaron* naturally have seats), and neither are the natural seats of the *diatessaron* to be found between the *finales* and *superiores* (where the species of *diapente* are naturally proceeding). Natural species, I say, existing between the letters of their names, as I said earlier, so that the first exists between the first notes and so forth.

30. Concerning the formal species.

It is now time to speak of the formal species. It is necessary to speak of formal species that have a form but are not natural, like .D. to .G., which has the form of the first species of *diatessaron*, having a semitone in the middle.[42] But since it does not exist between two first notes[43] but between first and fourth notes,[44] it must be called a first species in form but not in nature. A natural first species, however, is that which not only has a semitone in the middle but exists between two first notes, such as that between .A. and .D., of which one is the first of the *graves* and the other the first of the *finales*. Thus the species of *diapente* between .A. and .E. is a first species in its form but not a natural first species, because although like the natural first it climbs

tono, semitonio, ditono,[l] non tamen inter duas primas, sed inter primam constat ac[m] secundam, sicut illa quę est inter .D. finalem et .a. superiorem.

[31.] [a]Quod principales[b] chordę dicantur[c] quę constitutiue sunt troporum.[a]

Principales chordę dicuntur quę in troporum dispositionibus principatum sortiuntur, sicut in autento proto principales sunt istę: prima finalium, prima superiorum, prima excellentium. Finalis est merito principalis in primis, quia si secundum conuenientiam quam ipsa predocet cantum incipimus et usque ad finem procedere[d] non possumus, ostendit illum [e]aut esse[e] uitiosum aut iuxta alium modum gubernandum. Quidam cantant illam antiphonam [f]*Alliga Domine in uinculis*[f] [g]secundum tercium tonum,[g] secundum finalis conuenientiam incipientes eam in .G.,[h] sed quia defectus occurrit chordarum ut cantari non possit, cogitemus eam aut secundum alium modum iubilandam aut penitus esse mendosam. Sed falsam [i]esse dicere prius[i] non debemus quam secundum omnium finalium conuenientiam [j]incipientes exploremus, si in ullo[k] modorum [l]inoffensam reperiamus[l] eam, sicut istam iuxta[m] primi finalis conuenientiam[j] inchoantes in .F. sine scandalo percantabimus. Est quoque principalis ob hoc dicenda quod initium[n] cantus principiumque nonnumquam procedit ab[o] illa ut [p]*Ecce nomen domini*,[p] [q]*Ecce in nubibus celi*,[q] [r]*Ecce ueniet Deus et homo*,[r] [s]*Leua hierusalem*[s] et alia innumerabilia quę ad reperiendum sunt planissima. Est principalis quia distinctionum [t]interdum principia[t] interdum fines conuersantur in illa, aut aliqua musica proportione distant

[l] tono et tono *R*
[m] et *D1M₂*
[31.] [a–a] *om. W1*
[b] principes *M₂*
[c] *om. D1M₂*
[d] perducere *D1W1;* incipere *M₂*
[e–e] esse aut *R*
[f–f] Alliga domine in uinculis *D1;* Alliga domine in uinculis *S;* Alliga domine *W1*
[g–g] *om. R*
[h] .C. *M₂*
[i–i] dicere esse prius *S with* dicere *and* esse *marked for transposition;* esse prius dicere *W1*
[j–j] *om. S*
[k] nullo *M₂W1*
[l–l] reperiemus inoffensam *M₂W1*
[m] iuxtam *W1*
[n] incium *corr.* tercium *M₂*
[o] ex *R*
[p–p] Ecce nomen domini *D1;* Ecce nomen domini *M₂W1;* Ecce nomen domini *S*
[q–q] Ecce in nubibus celi *D1;* Ecce in nubibus celi *M₂;* Ecce in nubibus *S;* Ecce in nubibus *W1*
[r–r] Ecce ueniet Deus *D1;* Ecce ueniet Deus *M₂W1;* Ecce ueniet Deus et homo *S*
[s–s] Leua hierusalem *D1;* Leua ierusalem *M₂;* Leua hierusalem *S;* Leua hierusalem *W1*
[t–t] *om. S*

by tone, semitone, tone, and two tones, nevertheless it does not exist between two first notes, like that species between .D. of the *finales* and .a. of the *superiores*, but between a first note and a second note.

31. What the principal notes are called that constitute the tropes.

The principal notes are so called because they exercise prominence in the working of the tropes, just as in authentic *protus* the principal notes are as follows: the first of the *finales*, the first of the *superiores*, and the first of the *excellentes*.[45] The final note is deservedly first and foremost: since, if according to custom that teaches these very things, we begin the chant and cannot make continuous progress to the end, it shows itself either to be full of faults or requiring to be governed by another mode. Some sing the antiphon *Alliga domine in vinculis*[46] according to the third tone, beginning at .G. according to the custom of its final; but since a defect of the notes occurs that it is not possible to sing, we might think that either it is to be sung successfully in another mode or that it is thoroughly defective. But we must not say it is wrong before we attempt to begin according to the custom of all the finals, lest we find it inoffensive in any other mode—as beginning according to the first final at .F. we shall sing it through without fault. The final note is also to be called principal because the initiation and start of a chant always proceeds from it, as in *Ecce nomen Domini*,[47] *Ecce in nubibus caeli*,[48] *Ecce venit Deus et homo*,[49] *Leva Iherusalem*[50] and innumerable others that are plain to be apprehended. It is principal because the beginnings and ends of the phrases sometimes meet in it, or the rest differ from it in musical proportion—

ab illa,[u] id est aut tono uel[v] semitonio,[w] [x]siue semiditono, seu ditono,[x] an[y] [z]diatessaron, diapenteue[z] Principalis est merito cum omnis cantilenę finis [a]et requies sit in eius hospitio.[a]

Superiores chordę ideo principalitatis dignantur[b] nomine, quia principales autentorum partes diapente uidelicet ac diatessaron medietatis uinculo copulant, et quod ad eas nonnumquam pertingant neumę principales, principia dico distinctionum et[c] fines ac tonorum differentię. Excellentes [d]iure sunt[d] principales quę ita dominantur autentis ut in ipsis sit ascensionis eorum finis.

[32.] [a]Quę chordę sint principales in cantibus plagalibus[a]

In[b] plagalibus quoque eadem ratione dicuntur principales graues, finales, superiores, [c]qua in autentis finales,[d] superiores, excellentes.[c] Quapropter non est difficile inde huc[e] similitudinem[f] transferre.

[33.] [a]Quod principalitas chordarum discernenda sit.[a]

Principalitas chordarum accipi discretiue debet. Non ubiuis illa principalitas sed in sua specie consideretur sicut [b]prima grauium, prima finalium, prima superiorum[b] principales sunt in prima specie plagalium cantuum, id est in secundo tono, quę principaliter eiusdem sunt constitutiuę. Principaliter dico quia alię chordę cooperantur istę ut predictum est principantur, sicut in aulę constructione principales [c]partes sunt[c] columnę. Principales [d]quoque sunt[d] in secunda specie plagalium, [e]id est[e] [f]in quarto tono secunda grauium, secunda finalium, secunda superiorum[f] quę principaliter illum constituunt. Sic constituuę sunt tercię et quartę grauium, finalium, superiorum, tercię et quartę[g] speciei plagalium troporum, id est sexti et octaui toni.

[u] ipsa *W1*
[v] aut *D1*M_2*; om. W1*
[w] semitono *D1*M_2*;* semitonium *W1*
[x–x] siue semitono seu ditono *corr.* siue semiditono seu ditono *R;* siue semitono seu ditono *D1*M_2*S;* aut semiditono seu ditono *W1*
[y] an *corr.* aut *R*
[z–z] siue dyatessaron siue dyapente *W1*
[a–a] et requiescit in eius hospicio M_2*;* in eius | requiescit hosipcio *W1*
[b] signantur *W1*
[c] ac *R*
[d–d] sunt iure *S*
[32.] [a–a] *om. W1*
[b] <I>n *W1*
[c–c] *om. R*
[d] finalis M_2
[e] huic M_2*;* huius *W1*
[f] similitudine M_2
[33.] [a–a] *om. W1*
[b–b] prima grauium finalium superiorum *W1*
[c–c] sunt partes *S*
[d–d] sunt quoque *S*
[e–e] *om. W1*
[f-f] *om. R but added in text hand in right margin;* in quarto tono ii[a] grauium ii[a] superiorum ii[a] finalium *W1 marked with* a *and* b *to indicate correct order.*
[g] quarte et iiii[e] *R*

that is, either by a tone or a semitone, if not a semiditone or ditone, or perhaps a *diatessaron* or *diapente*. It is deservedly principal since the end and the resting of every chant are under its hospitality.

The notes of the *superiores* are also worthy of the name principal, since they join the principal parts of the authentic tropes—namely the *diapente* and the *diatessaron*—in the middle by a bond, and since, I say, it is to them that the principal shorter phrases, the beginnings and ends of the longer phrases, and the *differentiae* of the tones sometimes pertain. The *excellentes* are rightly principal because they so dominate the authentics that in themselves may be the end of their ascent.

32. Which notes are principal in the plagal chants.

In the plagals also, for the same reason, the *graves*, *finales*, and *superiores* are said to be principal, as with the *finales*, *superiores*, and *excellentes* in the authentics. Wherefore it is not difficult to transfer those similarities from here.

33. That the prominence of notes must be distinguished.

The prominence of the notes must be distinguished with care. That prominence is to be considered not where one pleases but in its own species, as the first of the *graves*, the first of the *finales*, and the first of the *superiores* are principal in the first species of plagal chant—that is, in the second tone—for they are the principal constituents of the same.[51] Principal, I say, since other notes help, but these as said are playing the principal role, as in the building of a hall the principal parts are the columns. There are also principal notes in the second species of plagal—that is, in the fourth tone the second of the *graves*, the second of the *finales*, and the second of the *superiores*—which are its principal constituents.[52] In the same way also the third and fourth of the *graves*, *finales*, and *superiores* are linked with the third and fourth species of plagal tropes—that is, the sixth and eighth tones.[53]

[34.] [a]De autentis[b] tropis.[a]

Prima finalium, prima superiorum, prima excellentium [c]principales sunt[c] in prima specie autenticorum[d] cantuum, id est in primo tono quem principaliter constituunt. Secunda finalium, secunda superiorum, secunda excellentium principales sunt in secunda autentica specie diapason, id est in tercio tono cuius principaliter sunt [e]constitutiuę. Sic de terciis tercia autentica[e] diapason constituitur, quarta de quartis.

[35.] [a]Quod principium similitudinis est in illis.[a]

Principales quoque dicuntur chordę quia principium sunt eiusdem habitudinis. Habitudinem autem appello ascensionis uel descensionis aut utriusque similitudinem. Qualis est intensio ab .A. in .D. talis est a .D. in .G.[b] et qualis est remissio a .G. in .D. talis est a .D. in .A., quia talis est concordia non solum quartis sed[c] quintis infra et supra, ut media alterius eleuationem alteriusque sumat depositionem. Et si ad quartam supra confertur cum eleuatione ad quintam superius respondet cum depositione; ac econtrario[d] cum quarta inferiori per remissionem cum quinta concordat per intensionem excepto graui deutero et superiori, qui[e] infra non inueniet diatessaron supra [f]se uero caret[f] diapente quamuis quinque sint chordę. Et[g] hinc monemur ut caute diffiniamus symphonias. Si aliquo[h] me interrogante quid est diatessaron uel diapente, respondebo quatuor chordę quinque chordę, [i]caute non[i] dixero cum quatuor [j]chordę sint[j] .a.♭.b.c.[k] et tamen non contineant nisi semiditonum,[l] cum quinque chordę sint .B.C.D.E.F. et non cohibeant nisi diatessaron et semitonium. Idcirco[m] dicamus[n] diatessaron est semitonium cum duobus tonis in nullo participantibus. Diapente est semitonium cum tribus[o] tonis in nullo participantibus. Hoc dico propterea quia tonus qui est ab [p].a. in .b.[p] cum illo tono qui est a .♭. in .c. participat spacium quod est a .♭. in

[34.] [a–a] *om. W1;* De autentis protis M_2R
[b] autenticis *R*
[c–c] sunt principales *R*
[d] autentorum *R*
[e–e] con||stiue. Sic de terciis tercia autentica *S. Originally the bottom line of fol. 121r read* |stitutiuę. Sic de terciis tercia autentica ||, *but was immediately erased and transferred to the top line of fol. 121v to preserve the ruling scheme of S.*
[35.] [a–a] *om. W1*
[b] .C. M_2
[c] sed etiam *W1*
[d] econtra *R*
[e] quia *W1*
[f–f] uero se caret $D1M_2W1$
[g] Ex M_2; ex *W1*
[h] autem aliquo *S;* aliquando $D1M_2W1$
[i–i] non caute *R*
[j–j] sint chordę *R*
[k] .A.B.♮.C. M_2; .a.b.♭.c. *R*
[l] semitonium $D1M_2S$; semitonium *corr.* semiditonum *R* (di *superscript and final* i *marked for expunction*)
[m] iccirco *D1W1;* icirco *M2*
[n] dicimus *S*
[o] duobus *W1*
[p–p] .A. in .b. M_2; .A. in .B. *W1*

34. Concerning the authentic tropes.

The first of the *finales*, the first of the *superiores*, and the first of the *excellentes* are principal in the first species of authentic chant—that is, in the first tone—which they principally constitute.[54] The second of the *finales*, the second of the *superiores*, and the second of the *excellentes* are principal in the second species of authentic *diapason*—that is, in the third tone—as they constitute its principal notes.[55] Likewise also the thirds constitute the third authentic *diapason*, and the fourths the fourth.[56]

35. That the beginning of the similarity lies in these things.

The principal notes are also so called because they are a foundation of the same pattern. This pattern I call the likeness of ascent or descent or of both. Such is extension from .A. to .D. as from .D. to .G. and such is remission from .G. to .D. as from .D. to .A.; for such is the agreement not only at the fourth note but also at the fifth note below and above, that the middle note takes up the ascent of one and the descent of the other. And if the *superius*[57] is connected to the fourth in ascent, it responds to the fifth in descent.[58] On the contrary, when the fourth below is connected by descent, the fifth is connected by ascent,[59] except *deuterus* of the *graves* and *superiores*, below which will not be found a *diatessaron* and above which will indeed be lacking a *diapente*, although there may be five notes.[60] Hence we are advised that we should define the intervals with caution. Should anyone ask me what is a *diatessaron* or a *diapente* and I were to respond saying "four notes" or "five notes," I should not be speaking cautiously with the four notes being .a. ♭.b.c. but spanning nothing more than a semiditone; or with the five notes being .B.C.D.E.F. and comprising nothing except a *diatessaron* and a semitone. On that account we say a *diatessaron* is a semitone with two tones in no way overlapping and that a *diapente* is a semitone with three tones in no way overlapping. I say this, moreover, that the tone which is from .a. to .b. with that tone which is from .♭. to .c. partakes of the space between .♭. to

.b., quod est maius toni spacium quod apotome dicitur, quia aliter poterit[q] probari et [r]semitonium esse[r] diatessaron et diatessaron esse diapente.

[36.] De similitudine diuitum et pauperum ad tropos utrosque.

Concordant discordantque autenti et plagales sicut diuites et pauperes, quia licet hi in alto [a]hi humili degant in loco,[a] quamuis isti ambulent[b] in tragedia illi musitent in comedia, unum tamen et equalem expectant[c] obitum et finem. Ita quamuis ascendant descendantque diuerse [d]eosdem tamen finales[d] sortiuntur autenti et plagales.

[37.] De similitudine uirilis femineique chori ad autentos et plagas.

Concordant discordantque autenti cum plagis quomodo si procederent de quatuor thalamis totidem nuptę modestę[a] cum suis sponsis, copularentque duos chorearum circulos ut ipsi thalami matronali choro essent centra, id est medietates [b]uirilibusque choreis[b] terminales, ut [c]etiam in hoc[c] euangelistarum exprimerentur uolumina; de quibus pronuntiat propheticus Ezechielis spiritus "quasi[d] sit rota in medio rotę," quia sicut euangelistarum opera[e] concordant discordantque ita autenti cum plagis. Nam quinque chordas habent communiter tres autem singulariter, ut duo circuli ita sibimet sint[f] implicati, ut utriusque extremitas centrum, id est medietatem alterius persecet; habent medium spatium commune altrinsecus [g]scilicet spatium[g] situm sine participatione.

[38.] De differentia autentorum et plagarum iuxta Horatium[a] Flaccum.

Differunt quoque autenti et plagę instar Horatianę sententię:
Vt festis[b] matrona moueri iussa diebus,
Intererit satyris[c] paulum pudibunda proteruis.
Non est enim suum matronalis incessus.
Saltantes satyros imitetur ut Alphesibeus.

Sicut cantus plagalis nec principia nec fines distinctionum tendit ad quintam cum etiam raro mittat ad quartam.

[q] potest *S*
[r–r] semiditonum *W1*
[36.] [a–a] hi in humili degnant loco *R*
[b] ambullentur *RS*
[c] exspectant *R*
[d–d] tamen finales *D1*
[37.] [a] honestę *D1*
[b–b] uirilibus choris *R*
[c–c] in hoc etiam *R*
[d] quasi si *D1S*
[e] *in marg. S*
[f] *om. D1RS*
[g–g] *om. D1S. Coinciding with the folio change at fol. 122rv in S.*
[38.] [a] oratium et *R*
[b] uestis *S*
[c] satyrus *S*

.b., which is the larger part of a tone and is called *apotome*,[61] since otherwise it could be proved that a semitone is a *diatessaron* and a *diatessaron* is a *diapente*.

36. Concerning the similarity of the rich and poor to each of the tropes.

The authentics and plagals are in concordance as well as discordance like the rich and the poor, since it is allowed that the former be in a high position and the latter in a low position.[62] However much the latter walk in tragedy and the former muse on comedy, nevertheless they both await one and the same death and end. Thus, although they ascend and descend differently, the same finals end the authentics and plagals.

37. Concerning the similarity of the male and female choirs to the authentics and plagals.

The authentics and plagals are in concordance as well as discordance, just as if they were to proceed from the four bedchambers of just so many modest brides with their respective bridegrooms[63] and join two circles of dance, so that the bedchambers themselves became the center—that is, the middle—of the wife's choir and the boundary of the man's choir. In this also one might perceive the volumes of the evangelists, about which the prophetic spirit of Ezekiel proclaims: "as if a wheel were in the midst of a wheel."[64] For just as the works of the evangelists concord as well as discord, so it is with the authentics and the plagals. They have five notes in common and three that are not shared: thus the two circles are joined in such a manner that the extremity of each dissects the center—that is, the middle of the other. They have the center space in common; the remainder, of course, is not shared.

38. Concerning the differences between authentic and plagal according to Horace.

The authentics and plagals also differ like these Horatian sentences:

Just as a lady provoked to dance on festal days,
Will join the brazen Satyrs with no small shame,[65]
It does not befit the gait of his wife
To imitate the Satyrs' capering steps like Alphesiboeus.[66]

Thus neither the beginnings nor the ends of phrases in plagal chant extend to the fifth, though they might occasionally reach as far as a fourth.

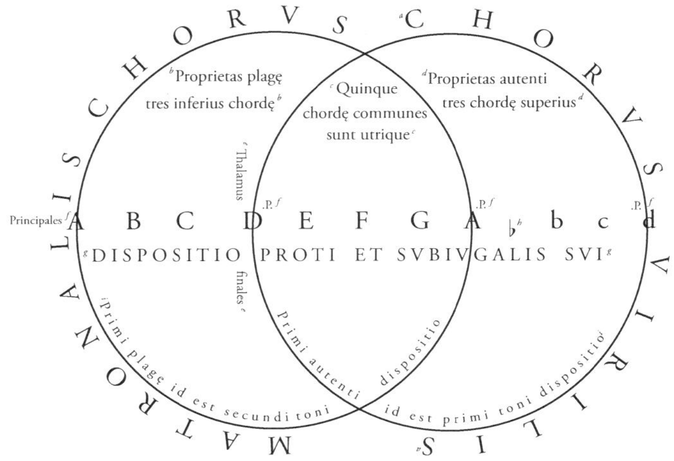

a–a VIRILIS CHORVS *M_2*
b–b propriae uoces subiugalis *M_2*
c–c Communes utriusque uoces *M_2*
d–d propriae autenti uoces *M_2*
e–e *om. M_2;* Thalamus id est finales *S*
f *om. M_2*
g–g *om. M_2*
h *om. S*
i–i Dispositio autenti proti et sui subiugalis *M_2*

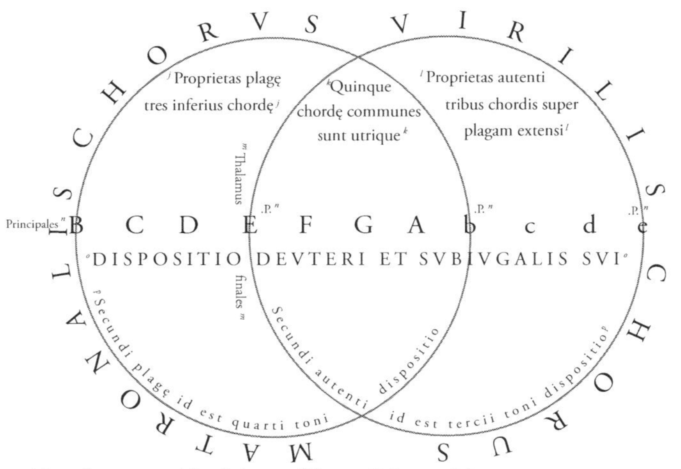

j–j proprie subiugalis uoces *M_2; S has a different version of this diagram, following R: see Appendix 1*
k–k Communes utriusque uoces *M_2*
l–l proprię autenti uoces *M_2*
l–l *om. M_2*
m–m *om. M_2*
n *om. M_2*
o–o *om. M_2*
p–p Dispositio autenti deuteri et sui subiugalis *M_2*

Diagram 2.1.

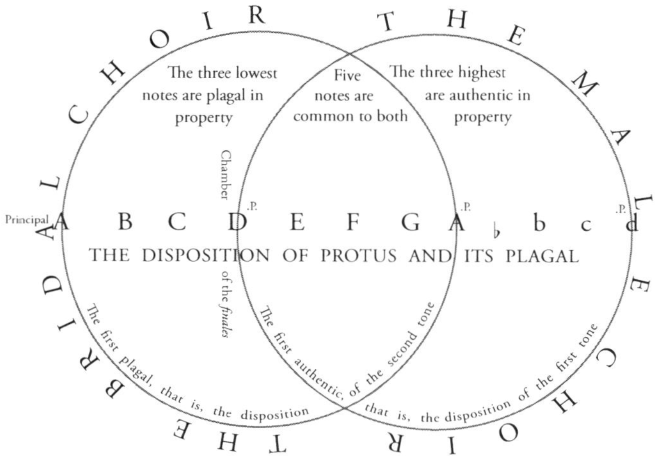

Diagram 2.2.

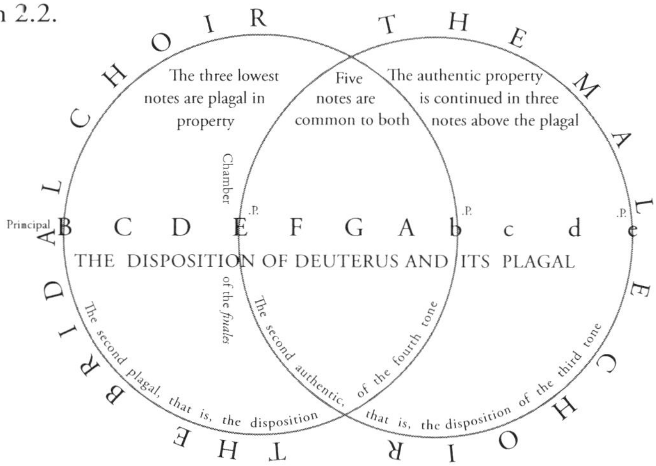

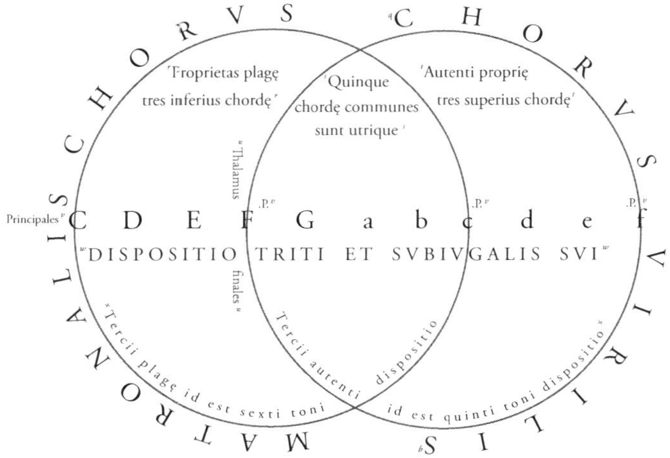

[q–q] VIRILIS CHORVS *M₂; S has a different version of this diagram, following R: see Appendix 1*

[r–r] proprie subiugalis uoces *M₂*

[s–s] Communes utriusque uoces *M₂*

[t–t] proprię autenti uoces *M₂*

[u–u] *om. M₂*

[v] *om. M₂*

[w–w] *om. M₂*

[x–x] Dispositio autenti triti et sui subiugalis *M₂*

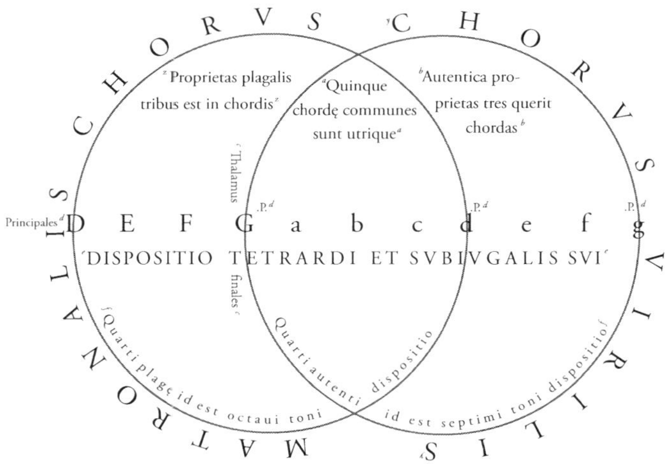

[y–y] VIRILIS CHORVS *M₂; S has a different version of this diagram, following R: see Appendix 1*

[z–z] proprię subiugalis uoces *M₂*

[a–a] Communes utriusque uoces *M₂*

[b–b] proprię autenti uoces *M₂*

[c–c] *om. M₂*

[d] *om. M₂*

[e–e] *om. M₂*

[f–f] Dispositio autenti tetrardi et sui subiugalis *M₂*

Diagram 2.3.

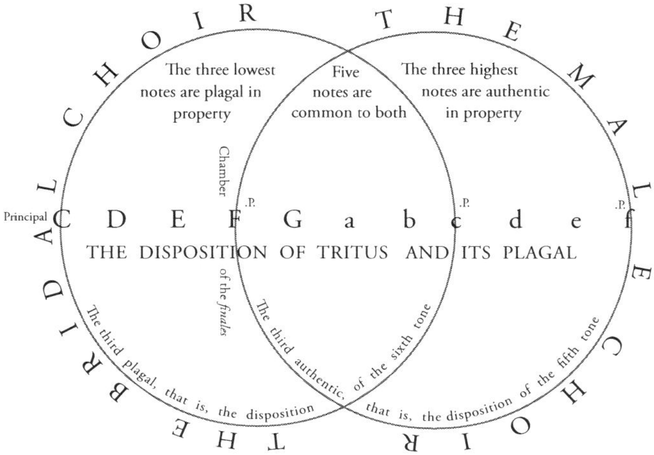

Diagram 2.4.

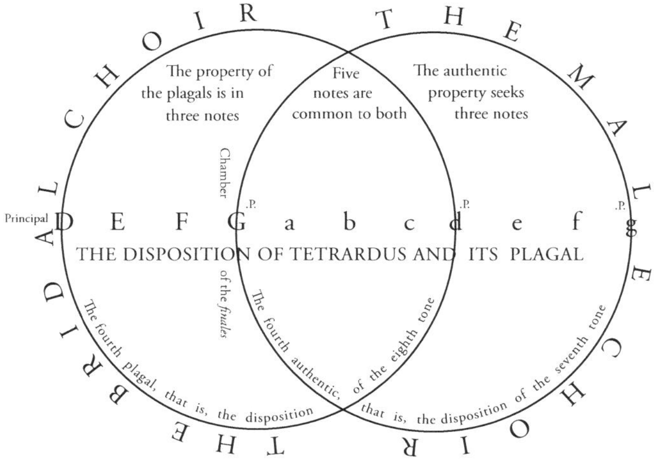

[39.] Iterum differentia tetrachordorum.

Tetrachordorum quoque differentia est nonnulla quia tetrachordum[a] grauium et superiorum claues sunt plagalium, tetrachordum finalium et excellentium claues sunt autenticorum.[b] Et medietatis uicem obtinent finales et superiores: finales plagalium, superiores autenticorum diatessaron et diapente conuincientes, ex hisque diapason componentes.

[40.] Quomodo tetrachordum grauium mystice pertineat ad Mattheum[a] [b]et ad humanitatem Christi.[b]

Tetrachordum grauium typice congruit saluatoris humanitati quam Mattheus describit, in qua Christus grauia quęque sustinuit, esuriendo sub infructuosa ficulnea, sitiendo et lassescendo super puteum, uulpibus pauperior et[c] uolucribus foueas ac nidos habentibus, cum non haberet ubi caput suum reclinaret.

[41.] Quomodo tetrachordum finalium saluatoris passioni congruat [a]et morti.[a]

Tetrachordum finalium uitalem Christi mortem figurat,[b] cum non solum ipse ad tempus uitam finiuit sed etiam ad finem tetenderunt templi uelum, soliditas petrarum, solis claritas, terrę stabilitas.

[39.] [a] tetrachordorum *R*
[b] autentorum *R*
[40.] [a] mattheu† † *S* (*the orange ink is so faded that is it impossible to tell whether this letter is* m *or* s)
[b–b] *om. S*
[c] ac *R*
[41.] [a–a] *om. S*
[b] significat *R*

39. Again a difference of the tetrachords.

There are also some differences between the tetrachords since the keys to the tetrachords of the *graves* and *superiores* are plagal, while the keys to the tetrachords of the *finales* and *excellentes* are authentic. The *finales* and the *superiores* occupy the middle: the *finales* occupy the middle of the plagals and the *superiores* occupy the middle of the authentics, joining the *diatessaron* and *diapente* and from these composing the *diapason*.[67]

40. How the tetrachord of the *graves* mystically pertains to Matthew and to the humanity of Christ.

The tetrachord of the *graves* accords figuratively with the humanity of the Savior that Matthew describes, in which Christ has borne all manner of lowly things: hungering below the unfruitful fig tree,[68] thirsting and growing tired above the well,[69] poorer than the foxes having holes or the birds having nests, since he had no place to rest his head.[70]

41. How the tetrachord of the *finales* accords with the passion and death of the Savior.

The tetrachord of the *finales* signifies the living death of Christ: since not only was he required to finish his life at the appointed time, but also at the end the veil of the temple, the solidity of the rocks, the brightness of the sun, and the stability of the earth were rent asunder.[71]

[42.] [a]Quodmodo tetrachordum superiorum Christi significet resurrectionem.[a]

Tetrachordum superiorum Christi gloriosam designat resurrectionem, in qua ad huius uitę superiora remeauit nobisque [b]supernę uitę[b] hereditatem delegauit.

[43.] [a]Quomodo tetrachordum excellentium Christi significet ascensionem.[a]

Tetrachordum excellentium typice iubilat excellentiam ascensionis Christi, in qua "ascendit Deus in" iubilatione et "Dominus in uoce tubę" ostendens se excellentissimum esse, "quoniam eleuata est magnificentia" eius "super cęlos."

[44.] [a]Quod duo tetrachorda ad humilitatem, duo ad Christi pertineant celsitudinem.[a]

Quorum tetrachordorum duo, id est grauium et finalium sicut sunt humilia, ita humilitatem Christi quę fuit in humanitate et passione designant; duo excelsa, id est superiorum et excellentium, celsitudinem saluatoris quę in resurrectione et ascensione patuit declarant.

[45.] [a]Item de discordia tetrachordorum et quod quedam incipiant quedam species finiant.[a]

Discordant tetrachorda quoniam quoddam est specierum diatesseron et diapente inceptiuum non finitiuum ut grauium, quoddam diffinitiuum non inceptiuum ut excellentium, quędam et inchoatiua et determinantia ut finalium et superiorum, quia finales determinant species diatesseron, incipiunt[b] species diapente; superiores finiunt species diapente, incipiunt[c] species diatesseron. Et hoc ita naturali ordine ut siue incipiat[d] seu terminet siue faciat utrumque inter primas prima, secundas secunda, tercias tercia [e]et inter[e] quartas quarta sit species uel[f] diatesseron seu[g] diapente.

[46.] [a]Quomodo graues sui nominis species diatesseron incipiatur.[a]

Prima grauium incipit primam speciem diatesseron, secunda secundam, tercia terciam. Quarta grauium, id est .D. quę biformis est, quartam speciem diatesseron incipit, quę et finit primam secundum quod prima finalis est.

[42.] [a–a] *om. S*
[b–b] uitę supernę *R*
[43.] [a–a] *om. S*
[44.] [a–a] *om. S*
[45.] [a–a] *om. D2S;* fini[u>a]nt *R*
[b] incipiunt autem *D2*
[c] incipiunt autem *D2*
[d] incipi[u>a]nt *D2*
[e–e] *om. D2*
[f] *om. D2*
[g] uel *D2*
[46.] [a–a] *om. D2S*

42. How the tetrachord of the *superiores* signifies the Resurrection of Christ.

The tetrachord of the *superiores* marks out the glorious Resurrection of Christ, in which he returned to the superiority of his former life and left to us the inheritance of life eternal.

43. How the tetrachord of the *excellentes* signifies the Ascension of Christ.

The tetrachord of the *excellentes* figuratively proclaims the excellence of Christ's Ascension, in which "God who is ascended in jubilation and the Lord with the sound of trumpet"[72] shows himself to be the most exalted, "since his magnificence has been raised above the heavens."[73]

44. That two tetrachords pertain to the humility and two to the celestial nature of Christ.

Two of the tetrachords—that is, those of the *graves* and *finales*—as they are lowly, signify the humility that Christ displayed in his humanity and in his Passion; the two higher tetrachords—that is, those of the *superiores* and *excellentes*—reveal the celestial nature of the Savior, which was made manifest in the Resurrection and the Ascension.

45. Also concerning the discordance of the tetrachords, and that certain species have their beginnings and certain species their endings in them.

The tetrachords discord, since one of them contains the beginning of the species of *diatessaron* and *diapente* but not the ending—namely, the *graves*; another contains their ending but not their beginning—namely, the *excellentes*; certain tetrachords contain both beginnings and endings—namely, the *finales* and the *superiores*, since the *finales* end in the species of *diatessaron* and begin in the species of *diapente*, whereas the *superiores* finish in the species of *diapente* and begin in the species of *diatessaron*.[74] And this is so according to natural order, that whether by beginning or ending or making, there may be a first species of *diatessaron* or *diapente* between the first notes, a second between the second notes, a third between the third notes, and a fourth between the fourth notes.

46. How the *graves* begin the correspondingly named species of *diatessaron*.

The first of the *graves* begins the first species of *diatessaron*, the second the second, the third the third. The fourth of the *graves*—that is, .D.—which is double functioned, begins the fourth species of *diatessaron* and ends the first, according to which it is the first of the *finales*.[75]

[47.] [a]Quomodo finales finiant et incipiant species.[a]

Prima finalis,[b] idem[c] uidelicet .D., finit primam diatesseron sed incipit primam diapente speciem. .E. secunda finalium secundam diatesseron et diapente speciem [d]finit et incipit.[d] .F. tercia finalium terciam[e] utramque speciem [f]finit et incipit.[f] .G. quarta finalium[g] quartam finit[h] quartam incipit.

[48.] [a]Quod contra legem finalium superiores finiant species et incipiant.[a]

E contrario prima superiorum id est .a., [b]finit primam[b] speciem diapente incipit primam diatesseron quam finit prima excellentium.

[49.] [a]Oppositio tetrachordi.[a]

Opposita sunt tetrachorda finalium et excellentium, tetrachorda[b] grauium et superiorum. Nam ista omnes diatesseron[c] incipiunt illa finiunt. Sed etiam media opponuntur, id est finalium et superiorum, quia omnes diapente species incipiunt finales finiunt superiores. Opposita [d]quoque sunt[d] ultima sicut media tetrachorda, quia grauium solummodo omnes diatesseron species incipit[e] excellentium[f] [g]easdem tantum[g] finit.[h] Finalium[i] omnes diapente species [j]incipit superiorum finit;[j] finalum[k] omnes[l] diatesseron species [m]finit superiorum incipit.[m]

[50.] [a]Quod tria sint in inchoando, tria in determinando, duo in utroque.[a]

Tria sunt [b]similia in inchoando:[b] grauium, finalium, superiorum; tria in determinando: finalium, superiorum, excellentium; duo in utroque: finalium, superiorum; singulariter ad incipiendum tantum grauium ad finiendum[c] dumtaxat excellentium.

[47.] [a–a] *om.* *D2S*
[b] finalium *D2*
[c] *om.* *D2*
[d–d] et incipit et finit *D2, marked, possibly for transposition*
[e] tercia *S*
[f–f] et incipit et finit *D2, marked, possibly for transposition*
[g] finales M_3; finalis *S*
[h] finit et *R*
[48.] [a–a] *om.* $D2M_3S$
[b–b] primam *om.* M_3; primam finit *R*
[49.] [a–a] *om.* $D2M_3S$
[b] tetrachordo M_3S
[c] Dyapente M_3
[d–d] sunt quoque M_3
[e] incipiunt *D2*
[f] Excellentes M_3, *beginning a new sentence*
[g–g] tantum easdem *marked with superscript* b *and* a *to indicate transposition* M_3
[h] finiunt *D2*
[i] Finales $D2M_3S$
[j–j] incipiunt superiores finiunt *D2*
[k] Finales $D2M_3S$
[l] *om.* $D2M_3S$
[m–m] finiunt superioru[m>e]s incipiunt *D2*
[50.] [a–a] *om.* $D2M_3S$
[b–b] in inchoando similia *R*
[c] definiendum *S*

47. How the *finales* begin and end the species.

The first of the *finales*, the same aforementioned .D., finishes the first species of *diatessaron* but starts the first species of *diapente*. The second of the *finales*, .E., ends and begins the second species of *diatessaron* and *diapente*. The third of the *finales*, .F., ends and begins the third of each of these species. The fourth of the *finales*, .G., ends the fourth and begins the fourth.[76]

48. That against the law of the *finales* the *superiores* end and begin the species.

On the contrary, the first of the *superiores*—that is, .a.—finishes the first species of *diapente* and starts the first species of *diatessaron*, which the first of the *excellentes* finishes.[77]

49. Opposition of tetrachords.

The tetrachords of the *finales* and *excellentes* are opposed to the tetrachords of the *graves* and *superiores*. For the latter begin all the species of *diatessaron* while the former end them. But those in the middle—that is, the *finales* and *superiores*—are also opposed, since all the species of *diapente* begin in the *finales* and end in the *superiores*. The outer tetrachords are also opposed like the middle ones: for the *graves* only start all of the species of *diatessaron* and the *excellentes* only end all of them; the *finales* start all of the species of *diapente*, the *superiores* end them; the *finales* end all of the species of *diatessaron*, the *superiores* begin them.

50. That three tetrachords contain endings, three endings and two both.

Three of the tetrachords are similar in containing the beginnings of the species: the *graves*, *finales*, and *superiores*. Three in containing their endings: the *finales*, *superiores*, and *excellentes*; two in containing both: the *finales* and *superiores*. Only the tetrachord of the *graves* exclusively contains beginnings and the tetrachord of the *excellentes* exclusively contains endings.

[51.] [a]Quod oppositio quoque sit in speciebus diatesseron et diapente.[a]

Vltimę quoque species [b]et medię[b] diatesseron et diapente sibimet sunt oppositę. Nam intensio primę remissio est quartę. Secundę ascensus [c]est tercię[c] descensus. Prima species diatesseron tono semitonio tono intenditur ab .A. in[d] .D., quarta eodem modo remittitur a .G. in .D. Secunda intenditur a .B. in .E. semitonio ditono, tercia remittitur ab .F. in .C. semitonio ditono.

[52.] [a]De oppositis diapente speciebus.[a]

Prima species diapente ascendit tono[b] semitonio ditono a .D.[c] finali in a.[d] superius. Quarta descendit[e] tono[f] semitonio ditono a .d.[g] superiori in .G. finalem. Secunda suspenditur ab .E. finali in .b. superius semitonio tritono. Tercia deponitur semitonio tritono a .c. superiori in .F. finalem.

[53.] [a]Quod oppositio specierum ad similitudinem fiat metricorum pedum.[a]

Species prima diatesseron constat ut amphimacrus ex longa et breui et longa, id est, ex tono semitonio tono. Secunda[b] intensa ut bachius ex breui et duabus longis. Remissa ut antibachius ex duabus longis et breui. Tercia species diatesseron constat secundum intensionem sicut secunda, iuxta remissionem ut antibachius; secundum remissionem[c] ut secunda, iuxta intensionem sicut[d] bachius. Quarta rursus ut insulę.

[54.] [a]De speciebus diapente ad pedum similitudinem se habentibus.[a]

Diapente prima species constat ex trocheo et spondeo suspensa ut liberabant,[b] deposita constat[c] ex spondeo et iambo ut conuenerant.[d] Secunda intensa ex epitrito primo[e] ut sacerdotes,[f] remissa ex spondeo et trocheo ut sacramenta.[g] Tercia ascendens ut secunda descendens ex spondeo et trocheo, descendens ut illa ascendens ex epitrito primo. Quarta ascendens ex spondeo et iambo ut prima descendit, descendens ut prima ascendens ex trocheo et spondeo.

[51.] [a–a] *om. D2M$_3$S*
[b–b] *om. D2*
[c–c] tercię est *D2*
[d] ad *D2*
[52.] [a–a] *om. D2M$_3$S*
[b] *om. M$_3$*
[c] .d. *R*
[d] .A. *M$_3$*
[e] ascendit *M$_3$*
[f] *om. M$_3$*
[g] .D. *M$_3$*
[53.] [a–a] *om. D2S. In place of chapters 53 and 54 M$_3$ reads:* Primo tono surgit species medioque; secunda tercia de tritono; | fons quartę ditonus extat. Quę tamen est epitritę tertia forma puellę.
[b] Secunda species *D2*
[c] remissionem uero *D2*
[d] ut *S*
[54.] [a–a] *om. D2S*
[b] Líbērábánt *D2*
[c] *om. D2*
[d] Cónuénēránt *D2*
[e] prima *S*
[f] sācérdótés *D2*
[g] sácráméntā *D2*

51. That opposition also exists among the species of *diatessaron* and *diapente*.

The final as well as the middle species of *diatessaron* and *diapente* are themselves opposed. For the extension of the first is the remission of the fourth. The ascent of the second is the descent of the third. The first species of *diatessaron* is extended from .A. to .D. by tone, semitone, and tone. The fourth in the same way returns from .G. to .D. The second is extended from .B. to .E. by semitone and two tones. The third returns from .F. to .C. by semitone and two tones.

52. Concerning the opposition of the species of *diapente*.

The first species of *diapente* ascends by tone, semitone, and two tones from .D. of the *finales* to .a. of the *superiores*. The fourth descends by tone, semitone, and two tones from .d. of the *superiores* to .G. of the *finales*. The second is suspended from .E. of the *finales* to .b. of the *superiores* by semitone and three tones. The third is brought back down by a semitone and three tones from .c. of the *superiores* to .F. of the *finales*.

53. That the opposition of the species occurs like that of the metrical feet.

The first species of *diatessaron* corresponds to the amphimacer of long, short, and long, that is, of tone, semitone, and tone.[78] The extension of the second species, like the bachian, consists of a short and two longs. Remission is like the antibachian, consisting of two longs and a short. The third species of *diatessaron* corresponds in extension to the antibachian, as does the second species in remission; in its remission to the bachian, as does the second species in extension. The fourth species likewise as *insulae*.

54. That the species of *diapente* have of themselves a similarity to the metrical feet.

The first species of *diapente* as it is extended consists of a trochee and spondee, like *liberabant*;[79] descending it consists of a spondee and iamb, like *convenerant*.[80] Extension of the second species consists of a first epitrite, like *sacerdotes*;[81] remission consists of a spondee and trochee, like *sacramenta*. The third ascending is like the second descending, and consists of a spondee and trochee; descending as the second ascends, with a first epitrite. The fourth ascends as the first descends, by spondee and iamb; it descends as the first ascends, by trochee and spondee.

[55.] [a]De speciebus diapason.[a]

Prima species diapason constat ex prima [b]diatesseron et diapente specie,[b] secunda de secundis, tercia de terciis, quarta de quartis. Et in his speciebus diatesseron,[c] diapente, [d]diapason naturalem merito[d] miramur ordinem, quia omnes in eandem desinunt ex qua incipiunt,[e] et [f]hę sunt[f] sui nominis.

[56.] [a]De quatuor speciebus diatesseron.[a]

Diatesseron species prima incipit a prima grauium .A., desinit in primam finalium .D. Secunda species diatesseron incipit a secunda grauium .B., desinit in secundam finalium E. Tercia species diatesseron incipit a tercia grauium .C., desinit in terciam finalium[b] .F. Quarta species diatesseron incipit et desinit a quarta et in quartam .D.G.

[57.] [a]Quod similiter incipiant et finiant omnes diapente species.[a]

Eodem modo species diapente inchoant et expliciunt. Prima a prima finalium et in primam superiorum .D.a. Secunda a[b] secunda et in secundam .E.b. Tercia a terciis, quarta constat a[c] quartis .F.c.G.d.[d]

[58.] [a]Quod ad eundem modum species diapason incipiant et finiant omnes.[a]

Prima species diapason constat a prima grauium, prima finalium, prima superiorum ita ut grauis et superior legitimi sint ascensus descensusque claues, finalis medium eiusdem diapason uinculum, in qua est .D. commissura diatessaron et diapente. Sic secunda species diapason secunda grauium, secunda superiorum clauditur .B.b. et secunda finalium [b].E. uinculatur.[b] Tercia terciis, quarta quartis et clauditur et dimidiatur .C.F.c.D.G.d.[c]

[59.] [a]Quod eodem modo ab aliis speciebus consistant autentice species sicut a prelibatis speciebus subiugales.[a]

Sicut istę quatuor species diapason, id est quatuor plagarum constant grauibus et superioribus dimidiantur autem finalibus prima primis, secunda

[55.] [a–a] *om. D2M$_3$S*
[b–b] specie diatessaron et diapente *D2*
[c] diatessaron et *D2*
[d–d] diapason quoque merito naturalem *D2*
[e] desinunt *R*
[f–f] hęc sunt *M$_3$S;* sunt he *marked with superscript* b *and* a *to indicate transposition R*
[56.] [a–a] *om. D2M$_3$S*
[b] finalem *RS*
[57.] [a–a] *om. D2M$_3$S*
[b] .a. *S*
[c] ex *D2*
[d] .f.c.g.d. *M$_3$*
[58.] [a–a] *om. D2D7M$_3$S*
[b–b] uinculatur .E. *M$_3$;* uel clauditur *marg. and interlinear in text hand M$_3$*
[c] .C.F.C.D.G.D. *D7;* a b c d e f g ♮ *S, in vacant space at line end in later gothic hand*
[59.] [a–a] *om. D7M$_3$S*

55. Concerning the species of *diapason*.

The first species of *diapason* consists of the first species of *diatessaron* and *diapente*, the second of the second species, the third of the thirds, and the fourth of the fourths.[82] And in these species of *diatessaron*, *diapente*, and *diapason* we deservedly admire the natural order, since all end in the same way that they begin, and from this they are of themselves named.

56. Concerning the four species of *diatessaron*.

The first species of *diatessaron* starts at the first of the *graves*, .A., and finishes at the first of the *finales*, .D. The second species of *diatessaron* starts at the second of the *graves*, .B., and finishes at the second of the *finales* .E. The third species of *diatessaron* starts at the third of the *graves*, .C., and finishes at the third of the *finales*, .F. The fourth species of *diatesaron* starts and finishes at the fourth and fourth, .D. and .G.

57. That all the species of *diapente* begin and end similarly.

In the same way the species of *diapente* begin and end. The first from the first of the *finales* to the first of the *superiores*, .D. to .a. The second from the second to the second, .E. to .b. The third from the third notes and the fourth from the fourth notes, .F. to .c. and .G. to .d.

58. That all the species of *diapason* begin and end in the same manner.

The first species of *diapason* consists of the first of the *graves*, the first of the *finales*, and the first of the *superiores*, so that the *gravis* and *superior*[83] are legitimately notes of ascent as well as descent, and the *finalis*[84] is a bond in the middle of the same *diapason* in which .D. joins the *diatessaron* and *diapente*. Thus the second species of *diapason* is encompassed by the second of the *graves* and the second of the *superiores*—.B. and .b.—with the second of the *finales*, .E., as the link. The third and the fourth species are encompassed and divided by the thirds and the fourths, .C.F.c. and .D.G.d.[85]

59. That in the same way the authentic species are comprised of the remaining species, just as the plagals are comprised of the aforementioned species.

As with these four species of *diapason*—that is, the four plagals consisting of the *graves* and the *superiores* divided indeed by the *finales* first by the firsts, second

secundis, tercia terciis, quarta quartis, sic quatuor sequentes ad autenticos pertinentes clauduntur finalibus et excellentibus dimidiantur [b]autem uel uinculantur[b] superioribus prima primis,[c] secunda[d] secundis, tercia terciis, quarta quartis, ut optime conseruatus[e] ordo naturalis Dei uoluntate[f] quę est rerum natura[g] collaudet [h]"quę illuminat[h] omnem hominem" quod in natura latuit uenatrices mentes inuestigare concessit.

[60.] [a]Vtrum sint "septima" uel octo "discrimina uocum" [b]cum synemmenon[b] uideatur octauum.[a]

Synemmenon octauum uocis discrimen non facit quia nunquam .b.[c] molle atque quadratum in unam conueniunt[d] neumam. Cum omne [e]uocis discrimen[e] fiat aut tono uel semitonio seu ex his compositis consonantiis, et inter .♭. et .b. nulla sit consonantia, patet profecto quod illę duę litterę [f]pro uno sint[f] discrimine. Illarum litterarum neumę nunquam in unum conueniunt, sicut Libra et Aries[g] pariter non uidentur: Consurgens[h] Aries Libram, Libra uellera mergit.

[61.] [a]Quod diuisio monochordi fiat aut per quantitatem aut per qualitatem.[a]

Monochordi diuisio fit bipartito. Cum enim dico totum monochordum in duas diuidi diapason uel duobus passibus fieri diapason, tribus diapente, quatuor diatessaron, tonum nouem,[b] quantitatis est et numeri ad mensuram pertinens[c] monochordi. Cum autem tetrachorda quędam dico intendi per tonum, semitonium, tonum, quedam uero remitti per ditonum et semitonium, designo qualitatem ad melodiam pertinentem. Quasi dicerem: cum tetrachordum grauium, finalium, superiorum, excellentium intendatur et remittatur per tonum, semitonium, tonum, potes quamlibet neumam [d]eodem modo se habentem[d] susum iusumque resultare. Sic et de illis quę[e] descendunt perpendas tetrachordis.

[b–b] aut uel clauduntur *M_3*
[c] primas *corr.* primis *M_3*
[d] secundis *corr.* secunda *M_3*
[e] conuersatus *corr.* conseruatus *M_3*
[f] uoluntatem *D7M_3RS*
[g] *om. S*
[h] quę in luminans *D7;* quę illuminans *M_3;* illuminans *R*
[60.] [a–a] *om. D7S*
[b–b] synemenon cum *marked with superscript* b *and* a *for transposition R*
[c] .B. *D7*
[d] conueniant *corr.* conueniunt *R*
[e–e] discrimen uocis *R*
[f–f] sint pro uno *R*
[g] ries *D7*
[h] sed consurgens *D7*
[61.] [a–a] *om. D7M_3S*
[b] nne *corr.* viiii *M_3*
[c] pertinentis *D7S;* pertinentes *M_3*
[d–d] *om. R*
[e] qui *S*

by the seconds, third by the thirds, and fourth by the fourths—so the following four pertaining to the authentics are encompassed by the *finales* and the *excellentes*, and divided or bound by the *superiores,* first by the firsts, second by the seconds, third by the thirds, and fourth by the fourths. In this the natural order best preserved by the will of God, which is the nature of things, rejoices "enlightening every man,"[86] so that which lies hidden in nature may be conceded to probing minds to seek out.

60. Whether there may be "seven" or eight "different notes,"[87] since *synemmenon* seems to be eighth.

Synemmenon[88] does not result in eight distinct notes, since soft .b. and square .b. never meet in a single phrase. Since every distinct note is made by either a tone or a semitone, or from these consonances having been put together, and since there is no consonance between .♭. and .b., it is perfectly obvious that those two notes may be treated as one. Phrases with those notes never meet together in one, as Libra and Aries are not seen together. Aries lifts up Libra, Libra dips the fleece.[89]

61. That the division of the monochord is made either according to number or according to quality of sound.

The monochord may be divided in two ways. When I say the monochord is divided into two *diapasons* or in two steps using the *diapason*, in three steps using the *diapente*, in four steps using the *diatessaron*, or in nine steps using the tone, it is a matter of the quantity and number pertaining to the measure of the monochord. When I say some tetrachords are extended by tone, semitone, and tone[90] but others are in fact remitted by ditone and semitone,[91] I designate it as the quality pertaining to melody. As if I might say: since the tetrachords of the *graves*, *finales*, *superiores*, and *excellentes* are extended and remitted by tone, semitone, and tone, you can treat any of the phrases having a rising and falling in the same manner. Thus also can you treat those tetrachords that descend.

[62.] [a]Vtrum idem modus qui dicitur dorius dicendus sit hypomixolidius propter .D.d. quod est biforme.[a]

Antiquitus erant quatuor tantum naturales[b] tropi. Quare autem quatuor naturales dicam tropos quęstionis scrutinio dignum est. Cum quiuis autenticus adiuncto sibi suo subiugali constet prima grauium, prima finalium, prima superiorum, prima excellentium, quid obstat quin sit unus modus cum de unis ut ita dicam fiat chordis, uidelicet omnibus primis. Sed secundum placitum facti sunt de quatuor octo, cogente tamen ratione. Cum quilibet cantus legitime uagari per undecim chordas potuisset, qui discursus cuilibet autento cum suo plaga composito deputatur, euenit sepe propter cantus prolixitatem ut aliquis uersus seu breuis psalmus adiunctus ab illo discordaret, cum omnem suum ascensum descensumue non potuisset implere. Tandem est excogitatum ut quiuis quatuor troporum in duos diuideretur, quorum uterque integra tantum diapason esset contentus, ut quidlibet sibi subiunctum suum posset equiparare discursum. Sicut nonnunquam propter infirmiorem comitis caballum uicinius petimus diuersorium.

[63.] [a]De hoc quod quadripertita figura et caprea sint imitatrices antiquitatis troporum.[a]

Quatuor[b] troporum naturalis antiquitas in quadripertita modernorum figura et in nostra patet caprea. Diuisionem autem eorum nostra circularis representat figura, quam de uirilibus femineisque choreis compinximus.

[64.] [a]De hoc quod quatuor tropi diuiduntur in octo.[a]

Maiores nostri perpendentes quemlibet troporum adhuc indiuisum quatuor principalibus ita chordis consistere ut altrinsecus collatę duas diapason species possent conficere, diuiserunt eos in autentos et plagas, autentos uocantes auctorales et digniores, plagas autem laterales et subiectos. Quod nomen subiectionis etiam greca sua testantur uocabula, quia primus tonus apellatur grece dorius, secundus uocatur hypodorius, id est subiugalis dorii, ita quartus et sextus hypofrigius et hypolidius dicitur.

Diuiserunt protum primam finalium cum altrinsecus posita prima[b] excellentium coniungentes et autentum primum, primum uidelicet tonum statuentes. Primam[c] grauium cum altrinsecus sita prima superiorum conferentes et primam[d] plagam tonum scilicet secundam componentes. In deutero secundam finalium cum altrinsecus locata secunda excellentium iunxerunt

[62.] [a–a] *om. D7S*
[b] *D7 ends here, mid-line, fol. 179r*
[63.] [a–a] *om. S*
[b] Quattuor *S*

[64.] [a–a] *om. S*
[b] cum prima *R*
[c] uero *added above R in a later hand*
[d] primum *RS*

62. Whether the same mode that is called dorian may be called hypomixolydian on account of .D. and .d. which have two functions.

In ancient times there were no more than four natural tropes. Why I say that there are four natural tropes is a question deserving of scrutiny. Since each authentic with its plagal having been joined to it consists of the first of the *graves*, the first of the *finales*, the first of the *superiores*, and the first of the *excellentes*, what prevents it from being a single mode, since I say that it is made of single notes, namely from all the firsts? But according as it was decided, there were made eight from four, reason nevertheless compelling this. Since any chant might legitimately wander over a range of eleven notes—and in so wandering might be considered to have constituted some authentic with its plagal—it often happens on account of the prolixity of chant that some verse or short attached psalm might be discordant with it, since it could not complete its whole ascent or descent. At length it was decided that the four tropes should be divided in two, each of which was to comprise a full octave, so that each joined to its plagal might be equipped to equal the range of the chant. Just as sometimes on account of the infirmity of a companion's horse we seek a closer lodging.

63. Concerning the fact that the quadripartite figure and *caprea* are imitators of the tropes of antiquity.

The natural antiquity of the four tropes is apparent in the quadripartite figure of the moderns and in our *caprea*. Our circular figure represents their division, which we have depicted by male and female choirs.

64. Concerning the fact that the four tropes are divided into eight.

Our ancestors, considering carefully that the principal notes of the hitherto indivisible four tropes might—being joined with their counterparts—yield two species of *diapason*, divided them into authentics and plagals, calling the authentics authoritative and more dignified but the plagals lateral and subordinate. The Greek words bear witness to the name subordinate, since the first tone is called dorian in Greek and the second tone is called hypodorian—that is, the plagal of dorian; so too the fourth and sixth are called hypofrigian and hypolydian.[92]

They divided *protus* so that the first of the *finales* being joined to its counterpart, the first of the *excellentes*, establishes the first authentic—namely, the first tone. The first of the *graves* being joined to its counterpart, the first of the *superiores*, composes the first plagal—namely, the second tone. In *deuterus* they joined the second of the *finales* with its counterpart, the second of the *excellentes*,

et secundam autentum, tercium quippe tonum, composuerunt. Secundam grauium cum secunda iunxerunt superiorum et secundam subiugalem, [e]quartum nempe tonum, statureunt.[e] In trito terciam finalium cum altrinsecus posita tercia excellentium et tercium autentum, quintum nempe tonum, confecerant. Similiter terciam grauium cum altrinsecus scripta tercia superiorum coniunxerunt et tercium plagalem, id est sextum tonum, posuerunt. Eodem modo in tetrardo quarta finalium,[f] id est .G., cum altrinsecus statuta quarta excellentium contulerunt et[g] quartum autentum, id est septimum tonum, composuerunt. Quartum grauium, id est .D., cum altrinsecus notata quarta superiorum, uidelicet .d., iunxerunt et quartum subiugalem, octauum quippe tonum, constituere uoluerunt. Sed quia eundem modum prius in proto autenticam [h]diapason speciem,[h] id est tonum primum, fecerunt, recusauerunt illum in tetrardo uel habere uel appellare plagalem, non prouidentes[i] quod .D.d. biformes sint litterę potentes naturaliter tam plagalem quam autenticam constituere speciem. Vnde ille biformis modus [j]qui est inter .D.d.[j] propter antiquorum inconsiderationem[k] non acquisiuit suę subiugali naturę debitum nomen, ut diceretur hypomixolidius, id est mixolidii septimi uidelicet toni subiectus.

[65.] [a]Quomodo iuniores eiusdem modi geminam intellexerint uim atque naturam.[a]

Sollertius autem prelibati modi naturam et efficatiam[b] iuniores intuentes plagales sibi formulas uel differentias attribuerunt. *Octo sunt beatitudines*. Seculorum amen. *In illa die* et cęteras. Seculorum amen. *Dum medium silentium*.

[66.] [a]Quod sanctus Gregorius eiusdem modi duplicem perspexerit operationem.[a]

Patet admodum sanctum[b] Gregorium totius pene ęcclesiastici cantus auctorem duplicem eius cognouisse operationem, qui in tetrardo[c] non potius autenticas quam plagales diligit odas. Cum autem aureo ipsius et sancti Ambrosii plagalis esse comprobetur testimonio, quid nobis est dubitandum quin ut est dicamus illum non solum dorium sed hypomixolidium.

[e–e] subiugalem statuerunt, quartum nempe tonum *S*
[f] finalis *R*
[g] *om. R*
[h–h] speciem diapason *R*
[i] peruidentes *R*
[j–j] *om. R*
[k] *om. R*
[65.] [a–a] *om. S*
[b] effecatiam *corr.* efficatiam *R*
[66.] [a–a] *om. S*
[b] beatum *R*
[c] autento *R*

and composed the second authentic, obviously the third tone. They joined the second of the *graves* to the second of the *superiores* and established the second plagal, indeed the fourth tone. In *tritus*, by joining the third of the *finales* to its counterpart the third of the *excellentes* they constructed the third authentic, truly the fifth tone. Similarly, they joined the third of the *graves* with the oppositely written third of the *superiores* and put in place the third plagal—that is, the sixth tone. In the same manner in *tetrardus* they brought together the fourth of the *finales*—that is, .G.—with its counterpart, the fourth of the *excellentes*, and composed the fourth authentic—that is, the seventh tone. They joined the fourth of the *graves*—that is, .D.—with its counterpart, the fourth of the *superiores*—namely, .d.—wishing to constitute the fourth plagal, which is the eighth tone. But because they had previously made the same mode in *protus* an authentic species of *diapason*—that is, the first tone— they refused to have it in *tetrardus* or to call it plagal, not foreseeing that the double-formed .D. and .d. are powerful letters naturally creating both a plagal and an authentic species.[93] Wherefore, on account of the inconsideration of the ancients, that double mode between .D. and .d. did not acquire the name appropriate to its plagal nature when it should have been called hypomixolydian—that is, namely, the plagal of the seventh mixolydian tone.

65. How the moderns have understood the force and nature of the same mode to be twofold.

The perceptive moderns, however, investigating more carefully the nature and efficacy of the aforementioned mode, have attributed to it plagal formulas or *differentiae*.[94] *Octo sunt beatitudines*.[95] *Saeculorum amen. In illa die*[96] and so forth. *Saeculorum amen. Dum medium silentium*.[97]

66. That St. Gregory[98] has perceived the two-fold operation of the same modes.

It is very manifest that St. Gregory, the author of almost all ecclesiastical chant, recognized its twofold operation, which in *tetrardus* does not love the authentic in preference to the plagal songs. But since it is proven to be plagal by the golden testimony of himself and St. Ambrose,[99] why should we doubt when as it is we may say that it is not only dorian but hypomixolydian?

[67.] [a]Quod idem modus habeat materiam plagalis.[a]

Cum idem modus habeat plagalis materiam, plagalem ex hac componamus formam, [b]aut negemus si naturaliter possumus[b] .D. non esse quartam grauium, .d. non esse quartam superiorum, aut esse concedamus. Si negabimus ab aduersario subsequente constringemur argumentatione: omnis chorda quę duorum synemmesis, id est coniunctio est tetrachordorum, alterius est finis [c]alteriusque principium.[c] Sed .D. synemmesis est tetrachordi grauium et finalium. Si finis est tetrachordi quarta est chorda. Sed finis est. Ergo quarta, quia omnis tetrachordi finalis quarta est. Argumentum a genera. Maxima propositio: quod in omnibus [d]ualet, ualet et in uno.[d] Ab argumento precendenti[e] possumus colligere quia si in tetrachordo finis est quarta chorda, principium est in eo prima chorda. Sed hoc est. Ergo .D. secundum hanc rationem et quarta est grauium et prima finalium. Hac ipsa argumentatione sit probatum quod .d. sit quarta superiorum, prima excellentium.

[68.] [a]Quod probatio ista pertineat ad materiam autenti et subiugalis.[a]

Iam probauimus quod modus sepe dictus inter .D. .d. constitutus tam materialis sit plagę quarto, id est octaua tono, quam autento primo; primo uidelicet tono quodque tam uere dicatur hypomixolidius quam dorius, quia cum constet quarta grauium, quarta superiorum, prima finalium, prima excellentium; probandum erit quarta grauium, quarta superiorum plagali esse materiales; aut adimamus si naturaliter possimus tribus grauibus .A.B.C. tribus superioribus .a.b.c. quod non sint constitutiuę et materiales tribus plagis, tono scilicet secundo quarto sexto, aut quartę grauium quartę superiorum concedamus ut materiales sint claues quarto plagalis, octauo denique tono. Sed impossibile est ut tribus prepositus grauibus et superioribus trium plagarum consititutionem adimamus. Ergo possibile est et uerissimum ut quartę grauium et superiorum quarti plagę, id est toni octaui, essentialem concedamus positionem.[b]

[69.] [a]De proprietate protorum, deuterorum, tritorum, tetrardorum.[a]

Proprietas est protorum ut concordent in eleuatione per diapente, in

[67.] [a–a] *om. S*
[b–b] aut si possimus, naturaliter negemus *R*
[c–c] alteriusque est principium *R*
[d–d] ualet in uno ualet et in uno *S*
[e] *At this point there is a misordering of the text in R, which jumps from fol. 23v to fol. 29v for its continuation. As this mistake does not coincide with a folio change, it cannot have been the result of a binding error. R, therefore, was copied from a source already possessing the misordering of the text. The misordering in that intermediate source was possibly the result of a binding error.*
[68.] [a–a] *om. S*
[b] *om. R*
[69.] [a–a] *om. S*

67. That this same mode may have plagal material.

Since this same mode may have plagal material, we may compose the plagal form from it, or, if we can, we might naturally deny that .D. is the fourth of the *graves* and .d. is the fourth of the *superiores*, or else we might grant this to be so.[100] If we deny it, we will be constrained by an opponent using the following argument: every note that is a *synemmesis*—that is, a conjunction of two tetrachords—is the end of one and the beginning of yet another. Now .D. is the *synemmesis* of the tetrachords of the *graves* and *finales*. If it is the end of the tetrachord, it is the fourth note. But it is the end and therefore the fourth, since every final of a tetrachord is fourth. Argument from genus. The maximal proposition: what holds for all holds also for one.[101] From the preceding argument we can gather that if in a tetrachord the final is the fourth note, the beginning of it is the first note. And this is the case. Therefore .D., according to this reasoning, is both the fourth of the *graves* and the first of the *finales*. From this argument itself it may be proved that .d. is the fourth of the *superiores* and the first of the *excellentes*.

68. That this proof should relate to the matter of the authentics and plagals.

We have already proved that the oft-mentioned mode between .D. and .d. is constituted as much of material from the fourth plagal—that is, the eighth tone—as of material from the first authentic. It is evident that in the first tone each may as truly be called hypomixolydian as it may dorian, since it consists of the fourth of the *graves*, the fourth of the *superiores*, the first of the *finales*, and the first of the *excellentes*. It will be proved that the fourth of the *graves* and the fourth of the *superiores* are of plagal material; on the one hand, if we naturally can, we might exclude from the three *graves* .A.B.C. and the three *superiores* .a.b.c. what is not constitutive or material to the three plagals—namely, the second, fourth, and sixth tones—while conceding that the fourth of the *graves* and the fourth of the *superiores* are material keys to the fourth plagal—that is, the eighth tone. But it is impossible for us to remove the substance of the three plagals from the three aforesaid *graves* and *superiores*. Therefore it is possible and most true that we should grant the essential character of the fourth plagal—that is, the eighth tone—to the fourth notes of the *graves* and the *superiores*.

69. Concerning the property of *protus*, *deuterus*, *tritus*, and *tetrardus*.

The property of *protus* is to concord in elevation by a *diapente*, in

depositione per tonum. Proprietas[b] est deuterorum cum integra diatessaron per intensionem, ditono per remissionem. Proprietas[c] est tritorum ut concordent intensione ditono, diatessaron remissione.[d] Proprietas[e] est tetrardorum ut protis opponantur quatenus[f] horum [g]eleuatio sit illorum depositio.[g]

[70.] [a]Quod non sit firmius argumentum quam proprietas.[a]

Quamuis satis sit probatum quod de plagali materia, uidelicet quarta grauium, quarta superiorum, quarta plagalis species, id est tonus octauus, possit conformari, nam inficiari uere non possumus, quin possit aureus de auro fieri stilus, tamen adhuc ipsi sufficientię uiolentiam uolumus inferre, etiam non necessariorum copiam ministrantes argumentorum. Efficacius argumentum ipsa proprietate non possumus inuenire. Neque enim temere proprietates troporum cogitauimus premittere. Videamus si .D.d. tam tetrardi quam proti proprietates possit habere. Tetrardorum est proprietas ut protorum intensio[b] sit illorum remissio. Sed .D. ita remittitur per tonum, semitonium, tonum, sicut .A. protus tono, semitonio, tono intenditur.

[71.] [a]Quod equaliter de se predicentur species et propria.[a]

Omnis homo risibilis est et omne risibile homo est. Omnis tetrardus per tonum, semitonium, tonum remissibilis est et omnis remissio toni, semitonii, toni tetrardus est. Sed .D. .d. remittitur tono, semitonio, tono. Ergo tetrardus est. Si tetrardus est, aut autentus aut plagalis. Sed necesse est ut sit plagalis, quia nullus autentus grauibus et superioribus constat. Irrefragabilibus transactis argumentationibus et prolixo naturę suę finitio scrutinio, baptizemus eundem modum nominantes eum hypomixolidium, ut sic sit binomius sicut eum biformem nouimus.

[72.] [a]Cur dicantur tropi.[a]

Tropi[b] dicuntur a reuersione, quia ubiubi cantus incipiat[c] quocumque ascendat seu descendat, ad ultimum in finalis reuertitur domicilium.

[b] <P>roprietas *S*
[c] <P>roprietas *S*
[d] horum eleuatio sit *added in R and marked underneath for correction/deletion*
[e] <P>roprietas *S*
[f] quatinus *RS*
[g–g] eleuatio istorum sit remissio *R*

[70.] [a–a] *om. S*
[b] intensione *R*
[71.] [a–a] *om. S*
[72.] [a–a] *om. S*
[b] <T>ropi *S*
[c] *om. R*

deposition by a tone. The property of *deuterus* is to make whole a *diatessaron* by extension, a ditone by remission. The property *tritus* is to concord in beginning by a ditone, in returning by a *diatessaron*. The property of *tetrardus* is to oppose *protus*, whose elevation is its remission.

70. That there is no sounder argument than that of property.

However much it may have been proved satisfactorily that it is possible to fashion the fourth species of plagal—that is, the eighth tone—from plagal material (namely, the fourth of the *graves* and the fourth of the *superiores*)—for, in truth, we are unable to deny it since it is only possible to make a gold pen from gold—we nevertheless wish to bring to bear the force of sufficiency, even though not furnishing an abundance of necessary arguments.

We cannot invent powerful arguments about their property. Neither have we thought rashly of overlooking the property of the tropes. Let us see if .D. and .d. can have the property both of *tetrardus* and of *protus*. The property of *tetrardus* is that the extension of *protus* may be its remission. But .D. is so remitted by tone, semitone, and tone in the same way that .A. of *protus* is extended by tone, semitone, and tone.

71. That species and properties predicate equally of themselves.

"Every man is capable of laughter and everything capable of laughter is a man."[102] Every *tetrardus* is remissible by tone, semitone, and tone, and everything remissible by tone, semitone, and tone is *tetrardus*. But .D. and .d. are remitted through tone, semitone, and tone. Therefore, they are *tetrardus*. If *tetrardus*, then they are either authentic or plagal. But it is necessary that they be plagal, for no authentic consists of *graves* and *superiores*. These irrefutable arguments having been transacted and the lengthy scrutiny of their nature having been finished, we may baptize this same mode in the name of hypomixolydian, so that it is doubly named, as he of the two forms with whom we have become acquainted.

72. Why tropes are so called.

The tropes are named by their returning; since wherever a chant begins, whithersoever it ascends or descends, in the end it returns home to its final.

[73.] [a]Vtrum trite synemmenon infra uel supra transductoriam ponenda sit lineam et utrum molle .♭. rotundumque sit magis necessarium minusue quam quadratum .b.[a]

Causa est antiquior quam effectus ut ignis combustionem precedit. Cum hiatus diezeuxis, id est disiunctionis tetrachordorum, patribus nostris plurima canendi pretendisset offendicula, quia tritus finalis .F. supra quarta, tritus excellens .f. infra caruit quinta, interposuerunt trite synemmenon ad emendandum iubilationis defectum. Ibi causa est diezeuxis, interpositio synemmenon effectus. Ergo posterior. Quę sit posterior in inuentione sit etiam posterior in sessione, sicut aduena "in domo aliena." Suscepta quidem sicut iambus

Spondeos stabiles in iura paterna recepit
Commodus et patiens non ut de sede secunda
Cederet aut quarta socialiter.

Ergo synemmenon infra collocetur non supra. Quę harum sit utilior chordarum perpendere possumus, si discernemus, cuius sit frequentior usus.

[74.] [a]Quod tritus maxime indigeat synemmenon, cum ipsa suppleat uicem superioris triti.[a]

Cantus quinti et sexti toni potissimum indigent synemmenon, cum ipsa sit uicaria triti superioris. In proto quoque succinit, sed rarissime, ut in *Ecce nomen Domini uenit de longinquo*. Quadratum autem .b. non solum in deutero, qui suus domesticus est, sed etiam in proto, in[b] tetrardo,[c] in ipso quoque trito conuersatur assidue, quamuis trito familiari non sit uicinitate coniunctum, quia nec a finali .F. nec ab excellenti .f. aliqua distat consonantia.[d] Hinc licet perpendere .♭. utile, .b. autem multum utilius esse, ideoque admodum esse commodiorem coniunctione disiunctionem. Qua[e] etiam ratione frequentioris utilitatis et rarioris possumus colligere infra .♭. supra .b. notandum esse in hunc modum:[f]

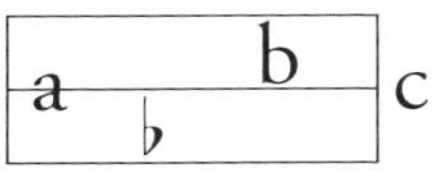

[73.] [a–a] *om. S*
[74.] [a–a] *om. S*
[b] *om. S*
[c] detrado *R*
[d] coniunctio *corr.* consonantia *R*
[e] Quam *eras.* Qua *R*
[f] 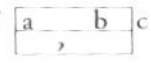 *R*

73. Whether *trite synemmenon* should be placed below or above the line of transfer, and whether soft as well as round .♭. is more necessary and valuable than square .b.

The cause is more ancient than the effect, as fire precedes burning.[103] The hiatus of *diezeuxis*, that is the disjunction of tetrachords, had been responsible for very many small errors in the singing of our forefathers: since a fourth above .F., the third of the *finales*, and a fifth below .f., the third of the *excellentes*, were lacking, they interpolated *trite synemmenon* to amend the defect in their praise.[104] Here the cause is *diezeuxis* and the effect is the interposition of *synemmenon*. Therefore it comes later. What is last in invention should also be last in assuming its place, like a stranger in "another man's house."[105] It was thus adopted like the iamb

> Admitted the steady spondees to its paternal rights,
> Being obliging and tolerant, but not so much as to
> Cede second or fourth places in its friendly ranks.[106]

Therefore, *synemmenon* is to be placed below, not above. Which of these may be the most useful note, we are able to consider carefully if we can determine which is used more often.

74. That *tritus* especially needs *synemmenon*, since it takes the place of *tritus* of the *superiores*.

Songs of the fifth and sixth tones especially need *synemmenon*, since it is the deputy of *tritus* of the *superiores*. In *protus* also it is sung, but very rarely, as in *Ecce nomen Domini venit de longinquo*.[107] Square .b., on the other hand, does not sound solely in *deuterus*, where it is at home, but also in *protus*, *tetrardus*, and likewise assiduously in *tritus*—although it may not be joined to *tritus* in close proximity because neither .F. of the *finales* nor .f. of the *excellentes* is a consonant interval away from it.[108] Hence it is permitted to conclude that although .♭. is useful, .b. is much more useful, for the disjunction is very much more useful than the conjunction. For reasons of more frequent or more rare use we gather that this .♭. is to be notated below and .b. above., in this manner:

Diagram 3.

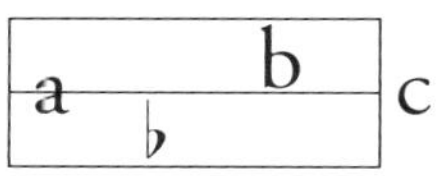

[75.] [a]Quod non sit dicenda quinta, sexta, septima, octaua species diapason quamuis sint octo.[a]

Licet [b]octo sint[b] species diapason, quintam tamen et sextam, septimam et octauam dici naturę ueritas non patitur. Cum enim omne totum de suis partibus nominetur[c] ueraciter, idem in tota diapason et in suis partibus, diatesseron scilicet ac diapente,[d] considerare debemus. Species diatessaron[e] et diapente non plures quam quatuor scimus esse. Sed cum species diapason constituantur de speciebus diapente et diatesseron, non possunt fieri plures quam partium species. Sed quoniam quatuor species diapason constituuntur ita ut diatesseron precedat diapente sequatur quę sunt plagales, quatuor autem ita ut diapente preuia diatesseron sit assecla quę sunt autenticę; patet profecto octo species esse, sed nullam earum quintam uere dici posse, cum neque diatesseron neque[f] diapente quinta species inueniatur esse. Quis dicit aulam ligneam de ligneis[g] partibus non constructam? Similiter quis dicit quintam speciem diapason de [h]quintis partibus[h] non consistentem cum nulla diapente sit quinta, nulla diatesseron, quę sunt constitutiuę partes diapason? Sed tamen octo species sunt diapason quamuis nulla quinta, quia octonarius ueraciter habetur ac computatur ubi quaternarius duplicatur. Quatuor species sunt diapason autenticarum,[i] quatuor plagalium, quę complent octonarium; nullam tamem, ut prediximus, quintam uere dicere possumus.

[76.] [a]De similitudine gemellipare quatuor uicibus geminos.[a]

Cogitemus aliquam in tantum esse fętosam ut quatuor uicibus sit gemellipara, quosdam germanorum primigenas, uel ut ita dicamus, secundigenas, tercigenas, quartigenas dicere possumus; nullum autem quintigenam cum eorum nemo[b] quinta uice sit genitus, quamuis octo tamen esse non dubitemus.

[77.] [a]Quod quidam unam musam, quidam duas, tres, quatuor, quinque, sex, septem, octo, nouem esse possint dicere secundum multiplices rationes.[a]

Vnam musam possumus asserere generale scilicet monochordum uocis humanę, [b]quę ex una fistula colli[b] efficacissime iubilat omnia melorum genera cui nullę hydraulię, nullę alię comparantur fistulę. Hęc cum cunctarum suppleat officium.

[75.] [a–a] *om. M3S*
[b–b] sint octo *M3R*
[c] nominetur *corr.* nominentur *S*
[d] dyapason *corr.* dyapente *M3*
[e] Dyapason *M3*
[f] nec *M3R*
[g] lignis *R*
[h–h] partibus quintibus *S*
[i] autenticorum *corr.* autenticarum *M3*
[76.] [a–a] *om. S*
[b] nomo *corr.* nemo *R*
[77.] [a–a] *om. S*
[b–b] quod ex nulla colli fistula *S*

75. That there should not be said to be a fifth, sixth, seventh, or eighth species of *diapason*, although there are eight.

Although there are eight species of *diapason*, nevertheless the truth of nature does not suffer it to be said that there is a fifth, sixth, seventh, or eighth. For since each whole is truly named from its parts, so we must consider that the same is true in the whole *diapason* and in its parts, namely the *diatessaron* and the *diapente*. We know the species of *diatessaron* and *diapente* to be not more than four. But since the species of *diapason* are constituted from the species of *diatessaron* and *diapente*, they cannot become more than the species of the parts.[109] Now since the four species of *diapason* are constituted so that with the *diatessaron* preceding and the *diapente* following they are plagal, on the other hand the four are such that with the *diapente* leading the way and the *diatessaron* following they are authentic. It is surely manifest that there are eight species; but none of them can truly be called a fifth, since neither a fifth species of *diatessaron* nor *diapente* is to be found. Who says that a wooden hall is not constructed from wooden parts?[110] Similarly who says that a fifth species of *diapason* does not consist of fifth parts, though no *diapente* or *diatessaron*, which are the constitutive parts of the *diapason*, may be of a fifth species? Nevertheless, there are eight species of *diapason*, however much there may be no fifth species, since the octernary is truly held and reckoned to be where the quaternary is duplicated. There are four species of authentic *diapason* and four plagals, which complete the group of eight; but as we said before, we can truly say that there is no fifth species.

76. Concerning the similarity of this to a mother of twins and four pairs of twins.

We might think, perhaps, that in a case of great fecundity, where a mother bears four pairs of twins and certain of the brothers are first born, we might also refer to a second born, third born, and fourth born; but there is none fifth born since none of them is born in the fifth place, however much we may not doubt that there are eight.

77. What one person says is one muse, another might say is a second, third, fourth, fifth, sixth, seventh, eighth, or ninth muse for a variety of reasons.[111]

We can maintain one muse to be the general range of the human voice, which from the pipe that is the throat most efficaciously utters every genera of melody and to which no water organ or other pipes are comparable, since this one supplies the function of all.

Duas musas possumus conicere in autentorum et plagarum esse dualitate, aut in pulsationis aut in flationis duplicitate, quarum altera cymbalis et chordis, altera fistulis seruit et tibiis; uel in bifida arsis et thesis, id est eleuationis et depositionis natura, sine qua non fit aliqua uox musica. Quid est musica? Motus uocum. Omnis autem uocis motus uel arsi fit aut thesi.

Tres musas intelligimus non absurde tria genera musicę: diatonicum, chromaticum, enarmonicum. Seu tres sunt musę, ipsa uox humana, pulsationis inflationisque mixtura, marinis in scopulis resultans syrena. Quę Grecum sortitur uocabulum: syrin enim Grece dicitur contrahere.[c] Vnde syrtes dicuntur ubi harenę contrahuntur. Hinc etiam comicus dicitur Syrus, quia[d] sua calliditate fugitiuum argentum traxerat ad se. Pauca sunt in fabulis quę non aliquo fonte diriuentur ueritatis. Ferunt syrenas cantatrices esse marinas[e] quę nautas interficiant inprouidos dulcioribus ad se modos[f] illectos. Quedam concaua saxa in mari sunt prominentia in quibus collisio procellarum dulcisonam imitatur melodiam. Quę dum dulcedine sua pretereuntes contrahit miserabili nonnumquam naufragio submergit, sicut huius mundi syrenę blandientes uidelicet illecebrę nostri similes periculosissimo[g] animarum submergunt naufragio.

Quatuor musas temere non arbitramur aut quatuor continuos antiquorum quos prelibauimus tropos, uel quatuor tetrachorda G. F. S. E. omnem melodiam possidentia. Siue Pythagoricos quatuor malleos quibus quatuor symphoniarum, toni, diatesseron, diapente, diapason reperit proportionem; seu quadripertitam monochordi distributionem, quę ascendendo primo [h]constitutiuo passu diatesseron, secundo diapente, tercio diapason constituit. Descendendo autem econtrario primo constitutiuo[h] passu diapason, secundo diapente, tercio diatesseron.

Quinque credimus musas quinque maiores symphonias: sesquiterciam, sesqualteram, duplam, triplam, quadruplam; aut quinque uocales sine[i] quibus non fiunt uoces litterales. Seu ad quinque referamus musas omnes penitus litteras quinque modis diuisas, quia

.i. .ii. .iii. .iv. .v.

quedam sunt uocales, quedam semiuocales, hę mutę, illę liquidę, duplices aliquę. Seu intelligamus quinque musas quinque sensuum noxias fenestras per quas anima bibit temporalium delectiones et musas.

[c] contrahrere *corr.* contrahere *R*

[d] qui *R*

[e] maritimas *R*

[f] modis *R*

[g] periculississimo *corr.* periculossissimo

[h–h] *om. S*

[i] sint *R*

We are able to perceive that two muses are in the duality of authentic and plagal, or in the duality of percussion and blowing, one of which is served by bells and strings,[112] and the other by tibia and pipes; or in the duality of arsis and thesis—that is, in the natural rising and falling without which there is no melody.[113] What is music? The movement of voices. However, the movement of all voices is made by arsis or by thesis.

It is not absurd of us to understand the three muses in the three genera of music: diatonic, chromatic, and enharmonic. Or there are three muses in the human voice itself, the mixture of percussion and blowing, and the reverberating sirens of marine promontories. This comes from the Greek word: siren in Greek means "to draw in." Whence sandbanks occur where sands are pulled together.[114] Hence also the comedian was called Syrus,[115] since by his cunning he drew in the fugitive silver. There are few things in stories that are not in some way derived from the font of truth. It is alleged that the sirens were maritime singers who killed the improvident sailors whom they drew to themselves by their very sweet melodies. There are certain rocky prominences in the sea at which the collision of the waves imitates the sweet melody. With its sweetness this melody lured those who passed by, sometimes sinking them in miserable shipwreck, just as the pleasant and flattering sirens of this world would similarly draw our souls into the most dangerous shipwreck.[116]

We do not rashly consider the four muses in either the four continuous tropes of the ancients, which we have already spoken about, or in the four tetrachords *Graves*, *Finales*, *Superiores*, and *Excellentes*, which possess all melody. Or in the four Pythagorean hammers,[117] which discover the proportion of the four symphonies of tone, *diatessaron*, *diapente*, and *diapason*; or in the quadripartite distribution of the monochord, which in ascent constitutes the *diatessaron* by its first step, the *diapente* by its second, and the *diapason* by its third. Descending, on the other hand, it constitutes the *diapason* by its first step, the *diapente* by its second, and the *diatessaron* by its third.

We believe the five muses to be the five greater symphonies: the sesquitertia,[118] sesquialter,[119] duple, triple, and quadruple; or the five vowels without which no letters can be voiced. Or if we call to mind five muses, virtually all letters may be divided in five categories, because certain are vowels, certain semivowels, some mutes, others liquids, and still more double.[120] Or else we may understand the five muses in the five noxious windows of the senses, through which the soul drinks the muses and temporal delights.[121]

Sex musas sex minores perpendamus esse consonantias: semitonium, tonum, semiditonum, ditonum, diatesseron, diapente; quibus omnis conformatur neuma regularis. Has sex dumtaxat dominus[j] Guido diligebat.

Septem musarum ad intellectum sumamus septem discrimina uocum, quia cętерę non additio sunt sed earumdem repeticio; uel septem planetas.

Octo musas octo tonos intelligamus quorum magisterio totum corpus cantionis disponimus[k] et gubernamus.

Nouem esse musas omnis consensit antiquitas imitatrix mundanę, quę nouem circulis continetur musicę. Cęli et terrę duo circuli, septem planetis adiuncti nouem perficiunt. Ad quam similitudinem in terrestri nostra musica nouem computauerant musas, nouem uidelicet consonantias: uoces unisonas, semitonium, tonum, semiditonum,[l] ditonum, diatesseron, diapente, diapente cum semitonio, diapente cum tono. Vnisonę uoces ut *Adiuua nos Deus salutaris noster*. Semitonium ut *Missus est Gabriel archangelus ad Mariam*. Sed puerile est de tam manifestis uti exemplis. De nouissimis tantum duabus exempla proponamus, id est de diapente cum semitonio, de diapente cum tono, quia hę et minus proportionales et minus usuales. Diapente cum semitonio sonat in illius ymni principio: *Mare fons ostium* et ibi *atque terra*.[m] Diapente cum tono in *Ad te leuaui animam meam Deus meus in te*, et in *Iam non estis hospites et aduene sed estis ciues sanctorum et domestici*.

[78.] [a]De simplici cymbalorum mensura sesquitercia et sesqualtera proportione intensa et remissa et cur [b]similis sit[b] monochordi cymbalorumque mensura.[a]

Arbitror idcirco eodem modo se habere mensuram monochordi cymbalorumque, quod pulsatio sonum excitat[c] utrimque, tinnitus chordę et cymbali ferit aerem liberum nullis circumstantiis clausum. Sed distat ab illis mensura fistularum fortassis propter aerem in ipsis coartatum. Qui dum se dilatandi[d] libertatem fistulę circumstantiis cohibitus non habeat, quęrit non solum longitudinis sed etiam grossitudinis adiectionem. Vnde in reperiendo tono non solum prioris[e] fistulę longitudinis sed[f] grossitudinis, id est diametri octauam partem assumimus, ut patebit in sequentibus. Sed ad cymbala redeamus.

[j] domnus *R*
[k] disposinimus *marked for correction to* disponimus *R*
[l] semitonum *S;* semitonum *corr.* semiditonium *by later hand R*
[m] *om. R*
[78.] [a–a] *om. D3*
[b–b] sit similis *W3*
[c] excitat id est et in monochordo et in | cymbalis *W3*
[d] dilatando *W3*
[e] priores *R*
[f] sed etiam *D3*

The six muses we may consider carefully to be the six lesser consonances—semitone, tone, semiditone, ditone, *diatessaron*, and *diapente*—to which every regular phrase conforms. Lord Guido dwelt upon these six with delight.[122]

The seven muses we may choose to be understood as the "seven different notes," since the rest are not an addition but a repetition of those;[123] or the seven planets.

The eight muses we may understand as the eight tones, by means of which we arrange and govern the whole body of chant.

All the ancients agreed there to be nine muses as in imitation of the world, which is contained in the nine circles of music.[124] Two circles of heaven and earth, having been joined to the seven planets, complete nine. As a likeness of this in our earthly music they have counted nine muses, namely the nine consonances: unison voices, semitones, tones, semiditones, ditones, *diatessarons*, *diapentes*, *diapentes* with semitones, and *diapentes* with tones. Unison voices as in *Adiuva nos Deus salutaris noster.*[125] Semitones as in *Missus est Gabriel archangelus ad Mariam.*[126] But it is childish to use such obvious examples. Let us put forward examples only of the last of these—that is, of the *diapente* with semitone and of the *diapente* with tone—since they are of lesser proportion and lesser use. The *diapente* with a semitone sounds at the beginning of this hymn: *Mare, fons, ostium*, and at *atque terra.*[127] The *diapente* with a tone in *Ad te levavi animam meam Deus meus in te*[128] and in *Iam non estis hospites et advenae sed estis cives sanctorum et domestici.*[129]

78. Concerning the simple measure of bells by the proportion of the sesquitertia in extension and the sesquialter in remission, and why the measurement of the monochord is similar to that of bells.[130]

I believe, therefore, that the monochord and bells are to be measured in the same way because a striking rouses sound in each—the ringing of the string or bell makes the air free and in no circumstances enclosed. But the measurement of pipes differs from these, perhaps on account of the air that is trapped within them, which while held in the pipe may not have the freedom to spread around and searches not only for an addition of length but also of breadth. Therefore, in discovering its pitch we take into account not only the length of the preceding pipe but also the breadth—that is, we add an eighth part of the diameter—as will be clear in what follows. But let us return to bells.

Propter toni tarditatem sesquitercia sesqualteraque proportione mensuram statui intendere et remittere. Octo cymbala sunt[g] ratione dimetienda.[h]

Reponderationes[i] cerę, quam ad primum cymbalum expendas, duas diligenter prouideas. Quarum alteram in duas, alteram in tres partes distribuas. Et isti quam in duas diuisisti propria medietate, illi tercia sui adiecta parte formes tibi duo cymbala, primo per diatesseron et diapente respondentia. Habeas quoque illius quam in duo distribuisti reponderationem. Quam diuidens in quatuor dimoueas quartam, de tribus partibus secundum cymbalum compositurus. Eiusdem secundi cymbali reponderationem cerę sumas et eius medietate[j] sibimet superposita formam sexti fingas cymbali. Cuius reponderationem quatuor partibus distribuens quartam secernens, de tribus tercium conformes cymbalum. Quod per medium diuidens tantumque ut est dimidium superaddens proponas septimum. Cuius reponderationem quadripertiens quartamque reiciens de tribus synemmenon conficias.

[79.] [a]Monochordi mensura eiusdem proportionibus constituta.[a]

Totum monochordum a gamma quatuor passibus diuidas et in primi fine .C., secundi .G., tercii .g. ponas. Post a gamma tribus passibus ascendas, ac in primi fine .D., secundi .d. constituas. Deinde remittas diatesseron ad .D. tribus, quarta uice .A. positurus, ascendas ab .A. tribus diapente intensurus. In primi fine ponas .E., in secundi .e. Iam remittas tribus diatesseron ad .E., quarta uice ponens .B., a[b] .C. diatesseron intendas, et in primi fine .F. scribe, secundi .c. Ex .F. diatesseron intendas, ut primo synemmenon secundo .f. inuenias, .a. .b. .$\frac{a}{a}$. residuę litterę dupla ab equiuocis inueniantur proportione. Eandem[c] remittas diapente duobus ad[d] .F. tercia uice inferius synemmenon scribe.

[80.] [a]Eiusdem mensurę epigramma.[a]

Passibus in primis totum partire quaternis
.Γ. gamma locans .C. .G. .g.[b] Diuide post tribus[c] ęque.
Inscribens[d] .D. .d.[e] Post hęc remeas tribus ad .D.

[g] sunt hac *D3W3*
[h] dimettenda *D3;* dimittenda *R*
[i] *Varied recension of last paragraph in D3W3.*
[j] medietatem *corr.* medietate *R*
[79.] [a–a] *om. S*
[b] .A. *W3*
[c] Tandem *W3*
[d] ab *W3*

[80.] [a–a] *om. S*
[b] .G. *W3*
[c] tribus qua circinus est uice quarta *S. The scribe of S made a copying mistake, taking text from two lines further on.*
[d] inscribe *R*
[e] .D. *W3*

On account of the cumbersomeness of measuring by tones, I have decided to measure using the proportions of the sesquitertia and sesquialter in extension and remission. The eight bells are to be measured according to rule.

By reweighing the wax that you use for the first bell you will be able to provide diligently for two more.[131] You should divide one of these in two parts and the other in three. To the former, which you have divided in two, add half again,[132] and to the latter add again one of its three parts,[133] so that you form for yourself two bells from the first bell, responding to the *diatessaron* and *diapente*. You will also have the weight of the bell that you divided in two. Dividing this in four, remove the fourth part; from the three remaining parts the second bell is to be made.[134] You should take the quantity of wax for this same second bell and by half of this having been added you fashion the form of the sixth bell.[135] Dividing the weight of the second bell in four parts and setting apart the fourth, form the third bell from the three remaining parts.[136] Dividing that in half and adding on half again, you produce the seventh bell.[137] By dividing this weight in four and setting aside the fourth part, you will find *synemmenon* from the three remaining parts.[138]

79. A measurement of the monochord constituted from the same proportions.[139]

You should divide all of the monochord from gamma in four steps and place the first ending at .C., the second at .G., and the third at .g. Afterwards you should ascend from gamma in three steps and establish the first ending at .D. and the second at .d. Then you should come back by *diatessaron* to .D. in three steps so as to place .A. in the fourth position and ascend from .A. in three steps by extension of the *diapente*. You should place the first ending at .E. and the second at .e. Now you should return in three steps by *diatessaron* to .E., placing .B. in the fourth place; from .C. extend by diatessaron, writing the first ending at .F. and the second at .c. From .F. extend by *diatessaron* so that you find in the first place *synemmenon* and in the second place .f. The remaining letters .a., .b., and .$\overset{a}{a}$. are found to be in double proportion from their equivalents an octave lower. Likewise you should return from the same by two *diapentes* to .F. and in the third step write the lower *synemmenon*.[140]

80. An epigram of the same measurement.

At the beginning all is divided in four steps
That place gamma (.Γ.), .C., .G., .g. Afterwards divide equally in three.
Inscribe .D. and .d. After these you should return by three steps to .D.

Scribatur grauis .A. [f]qua circinus est uice quinta.[g]
Ex .A.[f] suspendas tribus .E. Post .e. quoque[h] ponas.
Descendens et ad .E. tribus in quarta uice fac .B.
Bis binis ex .C. ueniens .F. scribe dehinc .c.
Sic synemmenon et .f.[i] totidem fac passibus ex .F.
Quicquid adhuc restet iam dupla proportio prestet.
.a.[j] .b. rursus et .$\overset{a}{a}$. sunt equiuocis statuenda.
.♭.[k] de .♭. legem reperire[l] [m]decet per eandem.[m]

[81.] [a]Alia monochordi[b] mensura ab acutis incipiens.[a]

Primus passus ab .$\overset{a}{a}$.[c] per diatesseron remittitur in[d] .e., secundus uacat, tercius in .a., quartus uacat, quintus in .E., sextus in .D., septimus et octauus uacant. Nonus in .A. Ab[e] .$\overset{a}{a}$. per diapente in .d.[f] remitte. Intende[g] a .d.[h] per diatesseron in .g.[i] Remitte a .g.[j] per diapente primum passum in .c., secundum in .G., tercius uacat, quartum[k] in .C., quintus uacat, sextus finit in gamma[l] .Γ.[m] Fiat ut .f. de .c. bis binis scandimus ęque. Ab .f. remitte per diapente primus passus in synemmenon, secundus tendit in .F., [n]tercius uacat, quartus in synemmenon inferius.[n] Ab .e.[o] remitte diatesseron[p] primus terminat in .b., secundus uacat, tercius in .E. prius inuentum, quartus uacat, quintus[q] in .B.

[82.] [a]Antiqua fistularum mensura quę intenditur.[a]

Mensuram duorum ordinum, id est sedecim fistularum hic dicere sufficiat secundum quam alios quotlibet[b] ordines quiuis adiciat. Primam fistulam tantę longitudinis ac latitudinis delibera quantam mediocritas cum arbitrio doceat. Longitudo autem[c] fistulę a[d] plectro sursum habetur, et latitudo est

[f–f] *om. RS;* qua circinus est uice quarta *supplied from S two lines before*
[g] quarta *SW3*
[h] *om. R*
[i] .F. *W3*
[j] .A. *W3*
[k] .B. *W3*
[l] require *R*
[m–m] de|cet eandem *S*
[81.] [a–a] *om. D3S;* Item alia ab acutis incipiens *W2*
[b] monochordii *R*
[c] .$\overset{a}{a}$. superacuto *D3*
[d] ab *S*
[e] Item ab *D3*
[f] .D. *W2*
[g] Inde *R*
[h] .D. *W2*
[i] .G. *W2*
[j] .G. *W2*
[k] quartus *R*
[l] *om. D3*
[m] *om. R*
[n–n] tercius uacat et quartus *D3*
[o] .E. *D3;* .f. *W2*
[p] per diatessaron *D3*
[q] *om. RS*
[82.] [a–a] *om. S*
[b] quot libeat *RW4*
[c] aut *R*
[d] ac *R*

.A. of the *graves* is written, whereupon you turn about for the fifth step.
From .A. you suspend .E. in three steps. Afterwards you may also place .e.
And descending to .E. in three steps make .B. in the fourth place.
Coming twice in two steps from .C. write .F. and then .c.
Make *synemmenon* and .f. in the same number of steps from .F.
Whatever yet remains will be apparent through a double proportion.
.a., .b., and again .$^{a}_{a}$. are to be established from their equivalents.
In the same way it befits to find .♭. from .♭.[141]

81. Another measurement of the monochord, beginning from the high notes.[142]

The first step downwards from .$^{a}_{a}$. to .e. is by *diatessaron*, the second is empty, the third is to .a., the fourth is empty, the fifth to .E., the sixth to .D., the seventh and eighth are empty. The ninth is to .A. Return by *diapente* from .$^{a}_{a}$. to .d. Extend by *diatessaron* from .d. to .g. From .g. return by *diapente* to .c. in the first step, to .G. in the second; the third is empty, to .C. in the fourth, the fifth is empty, and the sixth finishes at gamma (.Γ.). To make .f. from .c. we climb twice two steps equally. From .f. return by *diapente*: the first step is *synemmenon*, the second extends to .F., the third is empty, and the fourth is the lower *synemmenon*. From .e. return by *diatessaron*: the first ends at .b., the second is empty, the third ends at the .E. already found, the fourth is empty, and the fifth ends at .B.

82. An old measurement of pipes that involves extension.[143]

It suffices here to speak of the measurement of two series—that is, of sixteen pipes—from which one may add as many other series as may be needed. The first pipe should in length and breadth be according to a medium that judgment may teach. The length of the pipe is considered from the languid up, and the breadth is

ipsius concauitatis[e] capacitas, qua se in summitate in modum circuli aperit. Qui nimirum circulus non secundum ambitum suum, sed per medium duobus hemisperiis diuisus diametrum dicitur. Huius diametri longitudinem circino deprehensam statim post primę fistulę informationem in summitate eiusdem primę fistulę duabus lineis ęqualibus depinge, et unam earum[f] in octo, alteram in duas et in tres et in quatuor ęquas partes diuide; et post hęc tota mensura tibi erit facillima. Secundam autem a prima sumpturus octauam diametri eiusdem primę fistulę longitudini aufer, reliquum eius spacium usque ad plectrum in nouem partire, et nona in summitate reiecta habebis secundam. Terciam inuenturus secundę fistulę longitudini octauam diametri tolle, residuum eius spatium usque ad plectrum in nouem diuide, et nona parte in summitate pretermissa terciam inuenisti. Quartam quęsiturus primę fistulę longitudini terciam diametri adime, et quarta[g] parte ablata, quartam cum integro diatesseron addidisti.[h] Quintam reperturus[i] primę fistulę diametri medietatem disiunge, reliquum eius [j]spatium usque ad plectrum[j] in tria diuide, et tercia in summitate separata, quintam cum diapente aggregasti. Sextam appositurus secundę fistulę longitudini item medietatem diametri abscide, reliquum eius spatium in tres partire, et tercia relicta, sextam subiunxisti. Synemmenon ostensurus quartę fistulę terciam diametri reseca, residuum ad plectrum spatium in quatuor diuide, et quarta parte omissa, synemmenon designasti. Septimam inuenies si tercię medietatem diametri amputabis, et reliquum in tres diuides, et tercia in summitate reiecta, septimam finalem constituisti. His ita dispositis octauam a prima, nonam a secunda, decimam a tercia, undecimam a quarta, duodecimam a quinta, decimam terciam a sexta, inferius synemmenon a superiori synemmenon, decimam quartam a septima,[k] hoc modo facillime ordinabis ut unicuique superiorum integrum diametrum excipias, et reliquum eius spatium usque ad plectrum in duas partes diuidas, ac superiore declinata inferiorem, plectro dico contiguam pro octaua suscipias.

[83.] [a]Noua fistularum mensura que remittitur.[a]

Domnus Willihelmus prius Emmerammensis Ratisponę monachus, nunc autem alibi abbas uenerandus, fistularum nouam exquisiuit mensuram prioris intensionem conuertens in remissionem quam mecum communicauit. Nam meam dilexit paruitatem ultra paruitatis dignitatem qui est musicus

[e] cauitatis *W4*
[f] eorum *R*
[g] quarte *R*
[h] addisti *corr.* addidisti *R*
[i] respecturus *R*
[j–j] usque ad plectrum spacium *RW4*
[k] vi[a] *R*
[83.] [a–a] *om. S*

the size of that opening by which it opens in the form of a circle at the top. This, of course, is called a circle, not because of its circumference but from having its diameter divided in half by two semicircles. Immediately after the making of the first pipe measure the length of this diameter at the top with a pair of compasses. Let the same first pipe be represented by two equal lines: divide one of them in eight, and the other in two, three, and four equal parts; and after this all of the measurement will be easy for you. To calculate the second pipe from the first, subtract one-eighth of the diameter from the length of the same first pipe; dividing the remaining length to the languid in nine parts and by taking off one-ninth at the top, you will have the second pipe. In order to find the third pipe take away one-eighth of the diameter from the length of the second pipe, divide the remaining distance to the languid in nine parts, leave out one-ninth at the top and you will have found the third pipe. To search for the fourth pipe, take a third of the diameter from the length of the first pipe, subtract one quarter, and you will have added the fourth pipe, giving the complete *diatessaron*. To seek the fifth pipe, subtract half of the diameter from the length of the first pipe and divide the remaining distance to the languid in three parts, cut one-third from the top, and you will have added the fifth pipe, giving the *diapente*. In order to assign the sixth pipe, likewise take away half of the diameter from the length of the second pipe, divide the remaining distance in three, and by relinquishing the third, you will have uncovered the sixth pipe. To introduce *synemmenon*, take away one-third of the diameter from the length of the fourth pipe, divide the remaining distance to the languid in four, and by omitting one quarter, you will have designated *synemmenon*. You will come across the seventh pipe if you cut off half of the diameter from the length of the third pipe, divide the remainder in three, and by taking one third from the top, the seventh and last pipe will have been constituted. These things having been disposed of, you can easily work out the eighth pipe from the first pipe, the ninth from the second, the tenth from the third, the eleventh from the fourth, the twelfth from the fifth, the thirteenth from the sixth, the upper *synemmenon* from the lower *synemmenon*, and the fourteenth from the seventh in this manner: subtract the entirety of the diameter of each of the aforementioned pipes and dividing the remaining distance to the languid in two parts—the upper part having been taken away—you may adopt the lower part, continuous to the languid I say, for the eighth.

83. A new measurement of pipes that involves remission.[144]

Lord William, formerly a monk of St. Emmeram in Regensburg but now venerable abbot elsewhere,[145] has discovered a new measurement of pipes converting the extension of the former into remission, which he has communicated to me. For he who is greatest among musicians,

primus,[b] modernus uidelicet Orpheus et Pythagoras. Cuius [c]ista est[c] dispositio. Primę[d] ergo longitudo, sicut placuit domno Willihelmo, usque ad plectrum hęc est:[e]

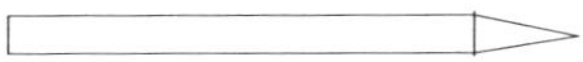

Grossitudinem autem,

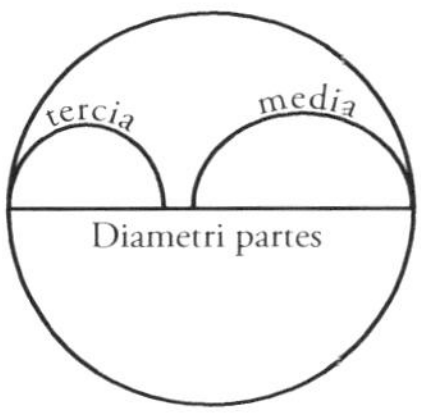

quę [f]omnibus ęqualis est,[f] iste designat circulus. Primę igitur fistulę quantitas in octo diuidatur, eique[g] octaua pars cum octaua diametri apponatur et erit secunda. Secundę[h] item longitudo in octo partiatur, additaque octaua cum diametri octaua erit tercia. Prima[i] item in tres diuidatur, additaque tercia cum tercia diametri, habebis diatesseron in ipsa quarta peractum. In hac ipsa incipit integer minor ordo priorque. Tercia item fistula in octo diuidatur, additaque octaua cum octaua diametri synemmenon reperitur. Item prima in duo diuidatur, additaque [j]medietate cum medietate[j] diametri [k]quinta perficitur. Secundę item longitudo[l] in duo partiatur, additaque medietate cum medietate diametri,[k] sexta peragitur. Tercia similiter in geminas partes diuidatur, appositaque altera cum altera diametri parte, septima producitur. Octaua a prima sic inueniatur. Prima duplicetur, insuper integrum diametrum apponatur, et octaua reperitur. Et sicut per primam inuenta est octaua, eodem modo omnes subsequentes facillime reperire poteris, tantum si singulis integrum diametrum apposueris.

[b] primas *SW4*
[c–c] est ista *R;* est ista *marked with superscript* a *and* b *for transposition W4*
[d] Primo *W4*
[e] *Diagram om. R*
[f–f] equalis est omnibus *RW4*
[g] eiusque *S; om. W4*
[h] <Se>cundę *W4*
[i] Primę *R*
[j–j] medietate *R*
[k–k] *om. W4*
[l] *om. S*

without doubt the Orpheus and Pythagoras of the moderns, has loved me beyond any worthiness that my poverty may possess.[146] This is his arrangement. As it pleased Lord William, therefore, the length of the first pipe continuously to the languid is this:

Diagram 4.

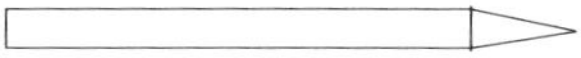

Moreover, this circle designates the size, which is equal for all:

Diagram 5.

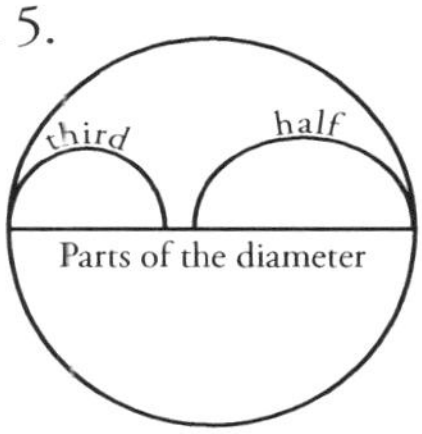

The length of the first pipe, therefore, is to be divided in eight, to which an eighth part with one-eighth of the diameter is added, and there will be the second pipe. The length of the second pipe is again divided in eight; and adding an eighth with one eighth of the diameter will give the third pipe. The first pipe is again divided in three: with the addition of one third plus one-third of the diameter you will have the *diatessaron* completed in the fourth pipe. From here the entire lesser and earlier series begins. The third pipe is also divided in eight: with the addition of one eighth plus one-eighth of the diameter, *synemmenon* is discovered. The first pipe is again divided in two, and with the addition of half plus half of the diameter the fifth pipe is completed. Again, the length of the second pipe is divided in two, and with the addition of half plus half of the diameter, the sixth pipe is made. The third pipe is similarly divided in two parts, and by adding to it one of the parts with its diameter, the seventh pipe is produced. The eighth pipe is found from the first in this way. The first pipe is doubled, and, moreover, the whole of its diameter is added giving the eighth pipe. And as through the first pipe the eighth pipe is found, in the same manner you can easily discover all subsequent pipes, if you merely add the entire diameter to each.

[84.] [a]Aribunculina fistularum mensura, nec in toto remissibilis nec in toto intensibilis sesquitercia et sesqualtera proportione.[a]

Nos autem in[b] utraque progredientes, modo hanc intendendo et abiciendo, modo illam remittendo et adiciendo,[c] sequentes in neutram partem[d] declinamus quia tonum per octo nouemue particulas reperire nolumus.[e] Non sine ratione quidem. Quanto enim mensura celerior tanto [f]est et uerior.[f] Alicuius[g] spacii quartam uel terciam dimidiumue octaua uel nona parte quęri certius et uelocius[h] pene patet omnibus. Vnde sesquitercia sesqualteraque[i] tendere susum[j] iusumque disposuimus proportione. Primę fistulę pars tercia cum tercia diametri sibimet addita format quartam. Item primę medietas cum diametri medietate sibi iuncta generat quintam. Quinta quarta sui parte cum tercia diametri deposita secundę staturam proponit. Secunda sui[k] diametrique medietate presumpta sexta[l] est mensura. Sexta quarta sui terciaque diametri reiecta terciam constituit. Tercię medietas cum diametri medietate sibimet superposita mater est septimę. Cuius quarta cum diametri tercia detruncata, quod restat fistulę synemmenon recinentis longitudinem prestat. Vela sollicitudinis deponamus quia iam securitatis portum occupamus. Prima duplex cum integro diametro reddit octauam, secunda nonam, tercia decimam, quarta undecimam, synemmenon aliud synemmenon, quinta duodecimam, sexta decimam terciam, septima decimam quartam, [m]octaua decimam quintam, nona decimam sextam, decima decimam septimam.[m] Totidem etenim[n] organicis fistulis uti placuit experientię domni Willihelmi, qui duobus ordinibus quatuordecim uidelicet fistulis tres adiecit, ut tetrachordum prestrueret, ut competens acumen in minimis et opportuna grauitas responderet in maximis.

[85.] [a]Organice dispositionis mensura.[a]

Ex .a. suspende primum diatesseron in .d.
Ex .a. rursus in .e. resupinam duc diapente.
Deponas et ab .e. passum diatesseron in .b.[b]
Rursus in .f. de .♭.[c] memor intendas diapente.
[d]Ex .f. depone speciem diatesseron in .c.[d]
Intendas a .c. contingens .g.[e] diapente.
A .d. suspendi debet diatesseron in Sy.

[84.] [a–a] *om. S;* Aribunculina fistularum mensura nec in toto intensibilis | nec in toto remissibilis *W4*
[b] inter *W4*
[c] abiciendo *W4*
[d] *om. R;* penitus *W4*
[e] uolumus *W4*
[f–f] et uerior est *R;* est uerior *W4*
[g] Ad cuius *S*
[h] uolocius *corr.* uelocius *R*
[i] sesqualtera *W4*
[j] susumque *R*
[k] sua *W4*
[l] sextę *SW4*
[m–m] *om. R*
[n] ergo *S*
[85.] [a–a] *om. D3S*
[b] .B. *D3RSW4*
[c] .B. *D3RSW4*
[d–d] *om. W4*
[e] *om. S;* .d. *D3*

84. Little Aribo's measurement of pipes, neither wholly by remission nor wholly by extension but by the proportions of the sesquitertia and the sesquialter.[147]

Though we may proceed with both this method of extending and contracting or that method of contracting and extending, we decline to follow either of them because we do not wish to discover the interval of a tone through eight or nine little divisions. And not, indeed, without reason. For the more rapid the measurement is, the truer it is.[148] That the quarter, the third, or the half of some interval is to be sought more assuredly and more quickly than the eighth or the ninth part is obvious to nearly all. We have decided, therefore, to extend the sesquitertia and the sesquialter up and down in proportion. The third part of the first pipe together with the third of the diameter having been added forms the fourth pipe. Again, half of the first pipe with half of the diameter having been joined to it produces the fifth pipe. The fifth pipe with a quarter of itself and a third part of the diameter having been taken away produces the second pipe. The second pipe having received both half of itself and its diameter is the sixth in measure. The sixth pipe, when a quarter of it and a third of the diametr have been taken away, constitutes the third pipe. Half of the third pipe with half of the diameter having been added to it is the mother of the seventh pipe. A quarter of this with a third of the diameter having been taken away, the remaining presents the length of the pipe retaining *synemmenon*. Let us put aside the veils of anxiety because we have now reached the harbor of safety. The first pipe doubled with its entire diameter produces the eighth pipe, the second the ninth, the third the tenth, the fourth the eleventh, *synemmenon* another *synemmenon*, the fifth the twelfth, the sixth the thirteenth, and the seventh the fourteenth. For just so many organ pipes fitted in with the experience of Lord William, who from two series added three to the fourteen pipes that he might construct the tetrachord, so that showing skill in small things he might respond with appropriate gravity in great things.[149]

85. A measurement of the arrangement of the organ.

From .a. suspend the first *diatessaron* to .d.
From .a. backwards to .e. lead back the reverse *diapente*,
And from .e. you should set down the step of the *diatessaron* to .b.
Remember that you should extend the *diapente* back from .f. to .♭.
From .f. set down the species of *diatessaron* to .c.
You may extend from .c. the *diapente* touching .g.
From .d. the *diatessaron* ought to be suspended to *synemmenon*.

[86.] [a]Qualiter ipse congruenter fiant fistulę.[a]

Sicut fistulę eiusdem sunt grossitudinis ita laminę de quibus fiant, eiusdem sint latitudinis. Prius iuxta domnum Willihelmum grossitudinis dipinximus circulum. Qui de qua latitudine possit prouenire, caute debemus perpendere. Dicit Macrobius de somnio Scipionis: Omne diametrum cuiusque orbis triplicatum cum adiectione septimę partis suę mensuram facit circuli. Hęc sunt uerba Macrobii. Vnde eius auctoritatem sequentes prescripti circuli diametrum triplicemus, septimamque diametri simul adiungamus: et secundum quantitatem lineę quę inde procedat,[b] omnium laminarum fistulis materialium latitudo fiat. Hę laminę in lateralibus extremitatibus attenuentur precipuę. Quę extremitates cum fabrili manu eas incuruante conueniant, non superponantur sibimet, sed osculo tantum collidantur coniunctissimo. Ad cuius osculi commissuram tegendam preparentur laminellę festucę tenuitatem et latitudinem habentes, que sibi tenacissimo conglutinentur stagno seu alio quod lentius diuturniusque perseueret lotario. Postquam autem in lamina adhuc patula cuiusque fistulę longitudo determinetur punctis utrimque in lateribus fixis, linea per transuersum de puncto tendat in punctum. Illa linea terminalis sit foramini et[c] ori fistulę. Quod os super ipsam ita excidatur lineam,[d] ut ad medietatem latitudinis fistulę aperiatur. In ipsam quoque lineam plectrum arctissime conglutinetur. A quo plectro subterius oris labrum mediocris festucę distet latitudine.

[87.] [a]De naturali musico et artificiali.[a]

Quamuis nihil ars primo nihil[b] natura inueniat postremo ut quidam asserit sapientium, expolitius tamen fiet per artem quam[c] incultum et hirtum naturę genitricis procedit ab utero. Ars enim ab artis quibus constringi conformarique debet dicitur regulis. Nobis admodum consanguineam et naturalem esse musicam precipue possumus ex hoc perpendere, quod quique histriones totius musicę artis expertes quaslibet laicas irreprehensibiliter iubilant odas, in uaria tonorum semitoniorumque positione nihil offendentes ad finalem chordam legitime recurrentes. Vnde quamuis non uere uerisimiliter tamen tractat Plato de animę genitura, dicens eam compositam musicis proportionibus. Cum enim dupla[d] proportio sesquitercia, sesqualtera, sesquioctaua iocunditatem mentibus intonat, potest a gentilibus credi non incongrue animas ex eisdem proportionibus consistere, cum similitudo sit amica, dissimilitudo odiosa.

[86.] [a–a] *om. S*
[b] proced[i>a]t *S*
[c] *om. W4*
[d] linea *W4*

[87.] [a–a] *om. SM₃*
[b] *om. R*
[c] quod *RM₃*
[d] duplam *corr.* dupla *R, possibly later*

86. How these pipes are suitably made.[150]

As the pipes are of the same size, so the metal sheets of which they are made are of the same width. Previously we have calculated the circumference of these pipes following Lord William. We ought to make cautious investigation about how the width may be established. Macrobius says concerning the dream of Scipio: the diameter of every circle, when tripled with the addition of a seventh part, gives the measurement of the circumference.[151] These are the words of Macrobius. Whence following his authority we triple the diameter of the aforesaid circle and add one-seventh of the diameter: and according to the measurement that results from this, the width of all the metal sheets to be used in the fabrication of the pipes will be known. These metal sheets should be made especially thin along their lateral edges. Their ends, bent around by the worker's hands, should not overlap but be brought face-to-face, just touching. To cover over this gap, metal strips having the slenderness and width of a straw are prepared, each of which is fixed most tenaciously with tin, or another adhesive that is applied more slowly and for a longer time. While each metal sheet is yet open, the length of the pipe is determined by points fixed at each end, and a transverse line is traced from one point to the other. The ends of that line may be the orifice and the mouthpiece of the pipe, which will be cut out above this line so that it lies midway across the breadth of the pipe. On this line also the languid will be affixed with great care. The upper lip of the mouthpiece will be separated from this lip by the width of a medium-sized straw.

87. Concerning the untrained musician and the educated musician.

Although art devises nothing at first and nature devises nothing at last, as a certain man of sense declares, that which uncultivated and rough proceeds from the womb of mother nature will nevertheless become polished by art.[152] For art is so called from having been subjected to rules,[153] by which it ought to be constrained and brought to conformity. We can especially conclude from this that music is exceedingly kindred and natural because stage performers who are expert in the whole art of music sing certain secular songs in a disreputable manner, causing no offence to the various positions of the tones and semitones, and lawfully running through to the final notes. Plato, dealing with the birth of the soul—although not yet truly in a manner resembling truth—says that it is composed of musical proportions.[154] For since the double proportion, the sesquitertia, the sesquialter, and the sesquioctave sound joyfully in the minds, it can be believed by the pagans, not incongruously, that minds consist of the same proportion since the familiar is friendly and the unfamiliar is hostile.[155]

Nam etiam boni bonos, reprobi [e]diligunt peruersos.[e] Sed histriones et cęteri tales musici sunt naturales, non artificiales. Artificialis autem musicus est qui naturalem omnium specierum diatessaron, diapente, diapason constitutionem intelligit subtiliter; qui dispositionem troporum naturę pedissequam cognoscit rationabiliter; qui principalium chordarum operationem perpendit efficaciter; qui troporum proprietates, quę in sex chordis consistunt tenet memoriter. Ipse quoque artis facultate optime sciat, legitima comprobare, uitiosa quęlibet emendare, irreprehensibiles persemet ipsum cantilenas excogitare.

[88.] [a]De musice artis moralitate.[a]

Ethicam id est moralem esse musicam quiuis ex hoc potest percipere quod, ut supra dictum est,[b] sua confert beneficia sine artis perceptione. Vnde eius usus arte possessus tanto nobis stabilior et perseuerantior quanto ipsa nobis est naturalior, ut diuturnius argento inheret aurum quam cupro. Moralis esse penitus ostenditur cum omnis sexus, omnis ętas in illa delectatur. Nec solum humanę sed etiam ferinę suam iocunditatem communicat naturę. Percepimus quippe autentica[c] uenatores foliis recinentes capreas aliasque feras ad se pellexisse; patetque non[d] penitus [e]fabulosum esse[e] Orpheum lyra Plutonem placasse, cum legamus Dauidem demoniacam Saulis feritatem cytharizando mitigasse. Nonne modulator Arion mortis euasit periculum, excutiens se super unum ad melodiam suam confluentium delphinorum? Musicę moralitatem etiam Plato demonstrat dicens: Animorum item placiditatem[f] constituebamus in delinimentis[g] et affabilitate musicę. Merito dicit Plato[h] placiditatem animorum esse in musica, cum nulla inquietudo cum assidua musicę conuersetur delectatione.[i] Est tamen ut legimus quidam expertus et in illa hoc satis esse ratum nihil omni parte beatum; qui quosdam modos infirmiores quosdam etiam sensit saniores: quem frigius ad quendam thalamum traduxit, hypofrigiusque penitentem reduxit. Nos quoque scimus quasdam species diatessaron et diapente aliis esse pulchriores[j] ut prima et quarta, secundę et tertię superant consonantiam. Prima et quarta semitonium habent in medio, ideo melius resonant; secunda et tercia semitonium habent hęc in principio illa in fine et ideo surdius sonant. Sed in diatessaron speciebus

[e–e] diuersos diligunt *M₃ with* diuersos *marked for correction*

[88.] [a–a] *om. SM₃*

[b] *om. R*

[c] autentica relatione *M₃*

[d] *om. S*

[e–e] esse fabulosum *M₃*

[f] placitatem *R*

[g] deliniamentis *S*

[h] *om. S*

[i] delectione *S*

[j] pulciores *M₃*

For even as the "good loves the good,"[156] the reprobate loves the perverse. But stage performers and all such kind of musicians are untrained and not educated. A musician is indeed educated who exactly understands the natural structure of all of the species of *diatessaron*, *diapente*, and *diapason*; who knows through reason that the disposition of the tropes is the servant of nature; who considers effectively and efficaciously the operation of the principal notes; who "holds in his memory"[157] the properties of the tropes that consist of six notes. He also knows best how to give his approval with lawful skill in the art, to emend any errors, and can work out the faulty chants by his own intelligence.[158]

88. Concerning the moral art of music.

That music pertains to ethics—that is to say, to morals—anyone can perceive from the fact that, as we said above, it confers its benefits without requiring knowledge of the art.[159] Therefore the more steadfastly and perseveringly we acquire that art the more natural it is to us, as gold with long usage adheres to silver rather than to copper.[160] It is shown to be entirely moral since every sex and every age delights in it. It communicates its pleasure not only to human nature but also to wild beasts.[161] We have indeed learned it to be true that hunters have attracted deer and other wild beasts by calling out from among the leaves, and it is clearly not entirely a myth that Orpheus placated Pluto with his lyre since we read that David eased the demonic ferocity of Saul by playing the harp.[162] Did not the singer Arion escape the risk of death by whisking himself away on one of the dolphins drawn to his melody?[163] Plato also demonstrates the morality of music saying, "We have established the tranquillity of minds according to the lineaments and for the love of music."[164] Plato rightly says that the tranquillity of minds lies in music since anxiety is incompatible with an assiduous delight in it. Nevertheless, it is as we read, and it must be borne in mind that nothing is entirely blessed in all its parts, as some have experienced who find that certain modes are weaker and also feel certain others to be stronger: whom the frigian mode brings into its bedchamber,[165] the hypofrigian brings back to penance. We also know certain species of *diatessaron* and *diapente* to be more beautiful than others, such as the first and the fourth, whereas the seconds and the thirds overwhelm concord. The first and the fourth have the semitone in the middle, on that account they sound sweetly. The second and the third have the semitone, the former at the beginning, the latter at the end, and on that account they sound duller. But in the species of *diatessaron*

tolerabilis est diuersitas in quibus ditonus [k]sequitur semitonium,[k] ut in secunda, uel precedit semitonium ut in tertia. In diapente autem secunda et tercia specie intolerabilis conturbante[l] nos tritono,[m] quem propter inconsonantiam[n] cantionem possumus alterum nominare Coridonem. Sed tamen est obsequio cantilenę nonnumquam necessarius,[o] sicut rusticus Coridon dominorum sumptibus.

[89.] [a]De oportunitate modulandi.[a]

Duplex est iubilandi dulcedo si ita proportionaliter conferantur neumę distinctionesque, sicut ipsę monochordi uoces dispositę, sicut domnus Guido docet, musicus quidem tempore nouissimus utilitate primus, [b]cuius merito[b] alios eiusdem artis preceptores ita comparamus ut mutas uocalibus.

Cuius hęc sunt uerba: "Ac summopere[c] caueatur talis neumarum distributio, ut cum neumę eiusdem soni repercussione tum duorum aut plurium conexione fiant, semper tamen aut in numero uocum aut in ratione tenorum[d] neumę alterutrum conferantur atque respondeant nunc ęquę ęquis, nunc duplę uel triplę simplicibus, atque alias collatione[e] sesqualtera uel sesquitercia."

"Item ut more uersuum[f] distinctiones ęquales sint, et aliquotiens[g] ęedem repetitę aut aliqua uel parua mutatione uariatę. Et cum perpulchrę fuerint duplicatę habentes partes non nimis diuersas. Et quę aliquotiens[h] ęedem transformentur per modos aut similes[i] intensę et remissę inueniantur. Item ut reciprocata neuma eadem uia redeat qua uenerat, ac per eadem uestigia.[j] Item ut qualem habitum uel lineam una facit saliendo ab acutis, talem altera inclinata e regione [k]opponat respondendo a grauibus.[k] Item aliquando una sillaba unam uel plures habeat neumas, aliquando una neuma plures diuidatur in sillabas."[l]

Quoniam quidem domnus Guido has preceptiones suas sine exemplis reliquit, quia eas ut sunt satis manifestas credidit, nos eas ualde simplicibus pro nostro captu exponemus. [m]Neumę nempe[m] unius soni fiunt repercussione cum[n] simplices sunt, id est, uel una uirgula uel una iacens, uel cum

[k–k] semitonium sequitur *M₃*
[l] conturbauit *R*
[m] tritono *corr.* tritonus *R*
[n] inconsonam *S;* [[ ]] *M₃*
[o] necessa[[ ]] *M₃*
[89.] [a–a] *om. M₃S*
[b–b] cui merito *Sf;* cui [[ ]] :ito *M₃*
[c] Summopere *M₃;* summo opere *Sf*
[d] tonorum *M₃RS*
[e] collationes *R*
[f] [[ ]] *M₃*
[g] aliquoties *S*
[h] aliquoties *S*
[i] [[ ]] *M₃*
[j] [[ ]] *M₃*
[k–k] respondendo a grauibus opponat *M₃*
[l] s[[ ]] *M₃*
[m–m] Nempe neumę *M₃*
[n] [[ ]] *M₃*

diversity is tolerable; in such cases the ditone follows the semitone, as in the second, or precedes the semitone, as in the third. But in the second and third species of *diapente*, however, the unbearable tritone disturbs us, which because of its discordant sound we call another Corydon.[166] But nevertheless it is not necessary in the service of chant because it is like the churl Corydon wearing the master's finery.

89. Concerning the opportuneness of singing.

The sweetness of singing praise is doubled if the shorter and longer phrases are brought together proportionally, just as the notes of the monochord are disposed; this Lord Guido teaches, who is indeed the most modern musician of the time, foremost in usefulness and with whose merit we compare other teachers of the same art as we do the dumb to the speaking.

These are his words: "Special care should be taken that shorter phrases, whether made by repeating the same note or by joining two or more, should always be arranged to correspond to each other either in the number of notes or in the relationship of the attenuations, so that some of them respond equally, some by two or three to one, or yet others by the proportion of the sesquialter and sesquitertia."[167]

"Also, that the longer phrases should be of the same length, as in the manner of verse, and should sometimes be repeated, either the same or varied by some little change. And if they are particularly beautiful they should be duplicated with their parts not too diverse. And at other times let them be transformed by the modes or similarly be subjected to extension and remission. Also, that a returning short phrase may come back by the same way it went and by the same path. Also, that when a short phrase crosses a certain place or line by jumping down from the high notes, another may respond similarly in the opposite direction from the low notes. Sometimes, too, let one syllable of the text be spread over one or more short phrases, and at other times let one short phrase be divided among more than one syllable."[168]

Because indeed Lord Guido has left these directions of his without examples, since he believed them to be sufficiently obvious, we will explain these things for the very simple as far as our ability permits. The short phrases are indeed made of one repercussion of sound when they are single—that is, either a *virgula* or a *iacens*—or when

duplices aut[o] triplices in eiusdem sunt soni repercussione. "Tum[p] duorum aut plurium conexione[q] fiant." Duorum aut plurium sonorum conexione fiunt omnes neumę, exceptis prescriptis: duę [r]duabus [r] [s]tres tribus [s] Et alię de amplioribus quas modo preterimus. "Semper tamen aut in numero uocum aut in ratione tenorum[t] alterutrum conferantur, nunc ęquę ęquis." Ęquę ęquis conferuntur cum simplices simplicibus, duplices duplicibus, triplices triplicibus opponuntur. Et hoc "aut in numero uocum" ut in ęquis [u]duę duabus, tres tribus[u] conferantur. In duplis duę uni .[v] Quatuor duabus .[w] Triplę simplis ;[x] "aut in ratione tenorum." Tenor dicitur mora uocis qui in ęquis est si quatuor uocibus duę comparantur, et quantum sit numerus duarum minor, tantum earum mora sit maior. Vnde in antiquioribus antiphonariis utrisque c. t. m. reperimus persepe, quę celeritatem,[y] tarditatem, mediocritatem innuunt.

Antiquitus fuit magna circumspectio non solum cantus inuentoribus, sed etiam ipsis cantoribus, ut quidlibet[z] proportionaliter et inuenirent[a] et canerent. Quę consideratio iam dudum obiit, immo sepulta est. Nunc[b] tantum sufficit ut aliquid dulcisonum comminiscamur non attendentes dulciorem [c]collationis iubilationem. "Item ut more uersuum distinctiones [d]ęquales sint,"[d] sicut in bene procuratis cantibus inuenimus quos metricos dicere possumus ut[e] *Non uos relinquam* [f] .i. *orphanos alleluia, uado*[c] *et uenio*[g] .ii. *ad uos alleluia, et gaudebit*[h] .iii. *cor uestrum alleluia*. Talis consideratio similis est rethorico colori qui compar dicitur, "qui constat fere ex pari numero syllabarum." "Hoc non de numeratione[i] [j]nostra fiet" dicit Tullius. "Nam id puerile est, sed tantum afferet usus." "Et aliquotiens[k] eedem repetitę uel parua mutatione[j] uariatę." Diuersitatem neumarum ostendit quia "similitudo mater

[o] uel M_3
[p] Cum M_3
[q] sonorum conexione M_3
[r–r] tribus M_3RSSf; *neumes om.* M_3
[s–s] *neumes om.* M_3
[t] tonorum M_3R
[u–u] *neumes om.* M_3
[v] *neumes om.* M_3
[w] *neumes om.* M_3
[x] *neumes om.* M_3
[y] celeritem *corr.* celeritatem *R*
[z] quilibet M_3R
[a] inuerent *corr.* inuenirent *R*
[b] Nunc autem M_3
[c–c] [[tionis iubelationem . . . Vado]] *lacking in Sf owing to later trimming*
[d–d] sint equales M_3
[e] ut antiphona M_3
[f] .i. *om.* M_3
[g] ueniam M_3R; .ii. *om.* M_3
[h] .iii. *om.* M_3
[i] murmuracione *R*
[j–j] *om.* M_3 *but supplied by text hand in bottom margin with reference*
[k] aliquoties *S*

in the same sound the repercussions are doubled or tripled. "When by two or more they are joined": all the shorter phrases are made by the connection of two or more sounds, except these prescribed—two by two, three by three, and others by more, which just now we pass over. "Always correspond to each other either in number of notes or in the relationship of their attenuations, now equally": the correspondence is equal when single is juxtaposed with single, double with double, or triple with triple. And this "or in the number of notes" so that when equal, double corresponds to double or triple to triple. When double, double corresponds to single or four to two. Triple to single or in the "relationship of the durations."[169] The attenuation is called a pause on a note, which is in equal proportion if four notes are being compared to two; and as much as the number of two is less, that much greater will be the delay on these notes. Whence in the more ancient antiphonaries we very often discover each of the letters c. t. m.,[170] which indicate a fast pace, a slow pace, or a moderate pace.

There was in ancient times a great circumspection not only among the inventors of chants but even among the cantors themselves so that anyone at all might compose and sing proportionally. This concern died out long ago—indeed, it is buried. Now, it suffices merely that we may devise something sweet sounding, not attending to the sweeter joy of the proportional combination. "Also, that the longer phrases should be of the same length, as in the manner of verse,"[171] such as we find in well-managed chant, which we can call metrical, as in *Non vos relinquam orphanos alleluia, vado et venio ad vos alleluia, et gaudebit cor vestrum alleluia*.[172] Such is considered to be similar to the rhetorical *color* that is called *compar*, "which consists of a virtually equal number of syllables."[173] To do this "we shall actually not count them" says Tully, "for that is childish, but only practice will bring it about."[174] "And sometimes be repeated the same or modified by some slight change."[175] This shows the diversity of the shorter phrases, since "likeness is the mother

est sacietatis" ut Tullius dicit. Exemplum sit istud. Eedem repetitę: *In Iherusalem* .[l] Vel parua mutatione uariatę:[m] *Putres suscitat mortuos membraque curat debilia, fluxum sanguinis constrinxit et satiauit quinque de panibus* [n]*quina milia.*[n] "Et cum perpulchrę[o] fuerint duplicatę" quasi efexegesis est et expositio priorum tamquam si diceret: "Eędem" sint "repetitę" sed tunc "cum perpulchrę fuerint." "Et quę aliquotiens eędem transformentur[p] per modos" ut[q] [r]*Festum nunc celebre.*[r] Semitonius est utrimque sed diuersi modi qualitatesque.[s] "Similes[t] intensę et remissę" ut [u]*Qui cogitauerunt.*[u] "Item ut reciprocata neuma[v] eadem uia redeat" qua uenerat ut [w]*Sidera Maria continens arua.*[w] "Item ut qualem ambitum[x] uel lineam una facit saliendo ab acutis, talem altera inclinata e regione opponat respondendo a grauibus" ut [y]*O admirabile.*[y] "Item aliquando una syllaba unam uel plures habeat neumas" ut [z]*Laudes Deo.*[z] "Aliquando una neuma plures diuidatur in syllabas" ut *Christi pugna.*[a]

Dicit item domnus Guido: "*Motus motui tum erit prepositus, id est in superioribus*[b] *positus; tum appositus, id est cum in eandem uocem unius finis erit alteriusque principium; tum interpositus, id est quando unus*[c] *motus infra alium positus et minus est grauis et minus*[d] *acutus; tum commixtus, id est partim interpositus partimque suppositus.* Quorum exempla sicut priorum ne simplicitas laboret aliquorum proponemus. Motus motui erit prepositus ut [e]*Clarum decus,*[e] appositus ut [f]*Ecce ego mitto uos,*[f] interpositus ut,[g] [h]*Nascetur nobis paruulus et uocabitur*[h] commixtus ut [i]*Vt a*[i] *dextris patris qui sedet spiritum mittat nobis semper.*"

[l] *neumes om. M3;* S; Sf
[m] uarietate *M3*
[n–n] quina milia *Sf*
[o] pulchre *M3*
[p] transformantur *marked for correction to* transformentur *M3*
[q] ut ymnus *M3*
[r–r] Festum nunc celebre magnaque gaudia *M3;* Festum nunc celebre *Sf*
[s] qualitatisque *RSf*
[t] Similis *R*
[u–u] *neumes om. M3;* Qui cogitaue *Sf*
[v] neumata *R*
[w–w] Sidera maria continens arua simul et uniuersa condita *M3;* Sidera Maria continens arua *S;* Sidera Maria continens arua *Sf*
[x] habitum *M3RSSf*
[y–y] O admirabile commertium *M3;* O admirabile *Sf*
[z–z] *neumes om. M3*
[a] pugna *Sf*
[b] simplicioribus *M3*
[c] unius *S*
[d] minus est *M3*
[e–e] *neumes om. M3;* Clarum decus *S;* Clarum decus *Sf*
[f–f] *neumes om. M3;* Ecce ego mitto uos *SSf*
[g] *om. M3*
[h–h] *neumes om. M3;* Nascetur nobis paruulus et uocabitur *S;* Nascetur nobis paruulus et uocabitur *Sf*
[i–i] [ ] us A *M3;* a *RSF*

of sufficiency," as Tully says.[176] Here is an example of being "repeated the same": *In Iherusalem.*[177] "Or modified by some slight change": *Putres suscitat mortuos membraque curat debilia, fluxum sanguinis constrinxit et satiauit quinque de panibus quina milia.*[178] "And if they are particularly beautiful they should be duplicated" like in the exegesis and exposition of the earlier texts, as though he might say: the "repetitions" are "the same," but then "if they are particularly beautiful."[179] "And at other times let them be transformed by the modes,"[180] as in *Festum nunc celebre.*[181] There is a semitone in both, but of different mode and quality. "Similar extension and remission,"[182] as in *Qui cogitaverunt.*[183] "Also a returning short phrase may come back by the same way it went,"[184] as in *Sidera maria continens arva.*[185] "Also that when a short phrase crosses a certain place or line by jumping down from the high notes, another may respond similarly in the opposite direction from the low notes,"[186] as in *O admirabile.*[187] "Also one syllable may be spread over one or more short phrases,"[188] as in *Laudes Deo.*[189] "And other times one short phrase may be divided among more than one syllable,"[190] as in *Christi pugna.*[191]

Lord Guido also says:[192] "*One melodic figure will either be placed over another—that is, among higher notes; or beside another—that is, when the final note of one will be the beginning of the other; or within another—that is, when one melodic figure is placed below another, and is less low and less high; or be mixed—that is, partly within and partly below another.*[193] We shall propose examples of these, as we did earlier, lest anyone's simplicity should have to labor. Let one melodic figure be placed above another as in *Clarum decus,*[194] beside another as in *Ecce ego mitto vos,*[195] within another as in *Nascetur nobis parvulus et vocabitur,*[196] or mixed as in *Vt a dextris patris qui sedet spiritum mittam nobis sanctum.*"[197]

[90.] [a]"De opportunitate motus qui dicitur prepositus et quod tantum sit ascensionis.[a]

Pręposítus erit opportunior si prior surgat per tonum et intermisso semiditono[b] prepositus iterum surgat per tonum, quia ita ambo in diapente constant ut[c] [d]*Clarum decus*[d]; aut per ditonum tendens prepositus ad principium prioris per diapente resultet, quia considerationem proportionis, id est collationis habere debemus in illis. Vnde pręposítus[e] per diatesseron et diapente non est formandus. Si autem prior surgat per semiditonum[f] interposito tono prepositus scandat per tonum, ut ita[g] principium eius et finis ad principium prioris per diatesseron et diapente, ad finem autem eius per tonum ditonumque resultet. Aliis modis minus erit commode, cum proportionis commoditas[h] et concinentia non consideratur. Idem quoque motus[i] tantum fit ascensione."

[91.] [a]"De commoditate apposita et quod tam ascendendo quam descendendo fit.[a]

Appositus[b] ut ascensioni ita est obnoxius et descensioni ut[c] [d]*Ecce ego mitto, Et dicent gloria tibi Domine.*[d] Item intensus [e]*Benedic Domine.*[e] Qui motus honestior erit si in proto ita fiat intensio, ut si prior surgat per tonum, appositus ascendat aut per semiditonum[f] trocheicum, id est cuius longum[g] toni spatium breue semitonii[h] precedit, quia semiditonus[i] est quidam trocheius, id est ex longa[j] et breui, quidam iambicus ex breui et [k]longa ut[k] .D.F.E.G. Ditonus uniformis est tantum spondeicus aut per diatessaron seu diapente. Sed diatessarontice melius ascendit appositus, quia eius principium et finis proportionaliter conferetur principio et fini precedentis. Finis principio et fini per diatessaron et diapente, principium fini per tonum. Sed diapenticus appositus tantum per finem fini precedentis respondet[l] per diapente, aut si prior surgit

[90.] [a–a] *om.* M_3S
[b] semitono M_3SSf; semitonio *R*
[c] ut ymnus M_3
[d–d] *neumes om.* M_3; Clarum decus *S*; Clarum decus *Sf*
[e] prepositus <u>prepositus</u> M_3
[f] semitonum M_3SSf; semitonium *R*
[g] *superscript* M_3
[h] commoditasque *R*
[i] modus M_3Sf
[91.] [a–a] *om.* M_3S; d<escendendo fit> *Sf*
[b] Oppositus *S*
[c] ut antiphonae M_3
[d–d] Ecce ego mitto, | Et dicent gloria tibi domine *Sf*
[e–e] Benedic domine *Sf. Sf end here, the rest of the text having been cut off.*
[f] semitonum M_3S; semitonium *R*
[g] longi M_3
[h] semitoni *S*
[i] semitonus M_3RS
[j] longo M_3RS
[k–k] longo *S*; vel ut *marked underneath with a line R*
[l] respondit *R*

90. "Concerning the effectiveness of the movement that is called *prepositus*, and that it merely pertains to ascent.

Prepositus will be more effective if the first phrase rises by a tone and, after a gap of a semiditone, *prepositus* again rises by a tone—since then both constitute a *diapente*, as in *Clarum decus*. Or if the first phrase rises by a ditone and *praepositus* results by *diapente* in comparison to its beginning, since we ought to consider proportion—that is, combination—in these things. Hence *prepositus* is not to be formed by *diatessaron* and *diapente*. If, however, the first phrase rises by a semiditone, then after a gap of a tone, *prepositus* should climb by a tone; thus the beginning and the end of the *praepositus* result by *diatessaron* and *diapente* in comparison to the beginning of the previous phrase, but by tone and ditone in comparison to the end of it. By other methods this will be less effective, since the effectiveness and elegance of proportion are not considered. This movement also relates only to ascent."[198]

91. "Concerning the convenience of *appositus* and that it may occur both ascending and descending.

Appositus is subject both to ascent as to descent, as in *Ecce ego mitto* and *Et dicent gloria tibi domine.*[199] Also extension in *Benedic Domine.*[200] In the case of *protus* this movement will be more honorable if its extension is made so that when the first phrase rises by tone the *appositus* will ascend by a trochaic semiditone—that is, a semiditone in which the long measure of the tone precedes the short measure of the semitone; for the semiditone is sometimes trochaic—that is, long followed by short as in .D.F.—and sometimes iambic—that is, short followed by long as in .E.G. The uniform ditone is only spondaic, whether by *diatessaron* or *diapente*. But *appositus* rises better by *diatessaron*, because its beginning and end relates proportionally to the beginning and end of the preceding phrase. Its end to the beginning and end by the *diatessaron* and *diapente*; its beginning to the end by the tone. But in *appositus* by *diapente* the end responds to the end of the previous phrase only by *diapente*; thus if the first phrase rises

per trocheium semiditonum[m] uel iambicum, appositus scandat per ditonum, qui duo modi diapente componunt. Posset secundum iudicium auditus prior per ditonum appositus per diatessaron surgere: sed principium precedentis finisque[n] sequentis nulla coniungitur proportione. Posset e contrario prior per ditonum appositus scandere per semiditonum[o] proportionaliter, quippe cum in diapason[p] ambo concludantur, sed integre non est euphonię."

[92.] [a]De interposito.[a]

"Interpositus necessario fiet intensus et remissus. In diatesseron tono semitonioue. In diapente autem ditono, semiditono,[b] tono, semitonio, quia diatesseron in medio aut tonum habet aut semitonium. Diapente uero ditonum[c] uel semiditonum,[d] siue tonum seu semitonium."

[93.] [a]"De conuenientia motus qui dicitur commixtus.[a]

Commixtus motus uenerabilior est omnibus. Ille autem duabus diapente diatesseronue[b] potest conuinculari susum et iusum et ditono et semiditono;[c] sed ita ut semiditonus[d] iambicus ascendat[e] non[f] descendat nisi si[g] duo semiditoni[h] conuinculentur: quia tunc uterque semiditonus[i] et trocheicus et iambicus intendentur remittenturque conuenientius."

[94.] [a]De distinctionibus cantuum et cur finales dicantur ac superiores.[a]

Quamuis principia presertim tamen fines distinctionum sunt considerandę quę [b]precipue debent finales[b] repetere, ut domnus Guido dogmatizat dicens: "Item ut ad principalem uocem, id est finalem pene omnes distinctiones currant." Hoc tamen rarius inuenitur quam crebrius. Inuenitur in hac

[m] semitonum *M_3RS; Textual misordering in R, fol. 40r, line 14. Continuation of chapter 91 on fol. 23v, line 16.*

[n] finis *S*

[o] semitonum *M_3S;* semitonum *corr.* semiditonum *R*

[p] diapente *M_3RS*

[92.] [a–a] *om. M_3S*

[b] semitono *M_3S;* semitono *corr.* semitonio *R*

[c] uel ditonum *M_3R*

[d] semitonum *M_3S;* semitonum *corr.* semiditonum *in later hand R*

[93.] [a–a] *om. M_3S*

[b] uel dyatessaron *M_3*

[c] semitono *M_3RS*

[d] semitonus *M_3RS*

[e] ascendat ascendat *S*

[f] et non *M_3*

[g] *om. M_3S*

[h] semitonii *M_3;* semitoni *RS*

[i] semitonus *M_3RS*

[94.] [a–a] *om. M_3S*

[b–b] finales precipue debent *M_3*

by trochaic or iambic semiditone, the *appositus* climbs by ditone, since both possibilities constitute a *diapente*. According to the judgement of the hearer, the first phrase can rise by ditone and the *appositus* by *diatessaron*: but the beginning of the first phrase and the end of the ensuing one will not be joined proportionally. It is possible, on the contrary, to raise the first figure by ditone and the *appositus* proportionally by a semiditone, since they both result in a diapason; but it is not entirely euphonius."[201]

92. Concerning *interpositus*.

"*Interpositus* necessarily involves extension and remission: in the *diatessaron* by tone or semitone, since the *diatessaron* has either a tone or a semitone in the middle. In the *diapente*, however, by the ditone, semiditone, tone, or semitone. For the *diapente* has either a ditone or a semiditone in the middle, or either a tone or a semitone."[202]

93. "Concerning the convenience of the movement that is called *commixtus*.

The movement of *commixtus* is the most venerable of all. It alone, by means of either a *diapente* or *diatessaron*, is able to connect rising or falling by a ditone or semiditone. For while an iambic semiditone may ascend, it may not descend unless two semiditones are joined together: then both the trochaic and iambic semiditone can be extended and remitted more conveniently."[203]

94. Concerning the phrases of chants and why the *finales* and the *superiores* are so called.

Although the beginnings of phrases are especially requiring of consideration, nevertheless the ends must also be considered because they particularly ought to reclaim the *finales*, as Lord Guido laid down by saying, "Also almost all the phrases proceed to the principal note—that is, the final."[204]

antiphona: [c]*Natiuitas tua Dei genitrix uirgo* , *Gaudium annuntiauit uniuerso mundo* 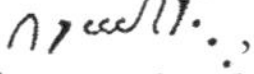, *Ex te enim ortus est sol iusticię Christus Deus noster* 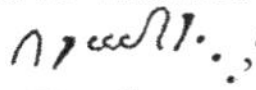, [d]*Et confundens mortem donauit nobis uitam sempiternam* 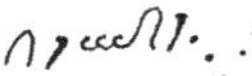.[c] Finales uoces triplici ex causa nuncupari uidentur: et quod finiunt legitimum autentorum ascensum,[e] et quod omnem determinant cantum et quod in easdem nonnumquam fines distinctionum perueniunt. Ideoque[f] dicimus nonnumquam quia non semper in illas sed in superiores et principia distinctionum pertingunt et fines et in primam sub finalibus in autenticis cantibus, in plagis etiam inferius. Superiores autem dicuntur, uel quia superiores plagalis cantilenę sunt claues uel quod superius sunt mediatrices autentorum diatesseron et diapente conuincientes, ex hisque autenticam diapason componentes, uel quod superiores sunt a finalibus quam finales a grauibus aut excellentes a superioribus.

[95.] De proti autenti speciebus diapente et diatesseron utilibus melodiam comminiscentibus.

Pręmissis modulationis utilitatibus cum domno Guidone nobis communibus, quia sua non [a]solum uerba[a] exposuimus, sed etiam commodiores motuum species quas ipse penitus reticuit proposuimus, ad singularia dona iubilandi nobis diuinitus concessa ueniamus.

Solum protum autentum sumamus nobis in exemplum ut modulandi commoditatem in allis modis reperire non desperemus quam in huius experiamus speciebus.

Protus autentus, id est primus tonus, quinque species diatesseron includit: unam primam formalem, unam secundam formalem, unam terciam naturalem, unam terciam formalem, unam primam naturalem. Quarum quinque unaqueque tres habet mutationes: saltatricem, continuam uel spissam, ternariam. Saltatrix duas ultimas tangit chordas, continua cunctas, ternaria tres. Saltatrix et spissa duplices sunt intendendo et remittendo. Ternaria quadrupla, utpote duplex intendendo, duplex remittendo. Quia quinque species sunt diatesseron, quarum quelibet[b] duas habet saltatrices, duas continuas, dicamus quinquies quatuor uel quater quinque uiginti sunt. Quoniam autem ternaria est quadrupla, multiplicemus quatuor per quinque et item erunt uiginti quę iunctę prioribus quadraginti componunt. In eodem quoque

[c–c] *Neumes only in RS. For* Ex te enim ortus est sol iusticię Christus Deus noster *and* Et confundens mortem donauit nobis uitam sempiternam *S has* 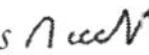

[d] *M_3 adds* Qui soluens maledictionem dedit | benedictionem, *which RS omit from the example.*

[e] *Remainder of M_3 lacking*

[f] Ideo *R*

[95.] [a–a] uerba solum *marked with superscript* b *and* a *for transposition R*

[b] quamlibet *S*

This, however, is rarely rather than frequently found to be the case. It is found in this antiphon: *Nativitas tua Dei genetrix virgo, gaudium annuntiavit universo mundo, ex te enim ortus est sol iusticiae Christus Deus noster, et confundens mortem donavit nobis vitam sempiternam.*[205] The notes of the *finales* seem to be so called for three reasons: because they end the legitimate ascent of the authentics, because they end every chant, and because the phrases sometimes reach their end in them. On that account we say that sometimes the beginnings and ends of the phrases do not always pertain to them but to the *superiores*, or to the first note below the *finales* in authentic chants and even lower in plagal ones. The *superiores*, therefore, are so called either because they are the keys to plagal chant, or because they mediate the binding together of the authentic *diatessarons* and *diapentes* out of which the authentic *diapasons* are put together; or because they are to the *finales* as the *finales* are to the *graves*, or the *excellentes* are to the *superiores*.

95. Concerning the useful species of *diapente* and *diatessaron* in contriving the melody of authentic *protus*.

Having set forth the useful ideas relating to melody that Lord Guido has shared with us, not only expounding his own words but also proposing more convenient types of movement about which he has kept thoroughly quiet, let us come to the special gifts of singing praises granted us by heaven.

We take as an example only authentic *protus* so that we may not despair of finding convenient types of melody in the other modes just as in these species in which we are experimenting.

Authentic *protus*—that is, the first tone—comprises five species of *diatessaron*: one formal first, one formal second, one natural third, one formal third, and one natural first.[206] Each of these five has three permutations: the leap, the continuation or the step, and the ternary. The leap touches the two outer notes, the continuation all of them, and the ternary three of them. The leap and the step are duplicated by virtue of extension and remission.[207] The ternary is quadrupled since there are two forms by extension and two by remission.[208] Since there are five species of *diatessaron*, each of which has two leaps and two continuations, we may say that five times four or four times five makes twenty. Since, however, the ternary is quadrupled, we may multiply four by five and again there will be twenty, which having been connected to the former ones makes forty. Since each of these

proto quatuor sunt species diapente. Quarum cum unaqueque duas habeat saltatrices, duas spissas, tres quaternarias, tres ternarias, multiplicatę per quatuor quadraginta fiunt. Quę totidem prioribus copulatę complent octoginta mutationes absque his quę in eodem tropo fieri possunt: ditono, semiditono,[c] tono, semitonio. Cognito numero principalium mutationum in proto, perpendendum est in primis, quia neumę ex predictis mutationibus natę non sunt omnes in eadem generositate, sed quedam primę, quedam secundę dignitatis sunt et tercię. Ex his generosiores ad olorinas musarum choreas sunt admittendę, cęterę non orpheis sed tytiris[d] sunt relinquendę. Omnes saltatrices laudabiles sed tamen nobis generosiores uidentur quam longobardis. Illi enim spissiori nos rariori cantu delectamur. Prima et secunda et quarta spissa diatesseron species intensa et remissa bene sonat sed tercia surdius. Ex eodem genere spissitudinis quarta species formalis in diapente, et prima ac[e] quarta naturalis satis sunt euphonię et intensę et remissę. Secunda uero et tercia propter innominati[f] tritoni raucedinem melibeis et ululis delegentur, excepta saltatrice quę in omnibus est ęqualis, nisi quod inest differentia grauitatis et acuminis. Ternaria diapente triplex est et aliquantulę sonoritatis. Ternaria diatesseron duplex est et minus sonora.[g] Reprobę sunt secundę et tercię species diapente excepta saltatrice. Vtiles colligamus ut earum numerum sciamus. Reprobatis de secunda et tercia specie diapente quatuor spissis sex quaternariis octo ternariis, de quinque speciebus diatesseron decem ternariis, utpote duabus de unaqueque[h] et insimul collectis duo de triginta de octaginta abiciemus et remanebunt quinquaginta due habiles cantilenas comminiscentibus et opportunę.

[96.] De uaria [a]neumarum oppositione.[a]

Interdum saltatrix contra saltatricem, spissa contra spissam, quaternaria contra quaternariam et cęterę contra equiuocales sunt constituendę. Interdum uariandę, ut spissa contra saltatricem uel quaternariam uel ternariam opponatur,[b] uel spissa diapente contra diatessaron, ut laudabilis similitudo uel dissimilitudo discernere scientibus commendetur; qui non solum hoc sed neumarum proportionem requirant ut triplex sit suauitas: una cantionis quę comprobetur ab auriculis, secunda proportionis uocum et neumarum ac distinctionum quę delectatio est rationis, tercia pulchrę similitudinis ac dissimilitudinis sex consonantiarum.

[c] semitono *RS*
[d] extiris *R*
[e] et *corr.* ac *R*
[f] inominati *RS*
[g] son[a>o]ra *S*
[h] unaquaque *S*
[96.] [a–a] oppositione neumarum *R*
[b] ponantur *S*

has two leaps, two steps, three quaternaries, and three ternaries, this multiplied by four becomes forty. Having been joined together with the previous ones, this completes eighty permutations without those made in the same trope by the ditone, the semiditone, the tone, and the semitone. The number of the principal mutations in *protus* having been ascertained, it must be considered in the first place that the melodic figures born of the aforesaid permutations are not all of the same nobility: some are of the first dignity, some of the second, and some of the third. Of these the more noble must be admitted to the swan-like choirs of the muses;[209] the others are to be left not to the Orphean but to the Tityran choirs.[210] All the leaps are praiseworthy, but nevertheless seem more noble to us than to the Lombards. They delight in the stepwise motion, whereas we prefer the more expansive chant.[211] Extension and remission by step in the first, second, and fourth of the species of *diatessaron* sound well, but in the third sound more dull. From the same genus of stepwise motion the fourth formal species in the *diapente* and the first and fourth natural species are most euphonious, both by extension and remission. The second and the third, however, on account of the hoarseness of the unmentionable tritone, are relegated to Meliboeuses and screech owls,[212] except for the leap which is equal in all, save for that which is inherent in the difference of low and high position. There are three ternaries in the *diapente*, which are of quite moderate sonority.[213] There are two ternaries in the *diatessaron* and they are of less sonority. The second and third species of *diapente* are disapproved of, excepting the leap. Let us gather together what is useful, so that we may know their number. Having rejected the four steps, six quaternaries, and eight ternaries from the second and third species of *diapente*, as well as ten ternaries from the five species of *diatessaron*, and having collected both lots together, we shall discard twenty-eight from eighty and there will remain fifty-two workable and appropriate for contriving chants.

96. Concerning the various juxtapositions of musical figures.

Sometimes a leap against a leap, a step against a step, a quaternary against a quaternary, and others against their equivalents must occur. Sometimes varied forms are juxtaposed, such as a step against a leap, a quaternary, or a ternary, or a stepwise *diapente* against a *diatessaron*, so that by discerning praiseworthy similarity or dissimilarity the chant may be commended to the learned. They require not only this but also a proportion in the figures, so that the sweetness may be threefold: first, in singing that may be proved to the ears; second, in the proportion of the notes and figures as well as the phrases, which is delectation to the reason; third, in the beautiful similarity and dissimilarity of the six melodic intervals.

[97.] De nobilitate et ignobilitate consonantiarum.

Sex consonantiarum tres nobiles tres sunt ignobiles. Nobiles: diapente, diatesseron, tonus quia originem et parentelam suam profiteri possunt quippe cum hęc sesqualterę, hęc sesquitercię, hęc sesquioctauę sit proportionis. [a]Ignobiles sunt ditonus, semiditonus,[b] semitonium, cum incertę sint gradationis,[c] id est proportionis.[a] Vnde etiam [d]credimus eas[d] esse minus dulcisonas.

[98.] De consideratione constitutiuarum[a] partium diatesseron et diapente.

Aliquotiens considerationem constitutiuarum[b] habeamus partium in diatesseron et diapente, aliquotiens specierum suarum, nonnumquam etiam interpositionis minorum consonantiarum. Constituiuę partes sunt diatesseron tonus et semiditonus,[c] uel ditonus et semitonium. Interdum partes preponamus interdum postponamus. Et si una uice preponamus uel postponamus istas alia uice illas. Aliquando quoque cingamus diatesseron partibus ipsa in medio uice dominę constituta. Constitutiuę partes preponuntur sequitur ipsa diatesseron in hunc modum: *Ecce ego mitto uos sicut.* Pręponitur tonus intensus: Ecce. Preponitur semiditonus[d] intensus et remissus: Ego. Sequitur diatesseron spissa per remissionem saltatrix per intensionem: Mitto uos sicut. Ambę partes diatesseron preponuntur tonus semiditonus.[e] Semiditonum[f] ditonus sequente diatesseron ut in hac *Rogo ergo te Pater ut.* Interdum totum preponitur partibus diuidendum ut hec *Surrexerunt.* Hęc consideratio non est inter contempnendas, cum in illa dialectica[g] luceat qualitas. Nam partium compositio totum facit, totius resolutio partes ostendit. Eadem obseruatio debet esse in diapente. Partes eius sunt tonus, diatesseron, semiditonus,[h] ditonus. Quibus premissis ipsa sequitur e[i] uestigio ut uenientibus sagmis domini sperantur. Hoc dicimus non ut ita semper inueniatur sed ut ita fieri oporteat naturaliter cum sine partibus totum non esse nec positis possit abesse.

[99.] De contubernio diatesseron et diapente.

Aliquotiens diatesseron et diapente commilitent ita ut si altera saltatrix intendatur altera spissa remittatur, aut si hęc quaternaria remittatur hęc ternaria intendatur. Tum diapente sibimet conferatur ut si hęc surgat spissa illa deponatur saltatrix uel quaternaria uel ternaria. Interdum per commixtum motum quem

[97.] [a–a] *om. R*
[b] semitonus *S*
[c] generati||tionis *S*
[d–d] eas credimus *R*
[98.] [a] constitutiuorum *RS*
[b] constitutiuorum *R*
[c] semitonus *RS*
[d] semitonus *RS*
[e] semitonus *RS*
[f] Semitonum *S;* Semitonium *R*
[g] dilectica *S*
[h] semitonus *RS*
[i] *om. R*

97. Concerning the nobility and the ignobility of the intervals.

Of the six intervals, three are noble and three ignoble. The noble ones are the *diapente*, the *diatessaron*, and the tone, since they are able to profess their own origin and parentage, and are, of course, in proportion with the sesquialter, the sesquitertia, and the sesquioctave. The ignoble consonances are the ditone, semiditone, and semitone, since they are of uncertain gradation—that is, proportion. Hence we also believe them to be less pleasing sounds.

98. Concerning the consideration of the parts that make up the *diatessaron* and *diapente*.

At various times we may consider the parts that make up the *diatessaron* and the *diapente*, at various times their species, sometimes even the interposition of the minor consonances. The parts that make up the *diatessaron* are the tone and the semiditone, or the ditone and the semitone. Sometimes we place these parts before and sometimes afterwards. And if on one occasion we were to place one before, on another occasion we might place one afterwards. Not infrequently also we surround the *diatessaron* with its constitutive parts while it itself maintains its place of lordship in the middle. The constitutive coming first, the *diatessaron* itself follows in this manner: *Ecce ego mitto vos sicut.*[214] A tone by extension precedes: *Ecce*. Then a semiditone by extension and remission precedes: *ego*. The *diatessaron* follows stepwise in remission, leaping by extension: *mitto vos sicut*. Both parts of the *diatessaron*—the tone and the semiditone—are placed first. A ditone and semiditone follows a *diatessaron* in *Rogo ergo te pater ut.*[215] Now and then the whole must be placed before the divided parts, as in *Surrexerunt.*[216] This consideration must not be among those that are despised since its quality shines in its logic. For the composition of the parts makes the whole and the resolution of the whole displays the parts. The same observation should be made in the *diapente*. Its parts are the tone, *diatessaron*, semiditone, and ditone. These having been set forward the *diapente* follows in their footsteps as the arrival of the emissary gives hope of the coming of the lord. We say this not that it is always to be found so but that it ought naturally to be made so, since without the parts the whole does not exist, neither can it be absent when they are in place.[217]

99. Concerning the comradeship of the *diatessaron* and the *diapente*.

Sometimes the *diatessaron* and the *diapente* are comrades, so that if one is extended by a leap, the other is remitted by step; or if one is remitted by a quaternary, the other is extended by a ternary. Then each of the species of *diapente* may be brought together, so that if one rises by step or by quaternary the other may fall by leap or by ternary. Now and then they are linked together by *commixtus*,

prelibauimus sibimet conuinculetur. Eodem modo diatesseron. Aliȩ quoque consonantiȩ aut pariter bis deponantur uel simul intendantur seu in commixto concatenentur. Et propter iocunditatem suam species illȩ gemellȩ diatesseron et diapente admodum in quibusdam cantilenis suum ostendunt contubernium.

[100.] De consideratione proportionum in his speciebus.

In his ergo omnibus considerationem proportionis obseruemus ut si diapente saltatrix sit in ista neuma in hac sit uel tonus uel alia saltatrix; siue sit in diapente siue in diatesseron, siue in ditono seu semiditono,[a] ut ȩqua sit responsio. Aut contra saltatricem ponamus aut spissam diatesseron aut diapente quaternariam ut dupla fiat proportio. Aut contra saltatricem constituamus ternaria diatesseron uel diapente aut ditonum semiditonumue[b] spissum ut sesqualtera fiat responsio, ut sine subtili collationis consideratione nihil temere fiat; ignoranterque penes omnes[c] qui histrionibus dulce iubilantibus ueram[d] iubilandi naturam comparationemque penitus ignorantibus admodum dissimiles esse debemus. Omnes saltatrices in omnibus consonantiis ȩqua proportione conferuntur et cum his tonus[e] ac semitonium. Diapente spissa contra sese ȩqua confertur[f] collatione aut contra saltatricem simul et ternariam, aut contra saltatricem simul et ditonum siue semitonum spissum, aut contra tonum siue semitonium cum ditono siue semiditono,[g] aut contra quaternariam et simplicem neumam, aut contra simplicem[h] et quatuor repercussas, aut contra tonum siue semitonium et tres repercussa. Quȩ consonantiȩ ȩqua[i] copulentur proportione pronum est perpendere. Proinde ad aliarum collationem[j] redeamus. Quaternaria ad ternariam ditonum, semiditonum,[k] sesquitercia est; ad tonum autem semitoniumue dupla. Ternaria ditonus semiditonus,[l] sesqualteram faciunt proportionem ad tonum semitoniumue.

[101.] De multiplicitate specierum.

Duplices sunt saltatrix et spissa utpote unam intensionem habentes et remissionem. Quaternaria in diatesseron non est quia non habet nisi quatuor chordas quȩ spissam faciunt. Ternaria in diatesseron octupla est, quadrupla intendendo quadrupla remittendo. Quaternaria in diapente decupla est, quia quinque intenditur quinque modis remittitur. Iam persoluimus quȩ cantilenarum auctoribus non nihil profore credidimus.

[100.] [a] semitono *RS*
[b] semitoniumue *RS*
[c] nos *R*
[d] uerum *R*
[e] tonis *R*
[f] conferuntur *R*
[g] semitono *RS*
[h] unam simplicem *R*
[i] aqua *S*
[j] collatione *R*
[k] semitonum *RS*
[l] semitonus *RS*

which we prefer. Likewise with the *diatessaron*. Other consonances too are correspondingly extended or remitted, or joined together by *commixtus*. And on account of its joyfulness, the species of that twin, *diatessaron* and *diapente*, display comradeship in certain chants to a very great degree.

100. Concerning the consideration of the proportions in these species.

In all these, therefore, we are to be mindful of proportion, so that if a leaping *diapente* is in this figure, a tone or another leap should be in that figure; or it may be by a *diapente*, or a *diatessaron*, or a ditone, or a semiditone, so that the response should be equal. Or against a leap we might place a stepwise *diatessaron* or a *diapente* in quaternary movement so that the proportion will be double. Or against a leaping figure we might fix a *diatessaron* or *diapente* in ternary motion or a stepwise ditone or semiditone to make a sesquialter in response, so that nothing is done rashly or ignorantly without a subtle consideration of proportion; we must be totally unlike all those who rejoice with sweetly rejoicing buffoons, thoroughly ignorant of true nature and proportion. All leaps are to be brought together in all the consonances by equal proportion, and the tones and semitones with them. The stepwise *diapente* is to be brought together in equal relationship against itself or against a leaping and a ternary *diapente* at the same time; or against a leaping *diapente* at the same time and a ditone or a stepwise semitone; or against a tone or a semitone with a ditone or a semiditone; or against a phrase of a quaternary and a single note; or against one single note and four repeated notes; or against a tone or a semitone and three repeated notes. It is easy to perceive that these consonances may be joined in equal proportion. In like manner let us return to another combination. A quaternary to a ternary or a ditone to a semiditone is a sesquitertia; a tone to a semitone is a double proportion. The ternary of the ditone and the semiditone makes the proportion of the sesquialter to the tone and the semitone.

101. Concerning the multiplicity of the species.

Leaping and stepwise motion are duplicated in that they have one extension and one remission. There is no quaternary motion in the *diatessaron* because it only has four notes, which make for stepwise motion. The ternary in the *diatessaron* is eightfold: fourfold in extension, fourfold in remission.[218] The quaternary in the *diapente* is tenfold, since extension is made in five ways and remission in five ways. We have already explained that we have not believed anything useful from the authors of the chants.

[a]Prima species diapente in proto autentico, id est tono primo[a]

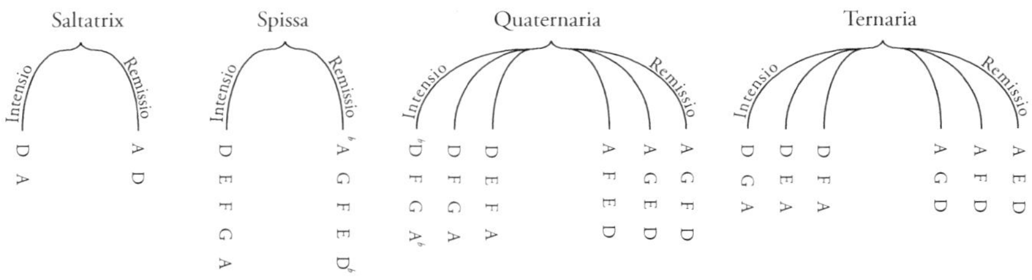

[a–a] *om. R*
[b–b] .A.G.F.E.D. *and* .D.F.G.A. *erased and replaced only with* .A.G.F.E.D. *S*

[a]Diapente species[a]

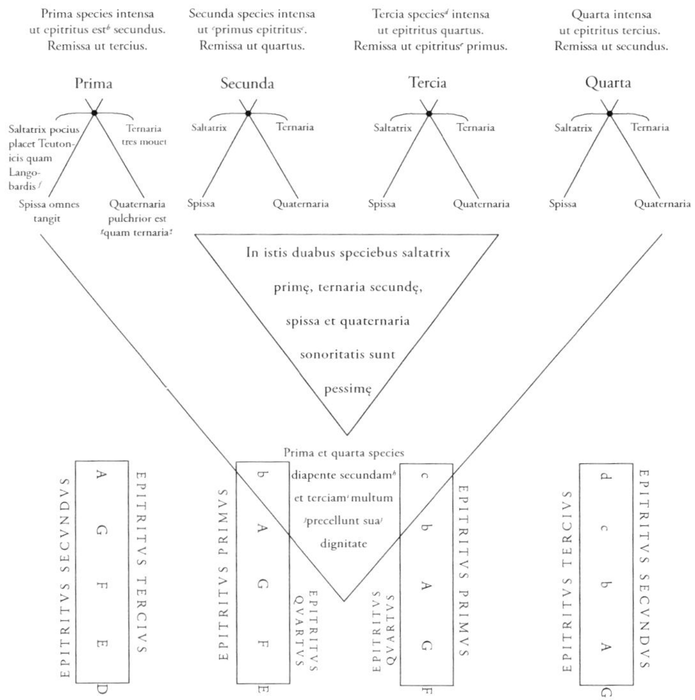

[a–a] *om. D4R*
[b] *om. D4*
[c–c] epitritus primus *D4*
[d] *om. S*
[e] *om. D4*
[f] barbaris *corr.* longobardis *R*
[g–g] omnibus *R*
[h] secunda *S*
[i] tercia *S*
[j–j] sua precellunt *D4*

Diagram 6.

The first species of *diapente* in authentic *protus*, that is the first tone

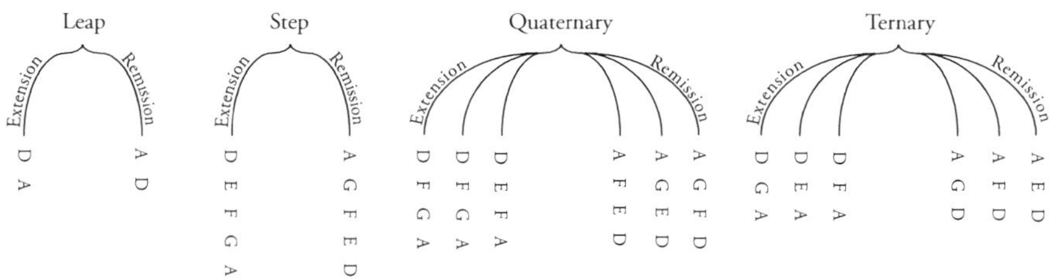

Diagram 7.

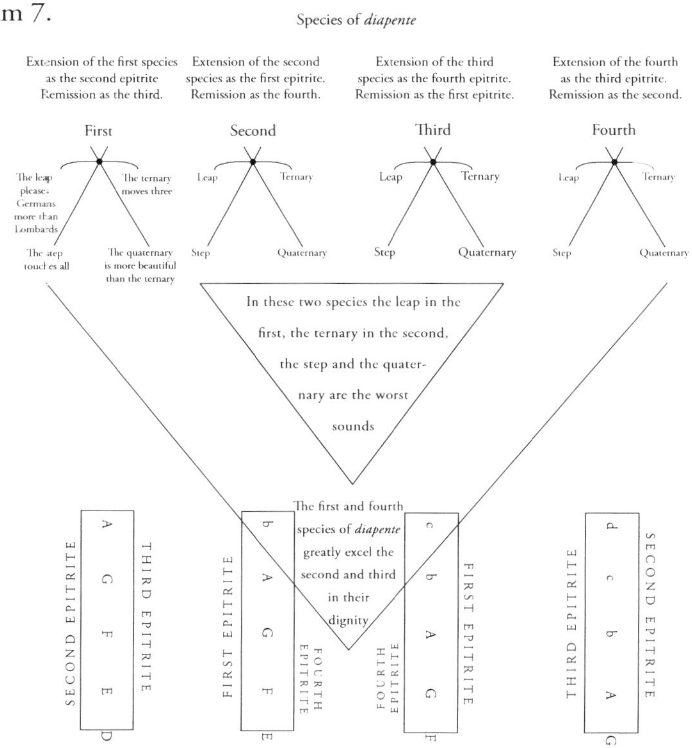

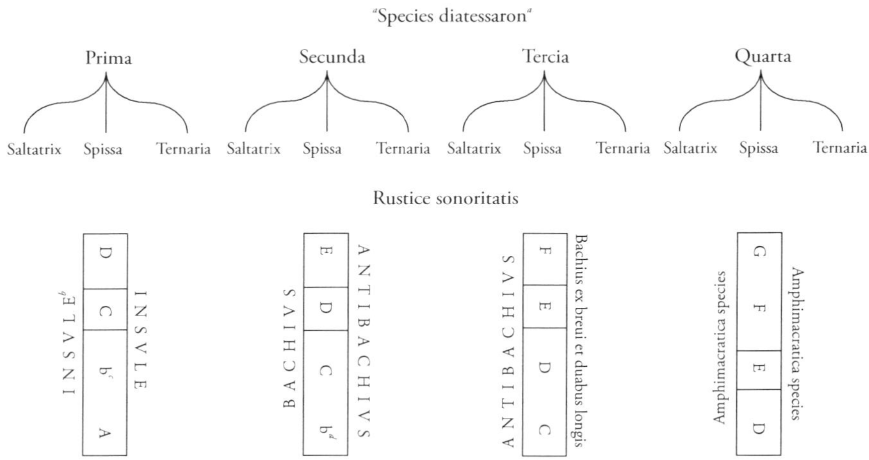

[a–a] *om. D4R*
[b] *om. D4*
[c] .B. *D4*
[d] .B. *D4*

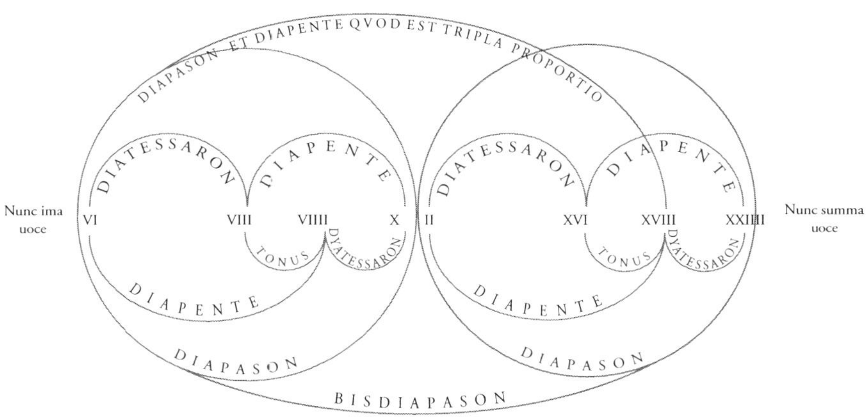

Diagram 8.

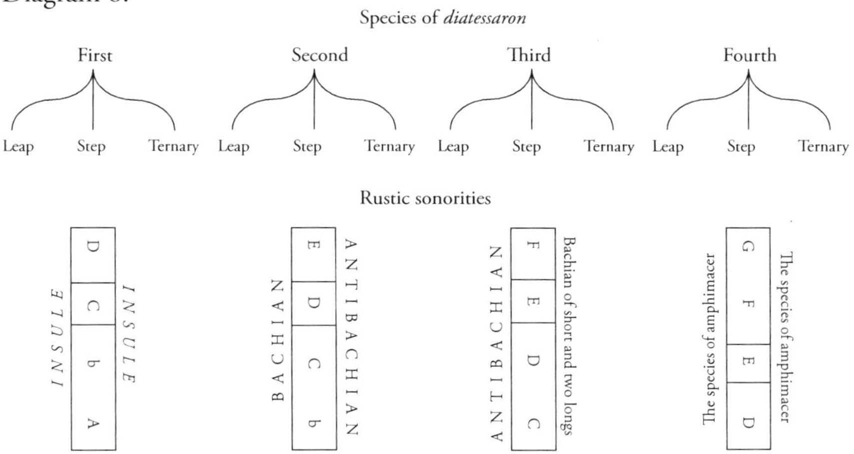

Diagram 9.

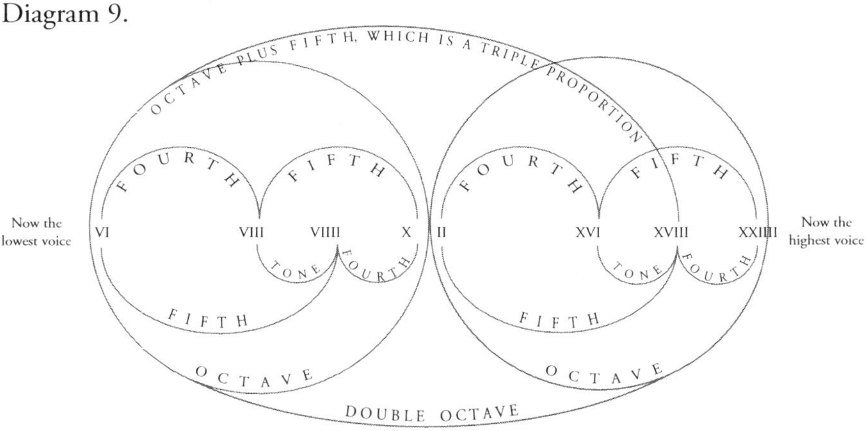

[a]Inter quas chordas et litteras quelibet sit consonantia[a]

Istam figuram sine inspectione memoriter[b] debemus scire ut iubilare possimus si ipsis forte litteris aliquis[c] ignotus[d] [e]nobis neumetur[e] cantus. Et ut

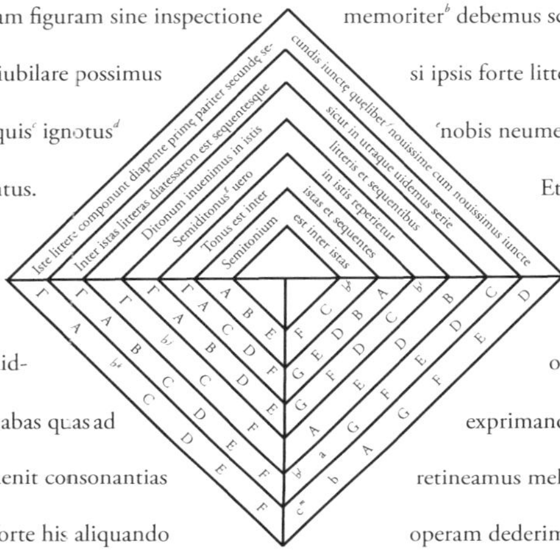

Guid- onis syllabas quas ad exprimandas inuenit consonantias retineamus melius si forte his aliquando operam dederimus.

[a–a] *om. R;* Inter quas chordas { } *S*
[b] memeriter *W5*
[c] aliquius *S*
[d] ignotur *W5*
[e–e] neumetur nobis *W5*
[f] et quelibet *R*
[g] Semitonus *RS*
[h] .B. *RW5*
[i] .B. *RW5*
[j] .B. *R;* synemmenon .B. *W5*
[k] .B. *RW5*
[l] .B. *R; om. S*
[m] *om. S*

[102.] [a]De caprea repeticio commendationis.[a]

Capream domine quam uobis obtuli in uestram commendo gratiam ut[b] ipsa natura uestrę experientię commendet eam. Euidentem troporum diuisionem ostendit, propter quadripertita penes modernos laudem promeruit. Sed si ipsa non naturaliter hoc faciens est gratiosa, caprea naturaliter idem conficiens non sit exosa. Si quadripertita in unam lineam omnes contra naturam monochordi conferens graues laudetur, nostra caprea in unam iuxta monochordi constitutionem colligens easdem non uituperetur. Quadripertita quarta grauium prima finalium quod primitiua dispositio renuit longe diuisit, nostra caprea collegit. Si autem illam peruersa diuisio commendet, istam naturalis collectio non condempnet. Si quadripertita protum acutissimum tetrardum faciens grauissimum celeberrima sit omnibus, capream non obscuret penitus, quod utique[c] naturalem grauitatem dedit et acumen. Easdem[d] litteras in nostra caprea contra se esse positas nemo reprehendat, sed

[102.] [a–a] *om. W6*
[b] si *SW6*
[c] utque *RS*
[d] uel eadem *S*

Diagram 10. Which intervals are between which notes and letters

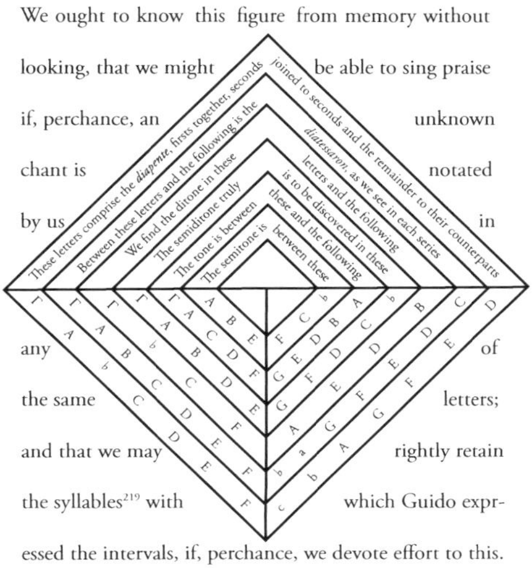

102. Concerning the repetition of *caprea*'s commendation.

I commend to your grace, my lord, *caprea* that I have offered to you, so that its very nature may commend itself to your experience.[220] It shows the manifest division of the tropes, on account of which the quadripartite figure has deserved praise among virtually all of the moderns.[221] But if the quadripartite figure is in everybody's graces when it does this unnaturally, *caprea* doing the same naturally ought not to be despised.[222] If the quadripartite figure brings together in one line all the *graves* against the nature of the monochord and yet is praised, then our *caprea* collecting the same in one according to the constitution of the monochord is not to be criticized.[223] The quadripartite figure divides far from one another the fourth of the *graves* and the first of the *finales*, which the primitive disposition of the monochord rejects, whereas our *caprea* collects them.[224] If indeed that perverse division commends the former, the natural collection does not condemn the latter.[225] If the quadripartite figure is most famous to all while making *protus* the highest and *tetrardus* the lowest, *caprea* will not fall into utter obscurity because it provides for the natural low and high positions. In our *caprea* nobody may find fault with the same letters having been placed against themselves; but

aliter secundum naturam fieri non posse perpendat, cum .A. grauis sit proti, qui secundum monochordum tono differt a graui deuteri .B. Si in dispositione deuteri non esset .A. contra .A., quod est in dispositione proti, fieret aut peruersa coniunctio aut peruersa disiunctio; si .B. opponeretur .A. esset peruersa coniunctio. Quam in quadripertita reprehendo grauibus duorum modorum in uno conuenientibus loco. Si autem gamma deuteri poneretur contra proti .a. peruersa fieret disiunctio, .A. grauem proti et .B. grauem deuteri ditono dirimente, penitus id natura monochordi renuente. Quid ulterius procedimus? In quo nostram capream quadripertita precellat ignoro, nisi in mensurę difficultate. Quę si merito laudibilior est facilitate, scio pluribus id admirationem generare. [e]Numquam aliud natura, aliud mea caprea dicit.[e]

[1.] Vtilis expositio super obscuras Guidonis sententias.

"*Et alię uoces ab aliis morulam duplo longiorem uel duplo breuiorem aut tremulam*[a] *habeant*, et paulo post: *Summopere caueatur talis neumarum distributio ut cum neumę tum eiusdem soni repercussione tum duorum uel plurium conexione fiant, semper tamen aut in numero uocum aut in ratione tenorum*[b] *neumę alterutrum conferantur et respondeant*. Vt mihi uidetur triplicem per hęc uerba designat cantilenę collationem: quia uult ut[c] proportionalis fiat aut intercapedo duarum uocum, quod notat dicendo *Et alię uoces morulam duplo longiorem uel duplo breuiorem aut tremulam habeant*; aut ut numerus[d] uocum proportionaliter consideretur,[e] quod his intimat[f] uerbis: *aut in numero uocum*; seu ut fiat comparatio: ut in ipsius uocis ultima protensione. Hęc tria ut apertius intelligantur sunt exemplificanda. Morula dupliciter longior est uel breuior, si silentium inter duas uoces [g]duplum est ad aliud silentium inter duas uoces.[g] Eodem modo morula dupliciter est breuior si taciturnitas inter[h] duas uoces simpla est ad aliam taciturnitatem inter duas uoces. Quod dicit *aut tremulam habeant*, puto intelligendum sic esse. Tremula est neuma quam gradatam[i] uel quilisma dicimus 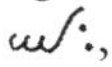, quę longitudinem, de qua dicit *duplo longiorem* cum subiecta uirgula denotat, sine qua breuitatem, quę intimatur[j] per hoc quod dicit *uel duplo breuiorem* insinuat.

[e–e] *written in orange S; om. W6*
[1.] [a] tremulant *S*
[b] tonorum *R*
[c] *om. R*
[d] numerum *R*
[e] consideremus *R*
[f] intonat *R*
[g–g] *in bottom margin S*
[h] in *R*
[i] gradatim *R*
[j] terminantur *R*

it must be considered that it cannot be done otherwise according to nature, since .A. of the *graves* may be of *protus*, which according to the monochord differs by a tone from the *deuterus* .B. of the *graves*. If in the arrangement of *deuterus* .A. were against .A., as in the arrangement of *protus*, there might occur either a perverse conjunction or a perverse disjunction. If .B. were to oppose .A., there would be a perverse conjunction. Thus I reject the quadripartite figure due to the *graves* of two modes meeting in one place. If indeed gamma in *deuterus* were to be put down against .a. in *protus* there would be a perverse disjunction: the low .A. of *protus* and the low .B. of *deuterus* separated by a ditone, which the nature of the monochord thoroughly rejects. How much further shall we proceed? In place of our *caprea* I do not know how the quadripartite figure excels, save in the difficulty of its measurement. If difficulty is more laudable than facility, I know that it generates admiration in very many people. By no means does nature speak of one thing and my *caprea* of another.

[*Sententiae*]

1. A useful exposition of some obscure sentences in Guido.

"*And some notes from others have a brief delay twice as long or twice as short or a trembling*,[226] and a little later: *Special care should be taken that the melodic figures, whether made by repeating the same note or by joining two or more, be always arranged to correspond to each other either in the number of notes or in the relationship of the durations*.[227] It seems to me that by these words he designates three relationships for singing: either because he wishes it to be done proportionally or by the spacing of two notes—which he considers saying *and some notes from others have a brief delay twice as long or twice as short or a trembling*—or that the number of the notes is to be considered proportionally, which he intimates by the words *either in the number of the notes*; or that a comparison may be made, as in the final delaying of the note itself. These three are to be analyzed so that they may be understood more clearly. A brief delay is twice as long or twice as short if the silence between two notes is double another silence between two notes. In the same manner, a brief delay is twice as short if the silence between two notes equals another silence between two notes. What he means by *or having a trembling*, I reckon to be understood thus: we call a trembling a graded figure or a *quilisma* , whose length—of which he says *twice as long*—is denoted with a horiz[illegible]l stroke without which shortness—which is suggested by what he terms *or twice as short*—is implied.

Secunda pars proportionis, quę describitur his uerbis *aut in numero uocum* hunc ut arbitror habet intellectum. Ipse uocum numerus inuicem est conferendus, ut neumę *nunc ęquę ęquis nunc duplę uel triplę simplicibus atque alias collatione sesqualtera uel sesquitercia respondeant.* Ęquę ęquis respondent ut [k]*Semen cecidit in terram bonam.*[k] Quinque uoces sunt in duabus distinctionibus prioribus [l]semen cecidit,[l] totidem in tribus sequentibus [m]in terram bonam.[m] *Nunc duplę simplicibus* ut [n]*Et obtulit fructum.*[n] In[o] [p]et obtulit[p] quatuor sunt uoces, duę in fructum.[q] Dupla ergo collatio. *Nunc triplę simplicibus* ut aliud;[r] a habet unam uocem, liud[s] tres, quia li duas[t] habet uoces in pedata neuma unam in ud. Tres ad unam[u] triplum faciunt. Atque alias collatione sequaltera ut centesimum, dimidia[v] dictio, id est cente[w] duas, alias[x] medietas, id est simum[y] tres habet uoces, unam in si, duas[z] in mum, quem conquiniscentem, id est inclinatiuam resultat. Ternarius ad binarium sesqualtera[a] uel sesquitercia collatione sicut est [b]Venite benedicti. Venite tres, benedicti[b] quatuor habet uoces. Quaternarius ad ternarium est sesquitercius. Tercia pars est proportionis quę describitur his[c] uerbis *aut in ratione tenorum neumę alterutrum conferantur et respondeant.* Tenor est ultimę uocis protensio quę ad inuicem confertur ita ut numerus uocum et interualla earum *nunc ęquę ęquis, nunc duplę uel triplę simplicibus, atque alias collatione sesqualtera uel sesquitercia.*

De quo tenore uel protensione domnus Guido dicit: *Tenor uero, id est mora ultimę uocis qui in syllaba quantuluscumque est amplior in parte, diutissimus uero in distinctione.* Dixit dominus mulieri chananeę.[d] Illam unam distinctionem Dixit habeatis syllabum,[e] Dixit dominus partem. Dixit dominus mulieri chananeę distinctionem. In Dixit, finalis xit [f]protendatur aliquantulum.[f] In Dixit dominus, finalis nus producatur amplius. In Dixit dominus mulieri chananeę, finalis[g] extendatur diutissime.

[k–k] Semen cecidit in terram bonam *S*
[l–l] Semen cecidit *S*
[m–m] in terram bonam *S*
[n–n] Et optulit fructum *S*
[o] *om. R*
[p–p] Et obtulit *S*
[q] fructum *S*
[r] aliud *S*
[s] liut *R*
[t] *Textual misordering in R, fol. 29v, line 23. Text of sententia 1 resumes on fol. 40r, line 14.*
[u] unam per *R*
[v] dimidium *R*
[w] cente *R*
[x] alia *S*
[y] simum *R*
[z] [al>d]uas *R*
[a] sesqualterat *RS*
[b–b] uenite benedicti. Venite .iii. Benedicti *R*
[c] *om. R*
[d] chaneę *S*
[e] syllabam *R*
[f–f] aliquantulum protendatur *R*
[g] finalis e *S*

The second part of the proportion, which is described by the words *either in number of notes* has, I believe, this meaning. The same number of the notes is to be brought together alternately, so that the figures *respond now equally, now by two or three to one, or yet others by the proportion of the sesquialter and sesquitertia.*[228] Equally as in *Semen cecidit in terram bonam*:[229] there are five notes for the first two gestures—*Semen cecidit*—the same in total as for the following three—*In terram bonam. Now by two to one* as in *Et obtulit fructum*:[230] there are four notes in *Et obtulit* and two in *fructum*, therefore the relationship is duple. *Now by three to one* as in *aliud*: *a* has one note and *liud* three, since *li* has two notes in the measured phrase and *ud* one. Three to one makes a triple ratio. *Or yet others by the proportion of the sesquialter* as in *centesimum*; the word divided in half—that is, *cente*—has two notes while the other half—that is, *simum*—has three, there being one for *si* and two for *mum*, from which a coalescence or an inclination together results. A ternary to a binary is a sesquialter or a sesquitertiary relationship as it is in *Venite benedicti*,[231] where *Venite* has three notes and *benedicti* four. A quaternary to a ternary is a sesquitertia. The third part is the proportion that is described by the words *be always arranged to correspond to each other either in the number of notes or in the relationship of their attenuations.*[232] The attenuation is a prolongation of the final note, which is so compared together alternately that the number of notes and their intervals respond *now equally, now by two or three to one, or yet others by the proportion of the sesquialter and sesquitertia.*[233]

About which attenuation or prolongation Lord Guido says: *An attenuation truly is a delay on the last note, which is very small for the syllable, larger for part of a phrase, and greatest for a whole phrase.*[234] *Dixit dominus mulieri Chananeae.*[235] Of that one phrase, let *Dixit* be the smallest part, *Dixit dominus* a larger part, and *Dixit dominus mulieri Chananeae* the entire phrase. In *Dixit* the final *xit* is a trifle prolonged. In *Dixit dominus* the final *nus* may be more prolonged. In *Dixit dominus mulieri Chananeae* the end may be prolonged for the longest time.[236]

Proponat sibi musicus quibus ex diuisionibus incendentem faciat cantum uel quę sint illę diuisiones. Sicut metrorum plurime sunt diuisiones, quia quedam sunt asclepiadea, quedam saphica, quedam alchaica et ad hunc modum ypponactica, nonnulla etiam gliconica; sic melodiarum neumę plurimas habent diuisiones, dum una sit diuisio ęquarum ad ęquas, altera et tercia duplarum triplarumque ad simplices, quarta quinta ut sesqualterarum sesquiterciarumque.[h] Distinctiones distinctionibus sunt equales ut in bene procuratis [i]apparet cantibus[i] sicut in illo responsorio *Ecce nunc tempus acceptabile* una distinctio, *Ecce nunc dies salutis* altera, *Commendemus nosmet ipsos* tercia; *In multa patientia* quarta; [j]*In ieiuniis multis*[j] quinta; *Per arma iustitię* sexta; *Virtutis Dei* septima. Quę omnes pene sunt commensurabiles.

Vt in modum currentis [k]*equi rarius*[k] *uoces ad locum respirationis*[l] *accedant. Spissim autem et raro prout oportet notę compositę huius rei poterunt indicium dare*. Equus dum currit crebrius ungulas figit, dum cessare cogitat rarius uestigia collocat; ita iuxta finem distinctionum ut rariores, id est tardiores uoces succedant est procurandum. Quod autem dicit *spissim autem et raro prout oportet notę compositę, huius rei poterunt indicium dare* artius est scribendi et neumandi[m] distinctio, donec [n]appropinquet ad finem.[n] Iuxta finem autem dissipetur scriptura cum neumis ut cantori sit indicium predictę tarditatis in hunc modum: *Miserere mei fili Dauid*. Sed hęc apertius se presentibus offerent colloquendo quam absentibus scribendo." Quod nobis inuidet commodum detestabilis intercapedo locorum.

"In sola enim ultima parte hoc argumentum reliquimus ut melum suo tetrardo conueniens redderemus." Recordari debetis, domine mihi[o] dilectissime uenerabilem Guidonem dixisse: "Has itaque quinque uocales sumamus, forsitan cum[p] tantum tribuunt concordię uerbis, [q]non minus[q] concinentię prestabunt et neumis. Supponantur itaque[r] litteris monochordi, et quia

[h] sesquiteriiamque *corr.* sesquiterciamque *R*
[i–i] cantibus ap|paret *R*
[j–j] *written over in brown ink by a late-medieval hand S.*
[k–k] equiramus *R:* ram *underlined for correction to* equi rarius
[l] respiramonis *corr.* respiracionis *R*
[m] neumanda *S;* neumanda *corr. by erasure* neumandi *R*
[n–n] ad finem appropinquet *R*
[o] mi *S*
[p] enim *R*
[q–q] quantum *R*
[r] atque *corr.* itaque *R*

Let the musician consider for himself with which of these proportions he will construct the chant,[237] or what will be their divisions. As there are many divisions in metrics—because certain are asclepiadian, certain sapphic, certain *alchacia*, and for that matter hyponactic or even glyconic—therefore the phrases of the melodies have many possibilities: whereas one melody may be divided up equally, a second or a third may be arranged two or three to one, and a fourth or a fifth arranged as a sesquialter or sesquitertia. The phrases are equal to the phrases, as it appears in well-managed chant, such as this responsory *Ecce nunc tempus acceptabile,*[238] where there is one phrase. *Ecce nunc dies salutis* is a second example; *Commendemus nosmetipsos* a third; *In multa patientia* a fourth; *In ieiuniis multis* a fifth; *Per arma iustitiae* a sixth; *Virtutis Dei* a seventh. Virtually all of these are commensurable.

As in the manner in which a horse gallops so the notes should be more widely spaced as they approach a breathing place. Spacing the notes close together or widely apart, as befits, is a good way to indicate this effect.[239] The horse while running places his hoofs close together, but while slowing down he thinks and places his steps more widely; thus near the ends of the distinctions spacing more widely apart is called for—that is, the notes may follow more slowly. Guido also says *spacing the notes close together or widely apart, as befits, is a good way to indicate this effect* in writing the longer and shorter phrases while approaching the end.[240] Close to the end, however, the writing is expanded with the phrases so that the cantor may indicate the said slowing down in this manner: *Miserere mei fili David.*[241] But these things show themselves more present in speaking than absent in writing."[242] That which is detestable to us grudges a convenient place of pause.

"Only in the last part did we abandon this argument so that we could lead the melody back properly to its *tetrardus*."[243] You ought to recall, my most dear lord,[244] what the venerable Guido has said. "Let us take these five vowels. Perhaps, since they bring such euphony to words, they will offer no less harmony to the musical phrases. Let them be placed in succession beneath the letters of the monochord, and since

quinque tantum sunt tamdiu repetantur, donec unicuique sono sua subscribatur uocalis," et ad istum dirigentur[s] modum.

A	E	I	O	V	A	E	I	O	V	A	E	I	O	V	A
Γ	A	B	C	D	[t]E	F	G[t]	a	b	c	d	e	f	g	aa
O	V	A	E	I	O	V	A	E	I	O	V	A	E	I	O[u]

Et quibusdam interpositis subiungit: "Sed ne grauis tibi imponatur[v] necessitas, quod ad hunc modum uix cuilibet[w] symphonię quinque accidant uoces, et ipsas transgredi sepe ad uotum non sufficiat ut tibi paulo liberius liceat euagari, alio item uersum subiunge uocalium. Sed ita sit diuersus ut a tercio loco prioris incipiat hoc modo."

o u a e i o u a e i o u a o u a e i
o u a e i o u a e i o[x]

Ecce quomodo[y] omnes syllabę contra suum[z] uocalem sunt positę excepta hau, quę est in hauriat, ultima uidelicet huius uersus parte, quia hau [a]posita est contra .F. Quę non habet *a* uocalem hau syllabę sed habet *u* et *e*.[a] Et musicus causam tradit cur ita mutauerit, quia conuenientius sonat hau in .F. quam in .G. quę tetrardi finalis debet esse.

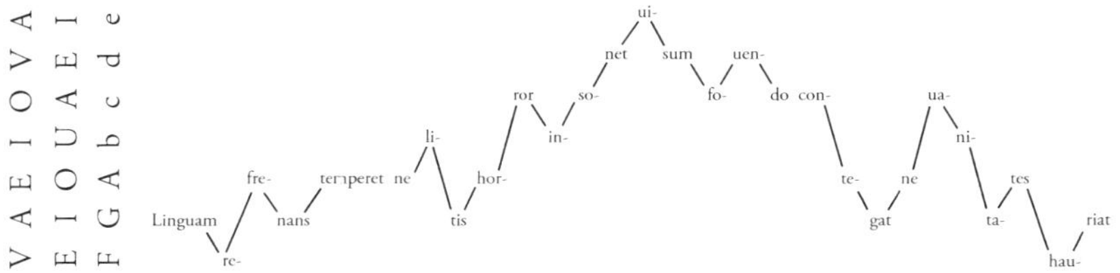

[2.] [a]Alia sententia utiliter explanata.[a]

"Quamuis autem duo semper toni in una sint littera uel una[b] uoce, tamen multo melius et frequentius conueniunt singulis neumis ac sonis formulę[c] toni secundi, quarti, sexti et octaui. Nam formulę primi, tercii, quinti, septimi non conueniunt nisi cum cantus descendit ab alto et in grauem deuenerit finem."

[s] dirigent *R*
[t–t] *originally omitted but added above R*
[u] *R adds* V *after*
[v] interponatur *S*
[w] quilibet *R*
[x] *om. R; vowels in orange S*
[y] quomodo moritur *R*
[z] suam *S*
[a–a] syllabę sunt habet .v. et e. *R*
[2.] [a–a] *title in orange in left-hand margin S;* Aribonis sententia *R*
[b] *om. R*
[c] formuli *R*

they are only five, let them be repeated until beneath each note its particular vowel is written" so that they will be arranged in this way.[245]

Diagram 11.

A	E	I	O	V	A	E	I	O	V	A	E	I	O	V	A
Γ	A	B	C	D	E	F	G	a	b	c	d	e	f	g	aa
O	V	A	E	I	O	V	A	E	I	O	V	A	E	I	O

And with certain things having been interposed below them: "So that no onerous necessity be laid on you—since by this method scarcely any tune would get less than five notes and there would be no way to get beyond these five according to your wish—if you wish to range about a little more freely, add another row of vowels below. But this should be different, so that it begins from the third place of the earlier row, in this way."[246]

o u a e i o u a e i o u a o u a e i
o u a e i o u a e i o

Behold how every syllable is placed against its note except *hau*, which is in *hauriat*, clearly the last part of our verse since *hau* is placed against .F. Though *a* does not have a note, *u* and *e* do. And musical cause hands down why it so changes, since it conveniently sounds *hau* at .F. rather than at .G., which ought to be the *tetrardus* of the final.

Diagram 12.

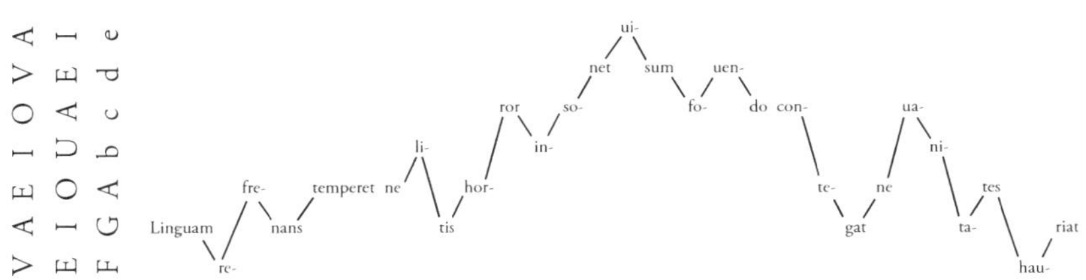

2. Another sentence usefully explained.

"However much each letter or sound always belongs to two tones, yet the patterns of the second, fourth, sixth, and eighth tones agree much better and more frequently in the individual melodic figures or sounds; for the patterns of the first, third, fifth, and seventh do not agree except when the chant descends from above and concludes with a low note."[247]

[d]Aribonis sententia.[d]

Quamuis cantus sit autenticus tamen plures eius neumę et soni uersantur in quinque eius chordis quę communes sunt autentis et plagalibus, quam [e]in tribus[e] quę autentis separatim deputantur, ideoque sepius et melius formulis plagalium etiam neumę autenticorum conueniunt, in quibus sepius morantur in antiphonis *Ecce nomen domini*. Quamuis sit autentica plures tamen eius neumę possunt plagales uideri quam autenticę ut puta *Ecce* et *nomen* et *domini* et *de longinquo* ac et *claritas* et *eius* et *replet* et *orbem* et *terrarum* sunt plagales, utpote[f] spacio plagalium currentes. Sola *uenit* est autentica, omnes tamen eius neumę plagales sunt dicendę, quia a finalis quinta non transcendit chordam. Sic in pluribus eadem ratio est habenda, de quibus modo non est dicendum per singula. Quando autem a finali chorda diapente transcendunt et sextam, septimam, octauam tangunt melodię, tunc autenticorum formulis quę altę extenduntur conueniunt. Et hoc est quod dicit "nisi cum cantus alto descendit et in grauem deuenerit finem."[g]

[d–d] Alia sententia utiliter explanata *R*
[e–e] uersibus *R*
[f] utpote *corr.* utpute *R*

[g] Explicit Musica Aribonis. In nomine summe et indiuiduę trinitatis Incipit Micrologus Guidonis in musicam *R*

Aribo's explanation.

However much a chant may be authentic, nevertheless many of its figures and sounds are situated in five of its notes, which are shared by authentic and plagal, than in three, which belong separately to the authentics. Additionally, the patterns of the plagals and the authentics meet more frequently and sweetly in those same figures, which more often feature in antiphons: *Ecce nomen domini*.[248] However much it may be authentic, nevertheless many of its figures appear to be plagal rather than authentic, so we reckon that *Ecce* and *nomen* and *domini* and *de longuinquo*, as well as *claritas* and *eius* and *replet* and *orbem* and *terrarum* are plagal, since they run in the range of the plagals. Only *venit* is authentic; yet all of its figures are said to be plagal, because it does not exceed a fifth from its final. Thus in many cases the same reasoning is maintained, which need not be explained individually. When, however, melodies exceed a fifth from the final and touch a sixth, a seventh, or an eighth, then they mix with the authentic patterns, which are extended from above. And so it is that he says *only when the melody descends from above and concludes with a low note*.

NOTES

1. Ellenhard, bishop of Freising from 1052 until 1078.

2. James 1:12. "Domno," "suo," "Ellenhardo," "dignissimo," "preclaro," "Aribo": similar cadence for words in the same case (*similiter cadens*) and similar endings for those not (*similiter desinens*). Aribo follows the advice of *Rhetorica ad Herennium* 4.20.28: "those who use these figures well generally combine them." Cf. Onulf of Speyer, *Colores rhetorici* 1.12–13, 2.12–13, ed. Linde, pp. 363–64, 376–77.

3. "Presentię . . . presentetur": repetition within phrases (*traductio*). Cf. *Rhetorica ad Herennium* 4.14.20; Onulf of Speyer, *Colores rhetorici* 1.4, 2.4, ed. Linde, pp. 358, 373.

4. Matt. 22:11–14. A pun is intended on the word "ragged" (*pannosus*) in the previous sentence. Aribo's pen—and by analogy the author himself—is unsuitable, as it lacks the appropriate vestige. Self-deprecation is a standard procedure in the *captatio benevolentiae* used in the introductions of letters and treatises in the Middle Ages. Cf. Alberic of Monte Cassino, *Flores rhetorici* 2.5, trans. Miller, pp. 138–39. On the relevance of Alberic's work in Germany, see McCarthy, "Literary Practice," p. 195.

5. "Iterum atque iterum": amplification through repetition (*conduplicatio*). Cf. *Rhetorica ad Herennium* 4.28.38; Onulf of Speyer, *Colores rhetorici* 1.21, 2.21, ed. Linde, pp. 370, 380.

6. Aribo's reference here is probably to the singing in the cathedral at Freising. His comment is a clear indication that he was familiar with the singing there, and supports the conclusion that he was a member of the cathedral chapter.

7. Virgil, *Eclogues* 3.50–54. The shepherd Palemon was called to act as judge in the poetic contest between Dameta and Menalca. Cf. Cassiodorus, *Institutiones* 2.1. The reference is a pun, referring to Ellenhard's episcopal role as both arbiter and shepherd.

8. A reference to the discussion that follows of the quadripartite figure and *caprea*.

9. "Intensionem . . . remissionem": a pun on the technical terms *intensio* and *remissio*, which occur frequently in *De musica*. "Seriarum," "rerum," "laboriosam," "intensionem," "blandientem," "remissionem": the device of similar endings (*similiter desinens*).

10. An indication that Aribo frequently encountered the figure drawn on monochords.

11. That is, the various letter names for the notes, which Aribo asserts are not arranged clearly on the quadripartite figure. Cf. Isidore, *Etymologies* 1.4.3–4, trans. Barney et al., pp. 40–41.

12. Inspired by Isidore, *Etymologies* 13.3.2 (trans. Barney et al., p. 272). The four modes—*protus*, *deuterus*, *tritus*, and *tetrardus*—mirror the four elements, which according to Isidore are joined among themselves with a certain natural logic and return to their origin. The Neoplatonic implications of the four modes returning to their origin are also evident in the music treatises by Bern and Herman of Reichenau: Bern of Reichenau, *Prologus in tonarium* 4, p. 40; Herman of Reichenau, *Musica* 2, p. 20: See McCarthy, *Music, Scholasticism and Reform*, pp. 156–58.

13. Influenced by William of Hirsau, *Musica* 15, 16, pp. 40–44. See below, nn. 75, 93.

14. An allusion to Horace, *Satires* 1.9.2. Most of the vocabulary in this couplet is drawn from book 1 of the *Satires*.

15. Perhaps an allusion to John 11:52. See also 2 Chronicles 11:23, Isaiah 11:12, and Ezekiel 36:19.

16. Parental imagery, which is also used by Bern and Herman of Reichenau, derives from Macrobius's *Commentarius in Somnium Scipionis* and, ultimately, from Plato's *Timaeus*. It is used by Aribo to show the discordance between the quadripartite figure and nature, while emphasizing the agreement between *caprea* and nature. See Bern of Reichenau, *Prologus in tonarium* 4, p. 40; Herman of Reichenau, *Musica* 2, p. 22; Macrobius, *Commentarius in Somnium Scipionis* 1.6.1; Plato, *Timaeus* 28a–29b.

17. "Quę habet . . . ": the device of repetition (*repetitio*) to begin three successive sentences. Cf. *Rhetorica ad Herennium* 4.13.19; Onulf of Speyer, *Colores rhetorici* 1.1, 2.1, ed. Linde, pp. 356, 373.

18. Perhaps an echo of Pope Leo I, *Sermo* 37, for Epiphany (PL 54:0257B).

19. A clever play on William of Hirsau's *theorema troporum*, which is, in fact, the quadripartite figure.

20. James 1:17; see also William of Hirsau, *Musica* 9, p. 26.

21. Psalm 113:1.

22. Genesis 27:20.

23. Genesis 27:31.

24. An allusion to 2 Peter 2:4, 2:9.

25. Cf. Appendix 2. Aribo's complaint possibly refers to the alignment of

.D.E.F.G. (tone-semitone-tone) on the bottom line of the quadripartite figure with .G.a.b.c. (tone-tone-semitone) on its top line.

26. A much-used biblical description, generally applied to the obduracy of the Israelites in the Old Testament.

27. Perhaps an echo of Jerome, *Commentariorum in Epistolam ad Galatas libri tres* 3.22 (PL 26:0419B).

28. Horace, *Odes* 27.1.

29. Perhaps an allusion to Virgil, *Georgics* 3.328.

30. Horace, *Satires* 1.1.106.

31. See Herman of Reichenau, *Musica*, p. 26; William of Hirsau, *Musica* 2, p. 14.

32. Though the tetrachords of the second group preserve consistency of intervals in ascent and descent, they are not symmetrical.

33. For a discussion of the meaning of the word *neuma*, see Desmond, "*Sicut in grammatica*." In the context of her comparative study, Desmond translates *neuma* as "sub-phrase." I have preferred to translate it with a less-defined meaning here. See above, p. xcvi.

34. The rhetorical color of *brevitas*. The device of *brevitas*—often called *epistolaris brevitas* from its use in letter writing—draws attention to the incompleteness of a given account and claims that further discussion would be futile since the consequences are obvious to all. For example, in a contemporary letter Archbishop Gebhard of Salzburg (d. 1088) claims that it is not necessary for him to list further a series of conciliar decrees because "they are well known to virtually everybody"; see Gebhard of Salzburg, *Epistola* 14, MGH Libelli 1, p. 269. See also McCarthy, "Literary Practice," 199.

35. See Introduction, p. xxvi.

36. .F.–.b. is an augmented fourth (tritone) and .B.–.F. is a diminished fifth; .♭. (and hence the *synemmenon* tetrachord .a.♭.b.c.) is required in each case to perfect the interval.

37. A complicated passage. The tetrachords of *hyperboleon*, *diezeugmenon*, *meson*, and *hypaton* are consistent in their extension (semitone and two tones) and their remission (two tones and semitone). But the extension and remission themselves are not symmetrical.

38. Juvenal, *Satires* 1.21.

39. In dialectical terms the order of tones and semitones constitutes a *differentia*—that is, an attribute that distinguishes a given species from other species belonging to the same genus. Consequently, the two groups are different species under the genus "tetrachord." This distinction is ultimately based upon Boethius's *De divisione*. See Boethius, *De divisione*, p. 16 (PL 64:0880). William of Hirsau (*Musica* 2, p. 14) and Frutolf of Michelsberg (*Breviarium de musica* 6, p. 51) also divided the tetrachords in this way.

40. Aribo is using Boethius as a generic term for "ancient." For Boethius's actual delineation of the tetrachords and note names, see *De institutione musica* 1.20, 4.3, pp. 206–12, 308–12.

41. That is .a.–.d., .b.–.e., .c.–.f., and .d.–.g. at the higher octave.

42. Aribo argues that the species of *diatessaron* between .D. and .G. is like the first species of *diatessaron* (.A.–.D.), because it has the form tone-semitone-tone. Although it may be a first species of *diatessaron* in its form, nevertheless it is not a natural first species, because it occurs between the first and fourth notes of the *finales* (.D. and .G.). The natural first, second, third, and fourth species of *diatessaron* occur between the corresponding ordinals of the *graves* and *finales*. A similar case obtains with the species of *diapente*.

43. The first notes of two conjunct tetrachords: for example, the first of the *graves* (.A.) and the first of the *finales* (.D.)

44. The first and fourth notes of the tetrachord of the *finales* (.D. and .G.).

45. The notes .D.a.d.

46. Lauds antiphon for Wednesday of Holy Week; *CAO* 1355.

47. Vespers antiphon for the First Sunday in Advent; *CAO* 2527.

48. Lauds antiphon for the Second Sunday in Advent; *CAO* 2515.

49. Office antiphon for Friday of the first week of Advent; *CAO* 2549.

50. Vespers antiphon for the Second Sunday in Advent; *CAO* 3606.

51. The notes .A.D.a.

52. The notes .B.E.b.

53. The notes .C.F.c. and D.G.d.

54. The notes .D.a.d.

55. The notes .E.b.e.

56. The notes .F.c.f. and G.d.g.

57. Any of the notes of the tetrachord of the *superiores*: .a.b.c.d.

58. A convoluted passage: in any of the authentic tones the top note of each set of three principal notes is a fourth (*diatessaron*) above the middle note. The lower note is a fifth (*diapente*) below the middle note. Taking authentic *protus*—.D.a.d.—as an example: the relationship between .a. and .d. is extension of a *diatessaron*, and the relationship between .a. and .D. is remission of a *diapente*.

59. Although Aribo does not make it clear, he is referring to the notes of the tetrachord of the *finales*: .D.E.F.G. In the plagal tones the top note of each set of three principal notes is a fifth (*diapente*) above the middle note, and the lower note is a fourth (*diatessaron*) below. Taking plagal *protus*—.A.D.a.—as an example: the relationship between .D. and .a. is extension of a *diapente* and the relationship between .D. and .A. is remission of a *diatessaron*.

60. There is no *diapente* above .B. (.B. to .F. is a diminished fifth), and no *diatessaron* below .b. (.b. to .F. is an augmented fourth).

61. On *apotome* (the major semitone), see Boethius, *De institutione musica* 2.30, pp. 263–64; trans. Bower as *Fundamentals of Music*, pp. 84–85.

62. The parallel imagery of high and low, rich and poor is probably an allusion to the chant *Aspiciens a longo*, the responsory for the First Sunday in Advent, which incorporates text from Psalm 48:3.

63. Psalm 18:6, Joel 2:16. The four chambers: the notes of the *finales* (.D.E.F.G.).

64. Ezekiel 10:10.

65. Horace, *Ars poetica* 232–33.

66. Virgil, *Eclogues* 5.73.

67. The species of *diapason* are composed from combinations of the species of *diatessaron* and *diapente*. See introduction, pp. xxii–xxvi.

68. Matthew 21:19.

69. A mistaken reference on Aribo's part. The word *puteum* is not used in Matthew and occurs only in John 4:11: "Dicit ei mulier, Domine neque in quo haurias habes et puteus altus est, unde ergo habes aquam uiuam."

70. Matthew 8:20.

71. Matthew 27:51; Mark 15:38; Luke 23:45.

72. Psalm 46:6. Cf. 3 Kings 1:41; Psalm 97:6.

73. Psalm 8:2.

74. The *superiores* (.a.b.c.d.) begin the species of *diatessaron* an octave above the *finales* (.A.B.C.D.). See introduction, pp. xxii–xxiii.

75. When .D. functions to begin the fourth species of *diatessaraon*, it is classified as the fourth note of the *graves* (.A.B.C.D.); when it functions to end the first species of *diatessaron*, it is classified as the first note of the *finales* (.D.E.F.G.). The insistence of Aribo and his German contemporaries on the double function of .D. opposes the teaching of Guido of Arezzo. See above, n. 13, and McCarthy, *Music, Scholasticism and Reform*, pp. 82–87.

76. See introduction, pp. xxii–xxiii.

77. The first species of *diapente*: .D.E.F.G.a.; the first species of *diatessaron* transposed up an octave: .a.b.c.d.

78. See Isidore, *Etymologies* 1.17, trans. Barney et al., pp. 47–49.

79. Trochee: the metrical foot consisting of long-short (-|˘). Spondee: long-long (-|-). See Fig. 7 below, p. 95.

80. Iamb: short-long (˘|-).

81. First epitrite: short-long-long-long (˘ -|- -).

82. See introduction, p. xxiv.

83. The first note of the *graves* (.A.) and the first note of the superiores (.a.).

84. The first note of the *finales* (.D.).

85. The function of the final note in each of these species is both to divide the *diatessaron* and *diapente* while simultaneously linking them as part of the octave (*diapason*). Their twofold nature is reflected in Aribo's use of *dimidio* and *uinculo* to describe their function.

86. John 1:9.

87. An allusion to Virgil, *Aeneid* 6.646. But its application to music is owed to Isidore, *Etymologies* 3.21.4. See n. 123 below.

88. The *synemmenon* tetrachord (.a.♭.b.c.). See introduction, p. xxvi.

89. An allusion to Macrobius, *Commentarius in Somnium Scipionis* 1.18. Aries and Libra are at opposite points of the zodiac and are only at equal positions in the sky at the equinoxes. At other times this seesaw arrangement means that one is higher or lower than the other.

90. The tetrachords of the *graves*, *finales*, *superiores*, and *excellentes*.

91. The tetrachords of *hyperboleon*, *diezeugmenon*, *meson*, and *hypaton*. See above, chapter 19, p. 14.

92. See introduction, p. xxv.

93. Aribo parallels William of Hirsau, who attacked Boethius on this point: William, *Musica* 16, pp. 42–44. See also above nn. 13, 75.

94. These formulas are the different cadence patterns available for the psalm tones, allowing them to be combined with a variety of antiphons in different modes.

95. The last of eight widely circulated didactic melodies designed to illustrate the different forms of the eight modes. See Hiley, *Western Plainchant*, pp. 331–33.

96. Lauds antiphon for the First Sunday in Advent; *CAO* 3244.

97. Antiphon for the First Sunday after Christmas; *CAO* 2461.

98. Pope Gregory I, "the Great," 590–604. Aribo repeats the common legend that Gregory was the author of the chant that bears his name. On Gregory and Gregorian chant, see Hiley, *Western Plainchant*, pp. 503–13.

99. St. Ambrose, bishop of Milan, 374–97. Like Gregory, he acquired a legendary musical reputation. David Hiley credits Aribo with starting the legend that Gregory created the four plagal modes in response to Ambrose's four authentic modes; see Hiley, *Western Plainchant*, p. 511.

100. "Negemus . . . non . . . non": Aribo is probably using the double negative for emphasis. The sense of the passage requires that it not be translated literally.

101. See Boethius, *In Topica Ciceronis commentariorum* 2 (PL 64:1081A). On Aribo's use of dialectic, see McCarthy, *Music, Scholasticism and Reform*, pp. 138–45.

102. Boethius, *De differentiis topicis* (PL 64:1175C).

103. Ibid. (PL 64:1179B).

104. .F.–.b. is an augmented fourth (tritone), while .b.–.f. is a diminished fifth.

105. Proverbs 5:10.

106. Horace, *Ars poetica* 256–58.

107. Advent antiphon, *CAO* 2527.

108. See n. 104 above.

109. Echoing Boethius, *De divisione*, p. 32. Aribo argues that since there are only four species each of *diatessaron* and *diapente*, there can logically be only four species of *diapason*: the eight species of *diapason* are really a duplication of the four species of *diapason*.

110. Echoing the maximal proposition "Quod in omnibus ualet, ualet et in uno" of chapter 67. The parallel question structure for this and the next sentence ("Quis dicit . . . ? / Similiter quis dicit . . . ?") combines the rhetorical colors of *repetitio* and *interrogatio*. The device frequently appears in the polemical literature of the eleventh-century Investiture Contest (the *Libelli de lite*). For parallel examples, see *libelli* by the royalist partisan Wenrich of Trier and the Gregorian apologist Bernold of St. Blasien: Wenrich of Trier, *Epistola sub Theoderici episcopi Virdunensis nomine composita*, MGH Libelli 1, p. 293; Bernold of St. Blasien, *Appollogeticus super excommunicacionem Gregorii septimi*, MGH Libelli 2, p. 161. See also McCarthy, "Literary Practice," 198–99.

111. Aribo was probably inspired by Isidore, *Etymologies* 3.14.1 (trans. Barney et al., p. 95): "Music is so called through derivation from the word 'muse,' for the muses (*musae*) were named from μάσαι, that is, from 'seeking,' because it was through them, as the ancients would have it, that the power of song and the modulation of the voice were sought."

112. The word *cymbala* generally referred to small handheld bell, rather than the tolling variety that was indicated by *campana*.

113. Derived in part from Isidore, *Etymologies* 3.19.9 (trans. Barney et al., p. 96): "Arsis is elevation of the voice, that is, the beginning. Thesis is lowering the voice, that is, the end." Also *Etymologies* 1.17.21 (trans. Barney et al., p. 48): "In each foot there occurs an arsis and a thesis, that is, a raising and lowering of the voice—for the feet would not be able to follow a road unless they were alternately raised and lowered. For example, in *arma* [arms], *ar-* is the raising, and *-ma* the lowering. Properly constituted feet are comprised of a distribution of these two."

114. The etymological connection between *syrtis* (sandbank) and *siren* (syren) is more apparent in the Latin than in the English. The allusion is to Isidore, *Etymologies* 13.18.6 (trans. Barney et al., p. 279): "The syrtes are sandy places in the sea. Sallust [*Jugurthine war* 78.3] says they are called syrtes from 'dragging' because they drag everything towards themselves, and they cling fast to whoever approaches the shallows of the sea."

115. A reference to Publilius Syrus, a famous mime actor of the late Republican period, who was better known in the Middle Ages as the author of a widely disseminated collection of *sententiae* (although many of the aphorisms in the collection were not actually by him).

116. Isidore, *Etymologies* 9.3.32. Cf. Peter Damian, *Letters* 31, 66, 112, vol. 1, pp. 303.21–304.2; vol. 2, p. 266.20–22; vol. 3, pp. 278.18–279.1.

117. The story of Pythagoras discovering the ratios of the consonances while passing by a smithy is told in Boethius, *De institutione musica* 1.8, p. 195. It is also related in less detail by Isidore, *Etymologies* 3.15.1, trans. Barney et al., p. 95.

118. The proportion 4 to 3.

119. The proportion 3 to 2.

120. See Isidore, *Etymologies* 1.4.1–9 (trans. Barney et al., pp. 40–41).

121. An allusion to Jerome, *Contra Jovianium* 2.8.

122. Guido of Arezzo, *Epistola ad Michahelem*, pp. 486–88.

123. Virgil, *Aeneid* 6.646. But the use of this allusion in music is probably owed to Isidore, *Etymologies* 3.21.4 (trans. Barney et al., p. 98). Aribo's comment that the notes at the higher octave "are not an addition but a repetition of those" echoes Herman of Reichenau, *Musica* 5, p. 29: " . . . sciendum est quod si quis ea quae dicta sunt in secundo diapason facere tentaverit, non aliam genituram diatessaron nasci, sed eam quae iam dicta est repeti."

124. Derived from Macrobius, *Commentarius in Somnium Scipionis* 2.3.1.

125. The ferial respond *Adiuva nos deus salutaris noster*, *CAO* 6040.

126. The Advent antiphon *Missus est Gabriel*, *CAO* 3794.

127. *AH* 50, p. 292. This hymn for St. Willibald, the founder and patron saint of Eichstätt, was apparently written by Bishop Heribert of Eichstätt, who died at Freising in 1042. The dissemination of the hymn was restricted to this area: Ilnitchi, *Play of Meanings*, pp. 77–78.

128. The introit for the First Sunday in Advent.

129. An alleluia verse from the Common of the Apostles. *TK*, p. 158, no. 197.

130. On measurement texts see introduction, p. xxxiii.

131. See Smits van Waesberghe, *Cymbala*, pp. 21–23. Beeswax was used to coat the bell mold over which a layer of loam was spread. When the mold had set the wax was melted and drained off, leaving a gap to be filled by the molten metal. The quantities of wax used to fashion the molds had to be weighed carefully according to the proportions of the monochord.

132. 1/2 + 1/2 + 1/2 = 3/2 = sesquialter = *diapente*.

133. 1/3 + 1/3 + 1/3 + 1/3 = 4/3 = sesquitertia = *diatessaron*.

134. By "the bell that you divided in two" Aribo must mean the bell for the *diapente* after the third half has been added: 3/2 ÷ 4 = (3/8 + 3/8 + 3/8 + 3/8). Removing the fourth part leaves (3/8 + 3/8 + 3/8), which gives 9/8, or the tone. The "second bell": the second bell in the series of the seven bells that correspond to the seven different notes of the scale.

135. The bell that forms the major sixth: 9/8 = 18/16. 18/16 + half (that is, 9/16) = 27/16, or the major sixth.

136. 27/16 ÷ 4 = (27/64 + 27/64 + 27/64 + 27/64). Three-quarters of this = 81/64, or the ditone (major third).

137. 81/64 = (81/128 + 81/128). Adding half again = 243/128, or the major seventh.

138. 243/128 = (243/512 + 243/512 + 243/512 + 243/512). Subtracting a quarter gives (243/512 + 243/512 + 243/512), which equals 729/512, or the augmented fourth (tritone) that will be situated between the *diatessaron* and *diapente*.

139. On this set of measurements, see Adkins, "Theory and Practice of the Monochord," pp. 146–49; Meyer, *Mensura monochordi*, p. 137.

140. See Theoger of Metz, *Musica*, trans. by Lochner in "Dietger," pp. 163–64; Meyer, "Organistrum et synemmenon grave," pp. 87–106.

141. That is, the lower *synemmenon* from *synemmenon* an octave above.

142. See Adkins, "Theory and Practice of the Monochord," pp. 166–68; Meyer, *Mensura monochordi*, p. 212.

143. See Sachs, *Mensura fistularum*, pp. 126–28. This set of measurements is also found—without attribution to Aribo—as part of a separate short treatise on organ pipes in a contemporary manuscript from Tergensee: Munich, Bayerische Staatsbibliothek, Clm 18914, fols. 39v–40r.

144. See Sachs, *Mensura fistularum*, pp. 86–89.

145. Abbot William of Hirsau (d. 1091). On William, see introduction, pp. xviii–xix, xxviii–xxx, xxxvi–xxxvii; and McCarthy, *Music, Scholasticism and Reform*, pp. 31–33.

146. For the significance of this comment see introduction, pp. xxviii–xxix.

147. See Sachs, *Mensura fistularum*, pp. 90–91.

148. As is the case with *caprea*. See above, chapter 12, p. 10.

149. An allusion to Matthew 25:21.

150. See also the contemporary account of Theophilus (possibly Roger of Helmershausen), *De diversibus artibus* 3.81–82. See Sachs, *Mensura fistularum*, p. 92.

151. Macrobius, *Commentarius in Somnium Scipionis* 1.20.16.

152. Cicero, *De natura deorum libri tres* 2.34.

153. Derived from Isidore, *Etymologies* 1.1.2.

154. See Plato, *Timaeus* 32C, 35B, pp. 29, 32; Boethius, *De institutione musica* 1.1, p. 180.

155. Derived from Boethius, *De institutione musica* 1.1, p. 180.

156. An allusion to Cicero, *Laelius de amicitia* 50.

157. An echo of Isidore, *Etymologies* 3.14.2 (trans. Barney et al., p. 95): "Sound, because it is something perceived by the sense, vanishes as the moment passes and is imprinted in the memory."

158. Agreeing with Herman of Reichenau, *Musica* 15, p. 47. See introduction, p. xx.

159. See Boethius, *De institutione musica* 1.1, p. 7–8.

160. Unidentified.

161. Inspired by Isidore, *Etymologies* 3.16.2 (trans. Barney et al., p. 95): "Music calls forth the very beasts to listen to its modulation, even serpents, birds, and dolphins."

162. 3 Kings 16:23. Cassiodorus, *Institutiones* 2.5.9; also Isidore, *Etymologies* 3.16.3.

163. Ovid, *Fasti* 2.79–96.

164. Plato, *Timaeus* 18A, p. 7.

165. Perhaps an allusion to the story of Pythagoras and Taormina told in Boethius, *De institutione musica* 1.1, p. 185.

166. Virgil, *Eclogues* 2.1.

167. Guido of Arezzo, *Micrologus* 15, pp. 164–65.

168. Ibid., pp. 168–69.

169. Ibid, p. 165.

170. Celeritas, tarditas, mediocritas.

171. Guido of Arezzo, *Micrologus* 15, p. 168.

172. Vespers antiphon for the First Sunday after Ascension; *CAO* 3941.

173. *Rhetorica ad Herennium* 4.20: "Conpar appellatur quod habet in se membra orationis, de quibus ante diximus, quae constent ex pari fere numero syllabarum."

174. Ibid.: "Hoc non denumeratione nostra fiet—nam id quidem puerile est—sed tantum adferet usus et exercitatio facultatis . . . "

175. Guido of Arezzo, *Micrologus* 15, p. 168.

176. Cicero, *De inventione* 1.76.

177. Alleluia verse for the First Sunday after Whitsun; *TK*, p. 141, no. 159.

178. The tenth verse from the Easter sequence *Laudes salvatori*; *AH* 53, pp. 65–66.

179. Guido of Arezzo, *Micrologus* 15, p. 168.

180. Ibid.

181. Matins hymn for Ascension; *AH* 50, p. 192.

182. Guido of Arezzo, *Micrologus* 15, p. 168.

183. A verse of the Good Friday tract *Eripe me* (Schlager, "Ars cantandi," p. 240), or a verse of the offertory *Custodi me* (Ilnitchi, *Play of Meanings*, p. 87).

184. Guido of Arezzo, *Micrologus* 15, p. 168.

185. From verse 9 of the sequence *Benedicta semper* attributed to Notker of St. Gallen (ca. 840–ca. 912).

186. Guido of Arezzo, *Micrologus* 15, p. 169.

187. Laudes antiphon for the Octave of Christmas; *CAO* 3985. Schlager, "Ars cantandi," suggests that it might be an antiphon for the office of St. Gregory (241).

188. Guido of Arezzo, *Micrologus* 15, p. 169.

189. Easter sequence by Notker of St. Gallen (ca. 840–ca. 912); *AH* 53, pp. 93–94.

190. Guido of Arezzo, *Micrologus* 15, p. 169.

191. Verse 11 of the Christmas sequence *Eia recolamus* by Notker of St. Gallen; *AH* 53, pp. 23–24.

192. Aribo copied the text from this point until the end of chapter 93 from *Commentarius anonymus in Micrologus Guidonis Aretini*. The Guidonian quotations, which are indicated here in italics, were taken from Aribo's copy of the anonymous commentary and not directly from *Micrologus*. See introduction, p. xxxviii.

193. Cf. Guido of Arezzo, *Micrologus* 16, p. 181.

194. Nocturns hymn for Quadragesima; *AH* 51, p. 57; *Monumenta monodica medii aevi* 1, p. 226.

195. Vespers antiphon for the Common of the Apostles; *CAO* 2512; *Monumenta monodica medii aevi* 5, p. 172, no. 1345.

196. Matins respond for the Fourth Sunday in Advent; *CAO* 7195.

197. Verse 17 from the Ascension sequence *Summi triumphum regis*; *AH* 53, pp. 65–67. *Commentarius anonymus*, ed. Vivell, pp. 83–84; ed. Smits van Waesberghe, p. 167 (Guido of Arezzo, *Micrologus* 16, p. 181).

198. *Commentarius anonymus*, ed. Vivell, p. 84; ed. Smits van Waesberghe, p. 167.

199. From the respond *Fundata est domus domini*, for the dedication of a church; *CAO* 6756.

200. Also from "Fundata est domus domini."

201. *Commentarius anonymus*, ed. Vivell, pp. 84–89; ed. Smits van Waesberghe, pp. 167–68.

202. *Commentarius anonymus*, ed. Vivell, p. 89; ed. Smits van Waesberghe, p. 168. Vivell, following Vienna, Österreichische Nationalbibliothek, Cod. 2502, fol. 18r, omits "semitonioue, in diapente autem ditono, semiditono, tono." The scribe of Vienna, Cod. 2502 skipped this line through homeoteleuton.

203. *Commentarius anonymus*, ed. Vivell, p. 89; ed. Smits van Waesberghe, p. 168.

204. Guido of Arezzo, *Micrologus* 15, p. 170.33

205. Vespers antiphon for the Birth of the Blessed Virgin Mary; *CAO* 3852.

206. See above, chapter 30, pp. 20–22.

207. That is, .D.G./.G.D. and .D.E.F.G./.G.F.E.D.

208. That is, .D.E.G./.G.E.D. and .D.F.G./.G.F.D.

209. A characterization derived from Isidore, *Etymologies*, 12.7.18 (trans. Barney et al., p. 265): "The swan is named for singing because it pours out a sweetness of song with its modulated voice. It is thought to sing sweetly because it has a long curved neck, and a voice forcing its way by a long and winding path necessarily renders varied modulations."

210. An allusion drawing partially on Virgil, *Eclogues* 8.55: "And let the screech-owls compete with the swans, let Tityrus be Orpheus, an Orpheus in the woods, an Arion among the dolphins." Aribo may well have known this passage from its quotation by Isidore in *Etymologies* 1.36.7 (trans. Barney et al., p. 59). He probably also remembered that *tityrus* was the name Isidore gave to a cross between a ewe and a billy-goat: Isidore comments that the *titryus*, like all such progeny, is the result of an unnatural combination (*Etymologies*, 12.1.61; trans. Barney et al., p. 251).

211. A reference to the melismatic nature of Milanese chant. Perhaps an observation prompted by firsthand experience on a visit to Lombardy.

212. Probably a reference to Virgil's shepherd Meliboeus from *Eclogue* 1 (a dialogue between Meliboeus and Tityrus in which Meliboeus's complaints and laments about his toil and duties are juxtaposed with Tityrus's rustic ease). See also Isidore, *Etymologies* 1.36.7.

213. That is .D.E.A., D.F.A., and .D.G.A.

214. For a discussion of Aribo's treatment of this chant, see Schlager, "Ars cantandi," pp. 241, 246–48.

215. Antiphon for the First Sunday after Whitsun; *CAO* 4666.

216. From the offertory *Eligerunt apostoli Stephanum* for St. Stephen's Day (December 26).

217. An allusion to Boethius, *De differentiis topicis* (PL 64:1188D).

218. See chapter 95, above pp. 86–87.

219. The Guidonian solmization syllables *Ut, re, mi, fa, sol, la,* representing the notes .C.D.E.F.G.a. Guido adopted the first syllables from each line of the hymn "Ut queant laxis" (as each line begins one step successively higher in pitch). See Guido of Arezzo, *Epistola ad Michahelem*, lines 120–28, p. 466.

220. Aribo employs the rhetorical colors of *traductio* (the repetition of the words "uestram" and "uestrę") and *similiter cadens* (produced by the accusative endings of "capream," "uestram," "gratiam," and "eam"). See *Rhetorica ad Herennium* 4.14.20, 4.20.28; Onulf of Speyer, *Colores rhetorici* 1.4 and 2.4, 1.12 and 2.12, ed. Linde, pp. 358, 373, 363, 376.

221. This sentence is constructed of two *membra*, or clauses supported by one another. The two clauses are divided by the conjunction "propter" and have virtually equal numbers of syllables (the color of *conpar*, or isocolon). Aribo achieves *similiter cadens* between "ostendit" and "promuerit." See *Rhetorica ad Herennium* 4.19.26; Onulf of Speyer, *Colores rhetorici* 1.10, 2.10, ed. Linde, pp. 362, 375–76.

222. The repetition of "naturaliter" employs *traductio*. As in the previous sentence, Aribo uses *conpar* to balance the two clauses, as well as *similiter cadens* between their conclusions. In addition, however, his juxtaposition of "graciosa" and "exosa" employs *contentio*, a style built on contraries. See *Rhetorica ad Herennium* 4.15.21; Onulf of Speyer, *Colores rhetorici* 1.5, 2.5, ed. Linde, 359, 374.

223. The juxtaposition of "quadripertita in unam" with "caprea in unam," and "contra naturam monochordi" with "iuxta monochordi constitutionem": the rhetorical device of reasoning through contraries (*contentio*). The transposition of the affirmative "laudetur" to the opening negative clause and the double negative "non vituperetur" to the subsequent affirmative clause: the figure of reciprocal change (*commutatio*). See *Rhetorica ad Herennium* 4.28.39; Onulf of Speyer, *Colores rhetorici* 1.23, 2.23, ed. Linde, pp. 371, 380.

224. "Renuit longe diuisit, nostra caprea collegit": a closely packed group of words expressing a complete thought (*continuatio*). See *Rhetorica ad Herennium* 4.19.27.

225. "Illam peruersa/istam naturalis": the figure of *contentio*.

226. Aribo copied text of *sententia* 1 until "quam absentibus scribendo" from *Commentarius anonymus in Micrologum Guidonis Aretini*. The Guidonian material, which is printed here in italics, he quoted from the commentary and not from *Micrologus*. Cf. Guido of Arezzo, *Micrologus* 15, p. 164.

227. Guido of Arezzo, *Micrologus* 15, p. 164.

228. Ibid., p. 165.

229. Antiphon for Sexagesima; *CAO* 4859.

230. From the antiphon *Semen cecidit in terram bonam*.

231. Office antiphon; *CAO* 5350.

232. Guido of Arezzo, *Micrologus* 15, p. 165.

233. Ibid.

234. Ibid., p. 163.

235. Vespers antiphon for the Second Sunday in Lent; *CAO* 2287.

236. See Desmond, "*Sicut in grammatica*," pp. 481–83.

237. Guido of Arezzo, *Micrologus* 15, p. 167.

238. Matins respond for the First Sunday in Lent; *CAO* 6600. All of the examples from *Ecce nunc dies salutis* to *Virtutis Dei* are taken from this responsory.

239. Guido of Arezzo, *Micrologus* 15, p. 175.

240. Ibid.

241. Antiphon for Quinquagesima; *CAO* 3776.

242. *Commentarius anonymus*, ed. Vivell, pp. 68–71; ed. Smits van Waesberghe, pp. 152–55.

243. Guido of Arezzo, *Mirologus* 17, p. 193.

244. A reference to Bishop Ellenhard of Freising.

245. Guido of Arezzo, *Micrologus* 17, p. 188.12.

246. Ibid., p. 190.21.

247. Guido of Arezzo, *Regulae rithmice*, lines 108–13, p. 432.

248. Advent antiphon; *CAO* 2527.

Appendices

Appendix 1

The circle diagrams transmitted by *R*(*S*)

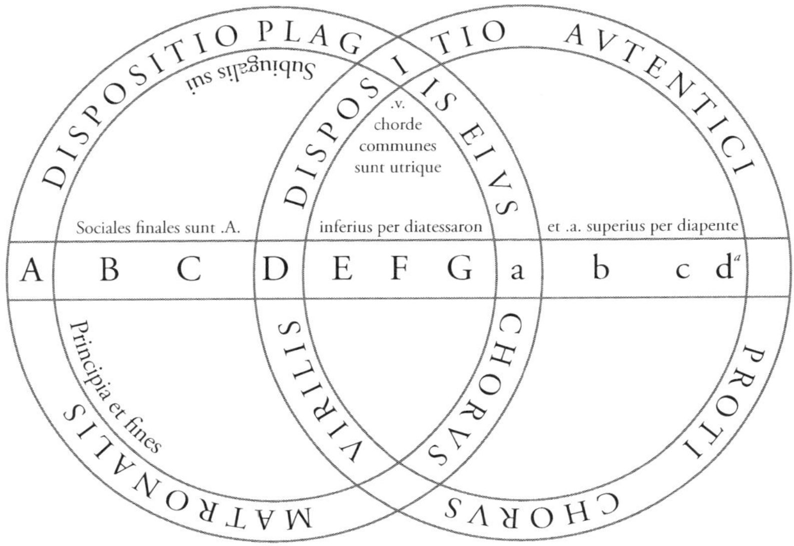

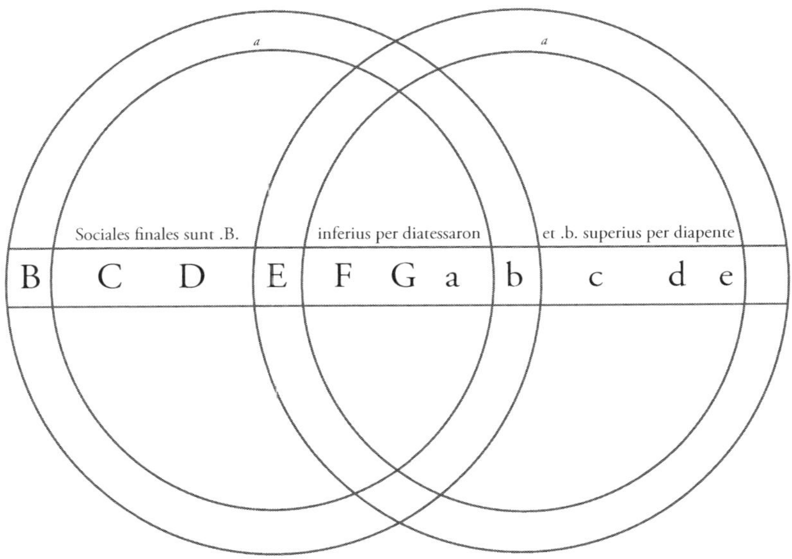

[a] *R has a mark correcting the placement of* .d. *to the right between the two concentric circles; this diagram transmitted only by R*

[a] *S lacks the inner concentric circle*

Diagram 1.

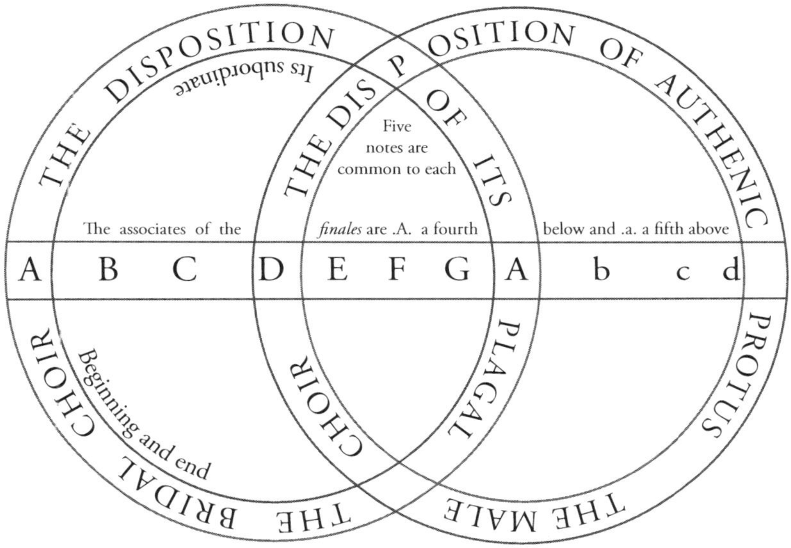

Diagram 2.

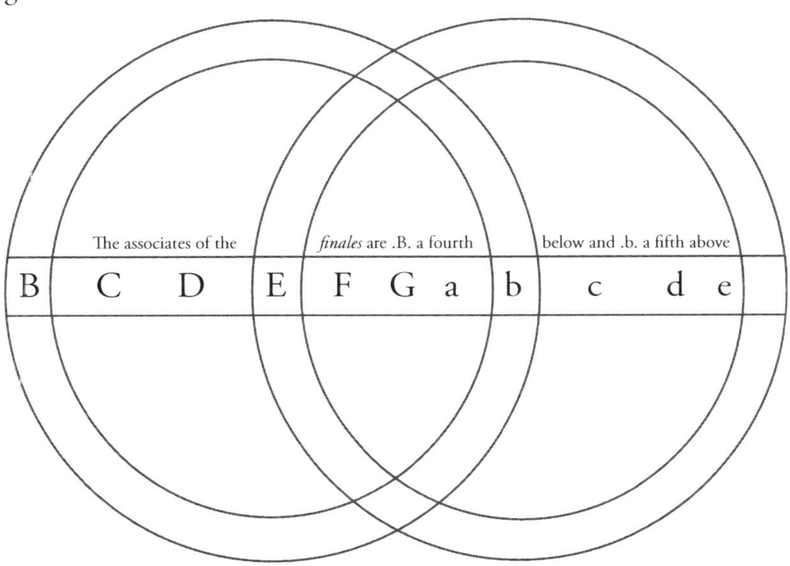

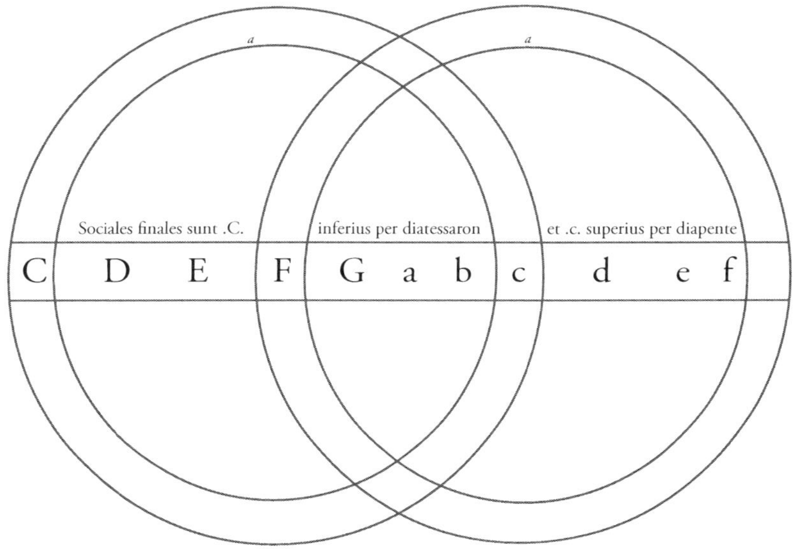

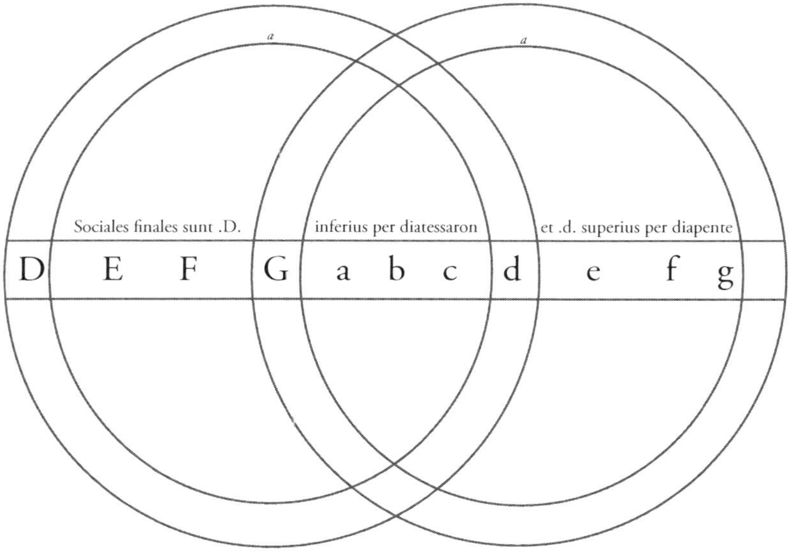

[a] *S lacks the inner concentric circle*
[a] *S lacks the inner concentric circle*

Diagram 3.

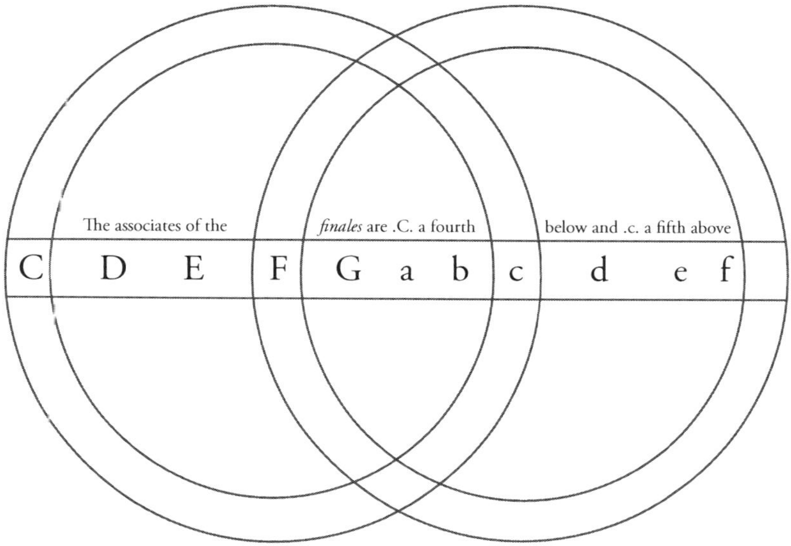

Diagram 4.

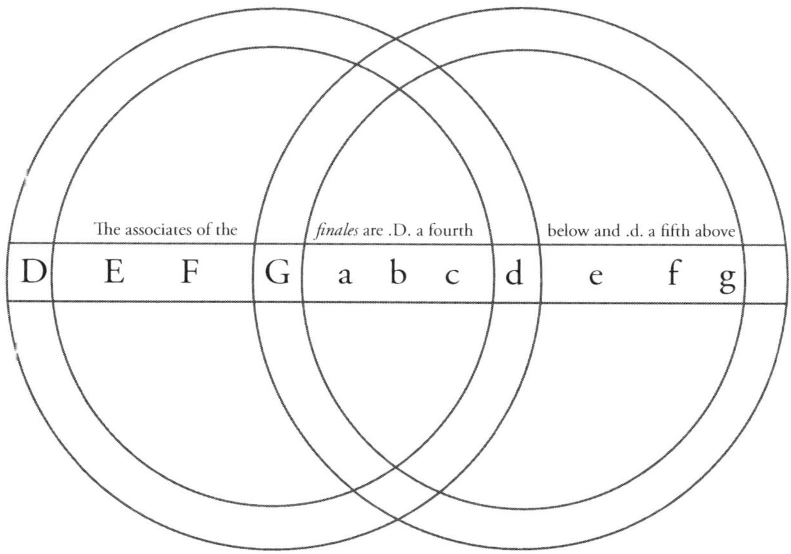

Appendix 2

The quadripartite figure transmitted by *D5*

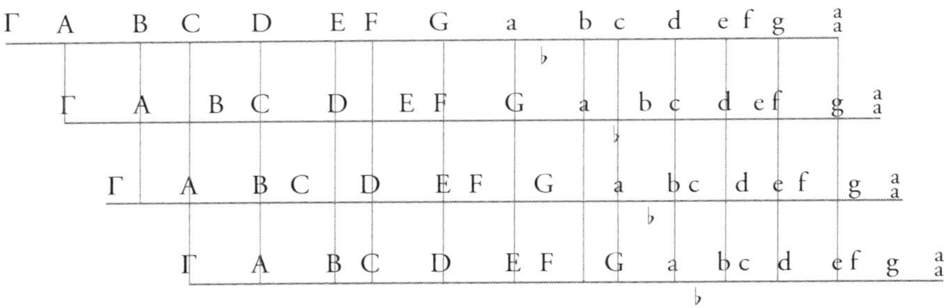

Bibliography

Primary Sources

Alberic of Monte Cassino. *Flores rhetorici*. Edited by D. M. Inguanez and H. M. Willard. Monte Cassino: Arti grafiche e fotomeccaniche Sansaini, 1938. English translation by Joseph M. Miller in *Readings on Medieval Rhetoric*, ed. Joseph M. Miller, Michael H. Prosser, and Thomas W. Benson. Bloomington: Indiana University Press, 1973.

Alia musica. Edited by Jacques Chailley in *Alia musica* (*Traité de musique du IXe siècle*): *Edition critique commentée avec une introduction sur l'origine de la nomenclature modale pseudo-grecque au Moyen-Age*. Publications de l'Institut de Musicologie de l'Université de Paris 6. Paris: Centre de documentation universitaire, 1968.

Analecta hymnica medii aevi. Edited by Guido Maria Dreves, Clemens Blume, and H. M. Bannister. 55 vols. Leipzig, 1886–1922. [Cited throughout as *AH*.]

Anselm of Laon. *Sententiae*. Edited by Odon Lottin in *Psychologie et morale aux XIIe et XIIIe siècles*, vol. 5, *Problèmes d'historie littéraire: L'école d'Ansleme de Laon et de Guillaume de Champeaux*. Gembloux: Duculot, 1959.

Aribo. *De musica*. Edited by Joseph Smits van Waesberghe as *Aribonis De musica*. Corpus scriptorum de musica 2. Rome: American Institute of Musicology, 1951. [Cited throughout as *Aribonis De musica*.]

Aurelian of Réôme. *Musica disciplina*. Edited by Lawrence Gushee as *Aureliani Reomensis Musica disciplina*. Corpus scriptorum de musica 21. Rome: American Institute of Musicology, 1975.

Bern of Reichenau. *Epistola de tonis, Prologus in tonarium, Tonarius*. Edited by Alexander Rausch as *Die Musiktraktate des Abtes Bern von Reichenau: Edition und Interpretation*. Musica mediaevalis Europae occidentalis 5. Tutzing: Schneider, 1999.

———. *Qualiter adventus Domini celebretur*. Edited by Philipp Jaffé in *Bibliotheca rerum Germanicarum*, vol. 3, pp. 365–71. Berlin: Weidmannos, 1866.

———. *Qualiter adventus Domini celebretur*. Edited by Franz-Josef Schmale in *Die Briefe des Abtes Bern von Reichenau*. Veröffentlichungen der Kommission für Geschichtliche Landeskunde in Baden-Württemberg Reihe A, Quellen 6, pp. 39–46. Stuttgart: Kohlhammer, 1961.

———. *Qualiter adventus Domini celebretur.* PL 142:1079–86.

———. *Qualiter quatuor temporum ieiunia per sua sabbata sint observanda.* PL 142:1085–88.

Bernard of Hildesheim (of Constance). *Liber canonum contra Heinricum IV.* MGH Libelli 1. Hanover: Impensis Bibliopolii Hahniani, 1891. Pp. 471–516.

Bernhard, Michael, ed. *Clavis Gerberti: Eine Revision von Martin Gerberts Scriptores ecclesiastici de musica sacra potissimum (St. Blasien 1784).* Bayerische Akademie der Wissenschaften. Veröffentlichungen der Musikhistorischen Kommission 7. Munich: Verlag der Bayerischen Akademie der Wissenschaften, 1989.

Bernold of St. Blasien (of Constance). *Apollogeticus super excommunicacionem Gregorii septimi.* MGH Libelli 2. Hanover: Impensis Bibliopolii Hahniani, 1892. Pp. 161–68.

———. *Chronicon.* Edited by I. S. Robinson in *Die Chroniken Bertholds von Reichenau und Bernolds von Konstanz, 1054–1100.* MGH SSrG NS 14. Hanover: Hahnsche Buchhandlung, 2003.

Boethius. *De differentiis topicis.* PL 64:1173–1216. Translated by Eleonore Stump as *On Topical Differentiae.* Ithaca, NY: Cornell University Press, 1978.

———. *De divisione.* Edited and translated by John Magee as *Anicii Manlii Severini Boethii De divisione liber: Critical Edition, Translation, Prolegomena and Commentary.* Philosophia antiqua 77. Leiden: E. J. Brill, 1998.

———. *De institutione arithmetica.* Edited and translated by Jean-Yves Guillaumin as *Boèce Institution Arithmétique.* Paris: Belles Lettres, 1995.

———. *De institutione musica.* Edited by Gottfried Friedlein as *Anicii Manlii Torquati Severini Boetii De institutione arithmetica libri duo, De institutione musica libri quinque: Accedit geometria quae fertur Boetii.* Leipzig, 1867; repr. Frankfurt am Main: Minerva, 1966). *Translated by Calvin M. Bower as *Fundamentals of Music: Anicius Manlius Severinus Boethius.* New Haven and London: Yale University Press, 1989.

———. *In Topica Ciceronis commentariorum libri sex.* PL 64:1039D–1174B.

Cassiodorus. *Institutiones.* Edited by R. A. B. Mynors as *Cassiodori senatoris Institutiones.* Oxford: Clarendon Press, 1937.

Chronicon Benedictoburanum. MGH SS 9. Hanover: Impensis Bibliopolii Avlici Hahniani, 1851. Pp. 210–38.

Commentarius anonymous in Micrologum Guidonis Aretini. Edited by Cölestin Vivell as "Commentarius anonymus in Micrologum Guidonis Aretini." *Akademie der Wissenschaften in Wien, Philosophische-historische Klasse, Sitzungsberichte* 185, no. 5 (1917): 5–92.

———. Edited by Joseph Smits van Waesberghe as *Expositiones in Micrologum Guidonis Aretini,* pp. 95–172. Amsterdam: North-Holland, 1957.

Corpus antiphonarium officii. Edited by René-Jean Hesbert. 6 vols. Rerum ecclesiasticarum documenta. Series Maior. Fontes 7–12. Rome: Herder, 1963–79. [Cited throughout as *CAO.*]

Donizo of Canossa. *Vita Mathildis.* MGH SS 12. Hanover: Impensis Bibliopolii Avlici Hahniani, 1861. Pp. 348–409.

Engelbert of Admont. *De musica*. Edited by Pia Ernstbrunner as *Der Musiktraktat des Engelbert von Admont (ca. 1250–1331)*. Musica mediaevalis Europae occidentalis 2. Tutzing: Hans Schneider, 1998.

Frutolf of Michelsberg. *Breviarium de musica*. Edited by Cölestin Vivell as "Frutolfi *Breviarium de musica* et *Tonarius*" in *Akademie der Wissenschaften in Wien, Philosophische-historische Klasse, Sitzungsberichte* 188, no. 2 (1919).

Gebhard of Salzburg. *Epistola ad Herimannum Mettensem episcopum data*. MGH Libelli 1. Hanover: Impensis Bibliopolii Hahniani, 1891. Pp. 261–79.

Gerbert, Martin, ed. *Scriptores ecclesiastici de musica sacra potissimum*. 3 vols. St. Blasien, 1784.

Glossa maior in institutionem musicam Boethii. Edited by Michael Bernhard and Calvin M. Bower. 3 vols. Bayerische Akademie der Wissenschaften. Veröffentlichungen der Musikhistorischen Kommission 9–11. Munich: Bayerische Akademie der Wissenschaften, 1993, 1994, 1996.

Guido of Arezzo. *Micrologus*. Edited by Joseph Smits van Waesberghe as *Micrologus Guidonis Aretini*. Corpus scriptorum de musica 4. Rome: American Institute of Musicology, 1955.

———. *Epistola ad Michahelem, Prologus in antiphonarium, Regule rithmice*. Edited and translated by Dolores Pesce as *Guido d'Arezzo's "Regule rithmice," "Prologus in antiphonarium" and "Epistola ad Michahelem": A Critical Text and Translation*. Wissenschaftliche Abhandlungen 73. Ottawa: Institute of Mediaeval Music, 1999.

Haimo of Hirsau. *Vita Willihelmi Abbatis Hirsaugiensis*. MGH SS 12. Hanover: Impensis Bibliopolii Avlici Hahniani, 1861. Pp. 209–25.

Henry of Augsburg. *Musica*. Edited by Joseph Smits van Waesberghe as *Musica domni Heinrici Augustensis magistri*. Divitae musicae artis collectae A/7. Buren: F. Knuf, 1976.

Herman of Reichenau. *Musica*. Edited and translated by Leonard Ellinwood as *Musica Hermanni Contracti*. Rochester, NY: Eastman School of Music, 1936.

Historia Hirsaugiensis monasterii. MGH SS 14. Hanover: Impensis Bibliopolii Hahniani, 1883. Pp. 254–65.

Hucbald of St. Amand. *Musica*. Edited by Y. Chartier as *L'Œuvre musicale d'Hucbald de Saint-Amand: Les compositions et le traité de musique*. Cahiers d'Études Médiévales 5. Montreal: Bellarmin, 1995.

———. *Musica*. Edited by Martin Gerbert as *De harmonica institutione* in vol. 1 of *Scriptores ecclesiastici de musica sacra potissimum*, pp. 103–25. St. Blasien, 1784; repr. Hildesheim: Georg Olms, 1963.

Isidore of Seville. *Etymologiae*. Edited by W. M. Lindsay as *Isidori Hispalensis episcopi Etymologiarum sive originum libri XX*. 2 vols. Oxford: Clarendon Press, 1911.

———. *Etymologiae*. Translated by Stephen A. Barney, W. J. Lewis, J. A. Beach, and Oliver Berghof as *The Etymologies of Isidore of Seville*. Cambridge: Cambridge University Press, 2006.

Jerome. *Contra Jovinianum*. PL 23:0211–338.

John. *De musica, Tonarius*. Edited by Joseph Smits van Waesberghe as *Johannis*

Afflighemensis De musica cum tonario. Corpus scriptorum de musica 1. Rome: American Institute of Musicology, 1950.

Macrobius. *Commentarius in Somnium Scipionis.* Edited by James Willis as *Ambrosii Theodosii Macrobii: In Somnium Scipionis commentarios selecta varietate lectionis ornavit Iacobus Willis.* 2nd ed. Bibliotheca scriptorum Graecorum et Romanorum Teubneriana. Leipzig: B. G. Teubner, 1970; repr. 1994.

Martianus Capella. *De nuptiis Philologiae et Mercurii.* Edited by James Willis in *Martianus Capella opera.* Leipzig: Teubner, 1983.

Monumenta monodica medii aevi. Vol. 1, *Hymnen.* Edited by Bruno Stäblein. Kassel: Bärenreiter Verlag, 1956.

Monumenta monodica medii aevi. Vol. 5, *Antiphonen im 1.–8. Modus.* Edited by László Dobszay and Janka Szendrei. Kassel: Bärenreiter Verlag, 1999.

Musica enchiriadis and Scolica enchiriadis. Edited by H. Schmid as *Musica et scolica enchiriadis, una cum aliquibus tractatulis adiunctis.* Bayerische Akademie der Wissenschaften. Veröffentlichungen der Musikhistorischen Kommission 3. Munich: Verlag der Bayerischen Akademie der Wissenschaften, 1981.

———. Translated by Raymond Erickson as *Musica enchiriadis and Scolica enchiriadis.* New Haven, CT: Yale University Press, 1995.

Notae necrologicae ecclesiae maioris Frisingensis. MGH NecG 3. Berlin: Weidmannos, 1905. Pp. 79–85.

Onulf of Speyer. *Colores rhetorici.* Edited by W. Wattenbach as "Magister Onulf von Speyer." *Sitzungsberichte der königlich Preußischen Akademie der Wissenschaften zu Berlin* 1 (1894): 361–86.

———. *Colores rhetorici.* Edited by J. C. Linde as "Die 'Rhetorici colores' des Magister Onulf von Speyer," *Mittellateinisches Jahrbuch* 40 (2005): 333–81.

Plato. *Timaeus.* Edited by J. H. Waszink as *Timaeus a Calcidio translatus commentarioque instructus.* 2nd ed. Plato Latinus 4. London: Warburg Institute, 1975.

Peter Damian. *Letters.* Edited by Kurt Reindel as *Die Briefe des Petrus Damiani.* 4 vols. MGH Briefe 4/1–4. Munich: Monumenta Germaniae Historica, 1983, 1988, 1989, 1993.

Porphyry. *Isagoge: Translatio Boethii.* Edited by Lorenzo Minio-Paluello. Aristoteles Latinus 1/6–7. Categoriarum supplementa, 5–31. Leiden: E. J. Brill, 1966.

———. *Isagoge.* Translated by Edward W. Warren as *Porphyry the Phoenician: Isagoge.* Toronto: Pontifical Institute of Mediaeval Studies, 1975.

Pseudo-Bernelinus. *Cita et vera divisio monochordi.* Edited by Martin Gerbert in vol. 1 of *Scriptores ecclesiastici de musica sacra potissimum,* pp. 312–30. St. Blasien, 1784; repr. Hildesheim: Georg Olms, 1963.

Pseudo-Odo of Cluny. *Dialogus de musica.* Edited by Martin Gerbert in vol. 1 of *Scriptores ecclesiastici de musica sacra potissimum,* pp. 251–64. St. Blasien, 1784; repr. Hildesheim: Georg Olms, 1963.

Quaestiones in musica. Edited by Rudolf Steglich as *Die Quaestiones in musica: Ein Choraltraktat des zentralen Mittelalters und ihr mutmaßlicher Verfasser Rudolf von St. Trond (1070–1138).* Leipzig: Breitkopf & Härtel, 1911; repr. 1971.

Quomodo de arithmetica procedit musica. PL 141:435–44.

Sachs, Klaus-Jürgen, ed. *Mensura fistularum: Die Mensurierung der Orgelpfeifen im Mittelalter.* 2 vols. Schriftenreihe der Walcker-Stiftung für Orgelwissenschaftliche Forschung. Stuttgart: Musikwissenschaftliche Verlags-Ges., 1970, 1980.

Smits van Waesberghe, Joseph, ed. *Cymbala: Bells in the Middle Ages.* Musicological Studies and Documents 1. Rome: American Institute of Musicology, 1951.

Theoger of Metz. *Musica.* Edited and translated by F. C. Lochner in "Dietger (Theogerus) of Metz and His 'Musica.'" PhD diss., University of Notre Dame, 1995.

Theophilus. *De diversis artibus.* Edited and translated by C. R. Dodwell. Oxford: Clarendon Press, 1986.

Udalric of Bamberg. *Codex Udalrici.* Edited by Philipp Jaffé in *Bibliotheca rerum Germanicarum,* vol. 5, pp. 17–469. Berlin, 1869.

Wenrich of Trier. *Epistola sub Theoderici episcopi Virdunensis nomine composita.* MGH Libelli 1. Hanover: Impensis Bibliopolii Hahniani, 1891. Pp. 280–99.

William of Champeaux. *Sententiae.* Edited by O. Lottin in *Psychologie et morale aux XIIe et XIIIe siècles.* Vol 5, *Problèmes d'historie littéraire: L'école d'Ansleme de Laon et de Guillaume de Champeaux.* Gembloux: Duculot, 1959.

William of Hirsau. *Musica.* Edited by D. Harbinson as *Wilhelmi Hirsaugiensis Musica.* Corpus scriptorum de musica 23. Rome: American Institute of Musicology, 1975.

Wipo. *Gesta Chonradi II imperatoris.* Edited by H. Bresslau in *Wiponis opera.* MGH SSrG 61. Hanover and Leipzig: Impensis Bibliopolii Hahniani. Pp. 1–62.

Wolf, J., ed. "Ein anonymer Musiktraktat des elften bis zwölften Jahrhunderts." *Vierteljahrschrift für Musikwissenschaft* 9 (1893): 186–234.

[Wolfger of Prüfening]. *De scriptoribus ecclesiasticis.* Edited by Emil Ettlinger as *Der sogenannte Anonymus Mellicensis De scriptoribus ecclesiasticisi.* Strassburg, 1896.

Secondary Sources

Adkins, Cecil Dale. "The Technique of the Monochord." *Acta Musicologica* 34 (1967): 34–43.

———. "The Theory and Practice of the Monochord." PhD diss., Iowa State University, 1963.

Alton, E. H., D. E. W. Wormell, and E. Courtney. "A Catalogue of the Manuscripts of Ovid's *Fasti.*" *Bulletin of the Institute of Classical Studies* 24 (1977): 37–63.

———. "Problems in Ovid's *Fasti.*" *Classical Quarterly,* n.s., 23 (1973): 144–51.

Angenendt, A. "Die Liturgie in der Vita des Johannes von Gorze." In *L'Abbaye de Gorze au X*[e] *siècle,* ed. Michel Parisse and Otto Oexle, pp. 193–211. Nancy: Presses universitaires de Nancy, 1993.

Arnold, K. "Admont und die monastische Reform des 12. Jahrhunderts." *Zeitschrift der Savigny-Stiftung für Reichsgeschichte* 89. *Kanonische Abteilung* 58 (1972): 350–69.

Atkinson, C. "'Harmonia' and the 'Modi, quos abusive tonos dicimus.'" In *Atti del XIV congresso della Società internazionale di musicologia: Transmissione e recezione delle forme di cultura musicale,* ed. A. Pompilio, pp. 485–500. Turin: EDT, 1990.

Autenrieth, Johanne. *Die Domschule von Konstanz zur Zeit des Investiturstreits: Die Wissenschaftliche Arbeitsweise Bernholds von Konstanz und zweier Kleriker dargestellt auf Grund von Handschriftenstudien.* Forschungen zur Kirchen- und Geistesgeschichte 3. Stuttgart: W. Kohlhammer, 1956.

Beach, Alison I. *Women as Scribes: Book Production and Monastic Reform in Twelfth-Century Bavaria.* Cambridge: Cambridge University Press, 2004.

Bernhard, Michael. "Das musikalische Fachschrifttum im lateinischen Mittelalter." In *Geschichte der Musiktheorie*, vol. 3, *Rezeption des antiken Fachs im Mittelalter*, ed. F. Zaminer, pp. 39–103. Darmstadt: Wissenschaftliche Buchgesellschaft, 1990.

———. "Überlieferung und Fortleben der antiken lateinischen Musiktheorie im Mittelalter." In *Geschichte der Musiktheorie*, vol. 3, *Rezeption des antiken Fachs im Mittelalter*, ed. F. Zaminer, pp. 7–36. Darmstadt: Wissenschaftliche Buchgesellschaft, 1990.

Bischoff, B. "Wolfger." In *Die deutsche Literatur des Mittelalters: Verfasserlexikon*, ed. Karl Langosch, vol. 4, cols. 1051–56. Berlin: DeGruyter, 1953.

Bower, Calvin M. "The Transmission of Ancient Music Theory in the Middle Ages." In *The Cambridge History of Western Music Theory*, ed. Thomas Christensen, pp. 136–67. Cambridge: Cambridge University Press, 2002.

Burnett, C. "Omnibus convenit Platonicis: An Appendix to Adelard of Bath's *Quaestiones naturales*." In *From Athens to Chartres: Neoplatonism and Medieval Thought; Studies in Honour of Edouard Jeauneau*, ed. Haijo Jan Westra, pp. 259–82. Leiden: E. J. Brill, 1992.

Buttenweiser, H. "Manuscripts of Ovid's *Fasti*: The Ovidian Tradition in the Middle Ages." *Transactions and Proceedings of the American Philological Association* 71 (1940): 45–51.

Cowdrey, H. E. J. *The Cluniacs and the Gregorian Reform.* Oxford: Clarendon Press, 1973.

———. *Pope Gregory VII, 1073–1085.* Oxford: Clarendon Press, 1998.

Czerny, Albin. *Die Handschriften der Stiftsbibliothek St. Florian.* Linz, 1871.

Desmond, Karen. "*Sicut in grammatica*: Analogical Discourse in Chapter 15 of Guido's *Micrologus*." *Journal of Musicology* 16 (1998): 467–93.

Donnat, L. "Vie et coutume monastique dans la Vita de Jean de Gorze." In *L'Abbaye de Gorze au Xe siècle*, ed. Michel Parisse and Otto Oexle, pp. 159–82. Nancy: Presses universitaires de Nancy, 1993.

Fichtenau, Heinrich von. "Wolfger von Prüfening." *Mitteilungen des Instituts für Österreichische Geschichtsforschung* 51 (1937): 341–51.

Gawlik, Alfred. *Intervenienten und Zeugen in den Diplomen Kaiser Heinrichs IV. (1056–1105).* Kallmünz: M. Lassleben, 1970.

Glauche, Günter. *Katalog der lateinischen Handschriften der Bayerischen Staatsbibliothek München: Die Pergamenthandschriften aus Benediktbeuern, Clm 4501–4663.* Wiesbaden: Harrassowitz Verlag, 1994.

Gümpel, K.-W. "Pseudo-Odo." In vol. 13 of *Die Musik in Geschichte und Gegenwart: Personenteil.* Kassel: Barenreiter and Metzler, 2005. Cols 1012–15.

Gushee, L. "Questions of Genre in Medieval Treatises on Music." In *Gattungen der Musik in Einzeldarstellungen: Gedenkschrift Leo Schrade*, ed. Wulf Arlt, E. Lichtenhahn, and H. Oesch, pp. 365–433. Munich: Francke, 1973.

Hallinger, Kassius. *Gorze-Kluny: Studien zu den monastischen Lebensformen und Gegensätzen im Hochmittelalter.* 2 vols. Studia Anselmiana philosophica theologica, fasc. 22–25. Rome: Herder, 1950, 1951.

Halm, C., F. Keinz, G. Meyer, and G. Thomas. *Catalogus codicum latinorum Bibliotheca Regiae Monacensis.* 4 vols. Munich, 1873–94.

Hauck, Albert. *Kirchengeschichte Deutschlands.* 4 vols. Leipzig, 1896, 1900, 1906, 1912; repr. Berlin: Akademie-Verlag, 1952–53.

Heinemann, Otto von. *Die Handschriften der Herzoglichen Bibliothek zu Wolfenbüttel.* 11 vols. Wolfenbüttel: J. Zwissler, 1884–1913.

Helssig, R. *Katalog der Handschriften der Universitätsbibliothek zu Leipzig.* Vol. 4, pt. 1. Leipzig: Otto Harrassowitz, 1901.

Hiley, David. *Western Plainchant: A Handbook.* Oxford: Clarendon Press, 1993.

Hirschmann, W. "Aribo." In vol. 1 of *Die Musik in Geschichte und Gegenwart: Personenteil.* Kassel: Barenreiter and Metzler, 2005. Cols. 905–8.

Holter, K. "Bibliothek und Archiv. Handschriften und Inkunabeln." In *Die Kunstsammlungen des Augustiner-Chorherrenstiftes St. Florian*, ed. V. Birke, pp. 29–92. Österreichische Kunsttopographie 48. Vienna: Schroll, 1988.

———. "Romanische Buchkunst aus der Stiftsbibliothek St. Florian." In *Geschichte und ihre Quellen: Festschrift für Fritz Hausmann*, ed. R. Härtel, pp. 545–78. Graz: Akademische Druck- u. Verlagsanstalt, 1987.

Hörberg, N. *Libri sanctae Afrae: St. Ulrich und Afra zu Augsburg im 11. und 12. Jahrhundert nach Zeugnissen der Klosterbibliothek.* Veröffentlichungen des Max-Planck-Instituts für Geschichte. Studien zur Germania sacra 15. Göttingen: Vandenhoeck and Ruprecht, 1983.

Huglo, Michel. "L'Auteur du Dialogue sur la Musique attribuée à Odon." *Revue de musicologie* 55 (1969): 119–71.

———. "Grundlagen und Ansätze der mittelalterlichen Musiktheorie von der Spätantike bis zur Ottonischen Zeit." In *Die Lehre vom einstimmigen liturgischen Gesang*, pp. 17–102. Geschichte der Musiktheorie 4. Darmstadt: Wissenschaftliche Buchgesellschaft, 2000

———. "Der Prolog des Odo zugeschriebenen 'Dialogus de Musica.'" *Archiv für Musikwissenschaft* 28 (1971): 134–46.

———. *Les tonaires. Inventaire, analyse, comparaison.* Publications de la Société française de musicologie 3, no. 2. Paris: Société francaise de musicologie, 1971.

Ilnitchi, Gabriela. "Aribo's De musica: Music Theory in the Cross Current of Medieval Learning." PhD diss., New York University, 1997.

———. *The Play of Meanings: Aribo's De musica and the Hermeneutics of Musical Thought.* Lanham, MD: Scarecrow Press, 2005.

Ineichen-Eder, Christine Elisabeth. *Mittelalterliche Bibliothekskataloge Deutschlands und der Schweiz.* Vol. 4, pt. 1, *Bistümer Passau und Regensburg.* Munich: Beck, 1977.

Jakobs, Hermann. *Die Hirsauer: Ihre Ausbreitung und Rechtsstellung im Zeitalter des Investiturstreites*. Kölner historische Abhandlungen 4. Cologne: Böhlau, 1961.

Jørgensen, Ellen. *Catalogus codicum Latinorum medii aevi Bibliothecae regiae Hafniensis*. Copenhagen: Hafniae, 1926.

Klemm, Elisabeth. *Die romanischen Handschriften der Bayerischen Staatsbibliothek*. Vol. 3, pt. 1 of *Katalog der illuminierten Handschriften der Bayerischen Staatsbibliothek in München*. Wiesbaden: Ludwig Reichert, 1980.

Klüppel, T. "Der heilige Aurelius in Hirsau. Ein Beitrag zur Verehrungsgeschichte des Hirsauer Klosterpatrons." In *Hirsau: St. Peter und Paul 1091–1991*, ed. Klaus Schreiner, 2:221–58. Stuttgart: K. Theiss, 1991.

Kreps, Joseph. "Aribon de Liège: Une légende." *Revue belge de musicologie* 2 (1948): 138–43.

Leitshuh, Friedrich, and H. Fischer. *Katalog der Handschriften der Königlichen Bibliothek zu Bamberg*. Vol. 1. Bamberg, 1898; repr. Wiesbaden: Harrassowitz, 1966.

Leyen, Friedrich von der, ed. *Deutsches Mittelalter*. Frankfurt am Main: Insel, 1980.

Lottin, O., ed. *Problèmes d'historie littéraire: L'école d'Ansleme de Laon et de Guillaume de Champeaux*. Vol. 5 of *Psychologie et morale aux XIIe et XIIIe siècles*. Gembloux: Duculot, 1959.

Markovits, Michael. *Das Tonsystem der abendländischen Musik im frühen Mittelalter*. Publikationen der schweizerischen Musikforschenden Gesellschaft 2nd ser., vol. 30. Bern: Paul Haupt, 1977.

Mayr-Harting, Henry. *Ottonian Book Illumination: An Historical Study*. 2 vols. London: Harvey Miller, 1991.

McCarthy, T. J. H. "Aribo's *De musica*, *Commentarius anonymus in Micrologum Guidonis Aretini* and Guido of Arezzo: Textual Correspondence and Scholastic Method." *Mediaevistik: Internationale Zeitschrift für interdisziplinäre Mittelalterforschung* 20 (2007): 141–61.

———. "Aribo's *De musica* and Abbot William of Hirsau." *Revue Bénédictine* 116 (2006): 62–82.

———. "Biblical Scholarship in Eleventh-Century Michelsberg: The *Glosa in vetus et novum testamentum* of MS Karlsruhe, Badische Landesbibliothek, 504." *Scriptorium* 62 (2008): 3–45.

———. *Chronicles of the Investiture Contest: Frutolf of Michelsberg and His Continuators*. Manchester: Manchester University Press, 2014.

———. "The Identity of Master Henry of Augsburg (d. 1083)." *Revue Bénédictine* 114 (2004): 140–57.

———. "Literary Practice in Eleventh-Century Music Theory: The *colores rhetorici* and Aribo's *De musica*." *Medium Aevum* 71 (2002): 191–208.

———. *Music, Scholasticism and Reform: Salian Germany, 1024–1125*. Manchester: Manchester University Press, 2009.

———. "The Origins of *Commentarius anonymus in Micrologum Guidonis Aretini* in the Medieval Glossing Tradition." *Revue d'Histoire des Textes*, n.s., 3 (2008): 217–27.

McGuire, Brian Patrick. *Friendship and Community: The Monastic Experience, 350–1250*. Cistercian Studies 95. Kalamazoo, MI: Cistercian Publications, 1989.

Meyer, Christian. "Aus der Werkstatt des Kompilators: Bermerkungen über zwei musiktheoretische Schriften des 11. Jahrhunderts." In *Quellen und Studien zur Musiktheorie des Mittelalters*, ed. Michael Bernhard, vol. 2, pp. 1–12. Veröffentlichungen der Musikhistorischen Kommission 13. Munich: Verlag der Bayerischen Akademie der Wissenschaften, 1997.

———. *Mensura monochordi: La division du monochord (IXe–XVe siècles)*. Publications de la Société Française de Musicologie 2nd ser., vol. 15. Paris: Société francaise de musicologie, 1996.

———. "Organistrum et synemmenon grave. Observations sur l'échelle acoustique dans l'espace germanique (XIe–XIIIe siècle)." In *Mittelalterliche Musiktheorie in Zentraleuropa*, ed. Walter Pass and Alexander Rausch, pp. 87–106. Tutzing: H. Schneider, 1998.

———. "La tradition du 'Micrologus' de Guy d'Arezzo: Une contribution à l'histoire de la réception du texte." *Revue de musicologie* 83 (1997): 5–31.

Meyer von Knonau, Gerold. *Jahrbücher des deutschen Reiches unter Heinrich IV. und Heinrich V.* 7 vols. Leipzig: Duncker & Humblot, 1890–1909.

Möser-Mersky, G., ed. *Mittelalterliche Bibliothekskataloge Österreichs*. Vol. 3. Vienna: A. Holzhausen, 1961.

Nightingale, John. *Monasteries and Patrons in the Gorze Reform: Lotharingia c. 850–1000*. Oxford: Clarendon Press, 2001.

Paulhart, H., ed. *Mittelalterliche Bibliothekskataloge Österreichs*. Vol. 5. Vienna: A. Holzhausen, 1971.

Perrot, Jean. *The Organ from Its Invention in the Hellenistic Period to the End of the Thirteenth Century*. Translated by N. Deane. Oxford: Oxford University Press, 1971.

Pfaff, M. "Abt Wilhelm von Hirsau." *Erbe und Auftrag* 48 (1972): 83–94.

Powitz, Gerhardt. *Die Handschriften der Stadt- und Universitätsbibliothek Frankfurt am Main: Mittelalterliche Handschriftenfragmente*. Katalog der Stadt- und Universitätsbibliothek Frankfurt am Main 10, no. 6. Frankfurt: V. Klostermann, 1994.

Robinson, I. S. *Authority and Resistance in the Investiture Contest: The Polemical Literature of the Late Eleventh Century*. Manchester: Manchester University Press, 1978.

———. "The 'colores rhetorici' in the Investiture Contest." *Traditio* 32 (1976): 209–38.

———, trans. *Eleventh-Century Germany: The Swabian Chronicles*. Manchester: Manchester University Press, 2008.

———. "The Friendship Circle of Bernold of Constance and the Dissemination of Gregorian Ideas in Late Eleventh-Century Germany." In *Friendship in Medieval Europe*, ed. Julian Haseldine, pp. 185–98. Stroud: Sutton, 1999.

———. *Henry IV of Germany, 1056–1106*. Cambridge: Cambridge University Press, 1999.

———, trans. *The Papal Reform of the Eleventh Century: Lives of Pope Leo IX and Pope Gregory VII*. Manchester: Manchester University Press, 2004.

———. "Zur Arbeitsweise Bernolds von Konstanz und seines Kreises: Untersuchungen zum Schlettstädter Codex 13." *DA* 34 (1978): 51–122.

Robinson, P. R. "The 'Booklet': A Self-Contained Unit in Composite Manuscripts." *Codicologica* 2 (1978): 46–60.

Rusconi, A. "L'insegnamento del canto liturgico nel *De musica* de Engelbert von Admont." In *Musicam in subtilitate scrudanto: Contributi alla storia della teorla musicale*, ed. Daniele Sabaino, pp. 129–67. Studi e testi musicali, n.s., 7. Lucca: Libreria musicale italiana, 1994.

Schmid, Karl. "Sankt Aurelius in Hirsau 830 (?)–1049/75: Bemerkungen zur Traditionskritik und zur Gründerproblematik." In *Hirsau: St. Peter und Paul 1091–1991*, ed. K. Schreiner, 2:11–44. Forschungen und Berichte der Archäologie des Mittelalters in Baden-Württemberg 10. Stuttgart: K. Theiss, 1991.

Schlager, Karl-Heinz. "Ars cantandi – ars componendi: Texte und Kommentare zum Vortrag und zur Fügung des mittelalterlichen Chorals." In *Die Lehre vom einstimmigen liturgischen Gesang*, ed. Michel Huglo, pp. 219–92. Geschichte der Musiktheorie 4. Darmstadt: Wissenschaftliche Buchgesellschaft, 2000.

———, ed. *Thematischer Katalog der ältesten Alleluia-Melodien aus Handschriften des 10. und 11. Jahrhunderts, ausgenommen das ambrosianische, ält-römische und ält-spanische Repertoire*. Erlanger Arbeiten zur Musikwissenschaft 2. Munich: W. Ricke, 1965. [Cited throughout as *TK*.]

Schrade, L. Review of Aribo, *De musica*, ed. Joseph Smits van Waesberghe. *Journal of the American Musicological Society* 9 (1956): 215.

Schreiner, K. "Hirsau und die Hirsauer Reform: Spiritualität, Lebensform und Sozialprofil einer benediktinischen Erneuerungsbewegung im 11. und 12. Jahrhundert." In *Hirsau: St. Peter und Paul 1091–1991*, ed. K. Schreiner, 2:59–84. Forschungen und Berichte der Archäologie des Mittelalters in Baden-Württemberg 10. Stuttgart: K. Theiss, 1991.

Schuba, L. *Die Quadriviums-Handschriften der Codices Palatini Latini in der Vatikanischen Bibliothek*. Kataloge der Universitätsbibliothek Heidelberg 2. Wiesbaden: Ludwig Reichert, 1992.

Smits van Waesberghe, Joseph. *Muziekgeschiedenis der Middeleeuwen*. Vol. 1, *De Luiksche muziekschool als centrum van het muziektheoretische onderricht in de middelweeuwen*. Nederlandsche muziekhistorische en muziekpaedagogische studiën, series A. Tilburg: W. Bergmans, 1936.

———. "Relazione inedita di una lezione di Guido d'Arezzo sulla teoria della musica." *Note d'Archivio per la storia musicale* 13 (1936): pp. 38–51.

———. "Some Music Treatises and Their Interrelation: A School of Liége *c.* 1050–1200?" *Musica disciplina* 3 (1949): 25–31, 95–118.

Smits van Waesberghe, Joseph, P. Ernstbrunner, Pieter Fischer, Christian Maas, Michel Huglo, Christian Meyer, N. C. Phillips, A. Rausch, and C. Ruini, eds. *The Theory of Music from the Carolingian Era up to 1400: Descriptive Catalogue of Manuscripts*. Répertoire International des Sources Musicales, series B 3/1–6. Munich: G. Henle, 1961–2003. [Cited throughout as RISM B.]

Steinböck, Walter. *Erzbischof Gebhard von Salzburg (1060–1088). Ein Beitrag zur Geschichte Salzburgs im Investiturstreit*. Vienna: Geyer, 1975.

Teeuwen, Mariken. *Harmony and the Music of the Spheres: The Ars musica in Ninth-Century Commentaries on Martianus Capella*. Leiden: E. J. Brill, 2002.

Vivell, Cölestin. "Ein anonymer Kommentar zum *Mikrologus* des Guido d'Arezzo." *Studien und Mitteilungen zur Geschichte des Benediktinerordens und seiner Zweige* 35 (1914): 56–80.

———. "Nachtrag zu den *Quaestiones in musica*." *Gregoriusblatt* 39 (1914): 51–53.

———. "Die *Quaestiones in musica*, ihre handschriftliche Quelle und ihr mutmaßlicher Verfasser." *Gregoriusblatt* 38 (1913): 51–76.

Weinfurter, Stefan. *Salzburger Bistumsreform und Bischofspolitik im 12. Jahrhundert*. Cologne: Böhlau, 1975.

Wisenbach, J. "Wilhelm von Hirsau: Astrolab und Astronomie im 11. Jahrhunderts." In *Hirsau: St. Peter und Paul 1091–1991*, ed. K. Schreiner, 2:109–54. Forschungen und Berichte der Archäologie des Mittelalters in Baden-Württemberg 10. Stuttgart: K. Theiss, 1991.

Worstbrock, Franz-Josef. "Ulrich von Bamberg." *Verfasserlexikon* 9 (1995): cols. 1245–47.

Worstbrock, Franz-Josef, Monika Klaes, and Jutta Lütten. *Repertorium der Artes dictandi des Mittelalters*. Münstersche Mittelalter-Schriften 66. Munich: W. Fink, 1992.

Index of Citations and Allusions

Index of Chants

General Index

Typeset in 11/13 Adobe Garamond Pro
Composed by Tom Krol

Medieval Institute Publications
College of Arts and Sciences
Western Michigan University
1903 W. Michigan Avenue
Kalamazoo, MI 49008-5432
http://www.wmich.edu/medieval/mip

Printed and bound in the United States of America

Western Michigan University